EDITORIALS

EDITORIALS

BY

LAFCADIO HEARN

EDITED BY

CHARLES WOODWARD HUTSON

BOSTON AND NEW YORK
HOUGHTON MIFFLIN COMPANY
The Riverside Press Cambridge
1926

The Riverside Press
CAMBRIDGE · MASSACHUSETTS
PRINTED IN THE U.S.A.

CONTENTS

FROM THE 'TIMES–DEMOCRAT'

CONTENTS

INTRODUCTION

THE miseries endured by Hearn in the early days
of his stay in New Orleans are fully set forth in
the pages of one of his latest biographers, Nina
H. Kennard, who draws upon various sources of
information.

But what she has no means of knowing and
cannot tell is the quantity, quality, and variety
of work he did for the *Item* from the day he was
engaged as its assistant editor to the day when he
left it to do kindred and yet different work for
the *Times-Democrat*.

It was only by delving tirelessly into the yellow
pages of its old bound volumes that, with the
help of my daughter, Ethel Hutson, I was able to
master the secret of that activity which made the
little *Item* for years a really readable journal and
a force in bringing about reforms for the community.

It is my purpose to show this by a selection
from his editorials; and my selection includes a
much smaller number from those he furnished
the *Times-Democrat*. For, though the Bakers
seem to have laid most stress on his ability as a
translator, they did avail themselves of his large
reading in current foreign literature to the extent

of opening the editorial columns of their Sunday edition to his pen on many occasions. Having both more time and space at his disposal, he wrote at much greater length for this paper than for the *Item*.

The dreamy student who elaborated the wild 'Fantastics,' took to heart the fate of the 'Little Red Kitten,' saw visions in the 'Coulisses' of a theater, made almost a fairy-tale of the arrival of Mark Twain in a riverside town, painted an idyll out of a visit to Grand' Isle, and turned a fan into a fantasy, could also reach out with unerring touch into the realms of only half-established science to foretell what might yet be its triumphs, discuss practical municipal questions with sanity and sense, and, above all, show that journalism and literature are not incompatible — a truth too often ignored even by the newspapers of to-day.

What I wish to make clear is that it was from deliberate choice that he labored to make himself the artist rather than the mere journalist; that he was perfectly capable of observing, recording, and criticizing the passing events of the day; and that even in so doing he had the prophetic vision of the seer and at times forestalled the accomplishments of science in his theories of future advance. For instance, while the mere scientist saw but a useless toy in the first efforts of Edison's genius, we see Hearn forecasting the wonders that were to come from his discoveries.

In those of his papers retained by Dr. Gould, besides the list of the translations published in the *Times-Democrat*, is a list of seventy-seven papers and a supplemental list of a few others contributed to the same paper. But we have a much longer list in a memorandum kept by the author and left in the possession of his landlady, Mrs. Courtney, to whom he was much attached, as she had been very kind to him. Indeed, there are unpublished letters of his to her and to her little daughter Ella still treasured by the family — letters of simple kindliness and affection, and of no literary value.

But all these lists cover only a few years of his work while he was connected with the *Times-Democrat*, and include no part of what he contributed to the columns of the *Item*. We have been able to add many more editorials to those authenticated by his memoranda.

Before taking up the question of these, there is a prejudice of the public in regard to which I have something to say.

It is always difficult for the public to believe that a man of genius can be practical, that a writer of the weird and the fanciful can pen sound and sane thoughts on matters of immediate interest, that an artist in words can also be a safe guide in municipal progress. Yet that the soaring spirit is incompatible with the keen intellect and the business sense has often enough been disproved to disabuse mankind of this prejudice. Shakespeare retired to his native town a gentleman of means; Voltaire amassed an independent fortune; Swedenborg the visionary was an able engineer before he became a seer; Sheridan, Bulwer, and Macaulay won parliamentary as well as literary fame. The truth is that excellence in one field of effort is far from precluding excellence in others.

Lafcadio Hearn has so long been looked upon as the masterly word-painter and the apostle of the exotic that it will be doubly hard to convince the reader that he could also produce admirable editorials of the best journalistic type. But this we hope to do by a simple selection of a few of those he furnished the *Item* and the *Times-Democrat* during his ten years' stay in New Orleans.

It will, of course, be asked how the unsigned articles of Lafcadio Hearn can be unerringly identified?

In the first place, the 'Fantastics' we know by abundant evidence to have been his. Bigney, the editor of the *Item*, in reply to the question of a brother editor in Claiborne, explicitly states the fact. One of those published in the *Item* without signature Hearn subsequently reproduced, with slight changes, in the *Times-Democrat* over his name. Lastly, he alludes to them again and again in his correspondence, and in a list meant to classify them for future publication in book form, he names several of them under the heading, 'Fantastics.'

The same thing is true of a large number of the papers he furnished the columns of the *Times-Democrat*, as has been already said: among his memoranda are found lists of articles he claimed as his.

But how is it with regard to the numerous unsigned articles not so authenticated, especially those in the *Item* for which there exist no such memoranda?

In brief, there are two infallible indexes that point to authorship by him and by him alone. One of these is the internal evidence; the other, the fact that no such matter is to be found in the paper before the time of his engagement with its editor nor after his retirement from the post of assistant editor.

He was emphatically *the* literary editor of the *Item:* we may say confidently, there was no literary editor on the staff of that paper before or after him. Bigney wrote the political editorials — the leading articles, and nothing else; and there is a fixed and definite place for these. Book reviews, dramatic criticisms, and literary and scientific editorials were Hearn's work; and his pen was busy every day, except when he had dengue fever and when he had trouble with his eyes — periods his letters to Watkin, Krehbiel, and others fix for us.

Certain subjects, then and afterwards, deeply interested him, and we can trace his pen very often simply by the tenor of the article. We find the same opinions expressed in these and in his published letters of much later date. Indeed, it is singular how little change his views on many subjects underwent.

Again, his extensive reading, especially in foreign contemporary literature, put him in advance of those around him on many matters; and we often find him considering subjects which are even now, or have but recently been, occupying the attention of our people. His near-sighted vision ʃ physical objects stood in singular contrast to his far-sighted vision for those of the spirit.

Still ag in, style betrays him. There are turns of expressio , selections of epithets, luminous and vivid phrases of the literary adept, which we say at once no other than Hearn could have penned then and there.

What has been said of his work in the *Item* is in a modified degree true of the work in the *Times-Democrat*. There were, it must be admitted, other writers employed by Page Baker capable of valuable literary work. But even there the distinctive quality of Hearn's touch is apparent in certain editorials. We have no hesitation, for instance, in attributing to his pen the editorial entitled 'Norodom the Last.' And, after marking it as his, we find it set down in the supplemental list in Dr. Gould's book thus:

'No. 406. Dorodom the Last. Editorial, probably in T. D. Undated.'

Moreover, it is also in the list contained in the scrapbook left with Mrs. Courtney, and there correctly given as 'Norodom the Last.'

It has thus the authentication of being among the author's memoranda.

In the case of the editorials in the *Item* which we attribute to him, we have not the advantage of this verification. But who can read the paper on 'French Journalism,' for instance, and doubt for a moment the authorship?

We track him in the *Item* as well as in the *Times-Democrat* by his passion for biology — doctors were his closest friends in New Orleans — by his never-ceasing interest in astronomy, meteorology, seismology, and cosmic phenomena in general, no less than by his fondness for archæology and the fascination far-away lands and races had for him — these subjects affording material for so many of the papers his memoranda claim as his. At all times his spirit seems to have soared, reaching out toward the unknown. But, besides these, the *Item* exhibits his deep interest in the city and people of his new environment, and there are many articles from his pen devoted to the Creoles. Until one has ransacked the columns of this little paper of the late seventies and the early eighties, one is wholly unaware of the extent of his fecundity and versatility.

Nor are these the only means of identifying his authorship. His very punctuation betrays him: the frequent use of the dash — to which his French and Spanish readings had accustomed him; his marked preference for the semi-colon — in the printing-room his sobriquet was 'Old Semi-colon'; and his practice of beginning a new series of paragraphs with a triangle of asterisks. Throughout both the papers with which he was connected here, these singularities are to be observed in all that he wrote.

Little need be said in regard to the editorials selected for this volume. Intrinsic merit has not been invariably the deciding factor in choosing them. 'Romanticism in Music,' for instance, was given a place chiefly as marking one of the many occasions Hearn seized upon to do honor to his friend, the musician Krehbiel.

Since it is in the *Item* that we seem to see him 'discovering' New Orleans, it occurred to the editor that preference should be given to such documents as indicate that phase of his interest; while in selecting from the *Times-Democrat* greater stress might well be laid upon the more philosophic side of his work.

On the 15th of June, 1878, he began his work on the *Item*. In the issue of the 16th appeared the beginning of his translation of 'The Mum-

my's Foot.' In less than a month we find him
contributing to the columns of the paper 'Pompeii,' 'Fantastic Possibilities of Invention,' 'Russia and Germany — A Possible Coalition,' 'Migrations of the Human Race,' 'Republican
France,' 'London,' 'How Poets Destroy their
own Poems,' 'Moresque Architecture for River
Steamboats,' 'Tobacco Shavings,' 'Saintly Legends,' 'The Question in Germany,' 'The Asiatic
Horizon,' 'North Sea Civilization,' 'Insect Politics,' 'Cyprian Antiquities,' 'Is the Sea Serpent
an Eel?' 'Poor Mummies!' 'Ancient and Modern Athletics.' Three of these appear the day
after he wrote to Watkin, 'Editor away and
whole paper on my hands.'

Many of these early editorials are included in
this selection, in order to show what a scholarly
air he at once gave to the little sheet which up to
that time was merely a political organ. It will be
seen that Bigney had soon learned to rely upon
him as an able and steady worker.

No less marked than the vigor and scholarli-
ness of his articles is the variety of the subjects
he treated of, and the range of his literary allu-
sions.

It will be seen from several of his *Item* articles
— notably 'Self-Supporting Wives,' 'Prevention
of Cruelty to Women,' 'Woman's Influence,'
'Woman Suffrage,' 'Human Monsters,' 'Penitentiaries and Punishments' — how early was

his interest in eugenics, in the humane treatment of convicts, in the betterment of woman's social condition, and in all kindred subjects.

'The Burning of the Dead,' taken from the *Times-Democrat*, shows a like interest in sanitation; but there were many articles bearing on sanitation and hygiene contributed to the *Item* years before, which regard for space has shut out from this selection.

In 'The Secrets of the Infinite,' 'The Electric Light,' 'What is Light?' 'As If Painted by Lightning,' 'Sun-Spasms,' and 'The Destiny of Solar Systems,' we see how eager he was to welcome the latest scientific discoveries and inventions and to forecast their possible consequences. His paper on 'Sun-Spasms' is significant just now in view of the fact that the same phenomena were observable, when another great war was in progress.

His delight in ethnic, linguistic, and archæologic discovery is manifested in the papers on 'A New Pompeii,' 'Norodom the Last,' and 'Archæology in Cambodia'; while literary and artistic topics find treatment in 'Literary Demoralization,' 'French Journalism,' 'The Sexual Idea in French Literature,' Baudelaire's version of Poe, 'A Mad Romantic,' 'L'Arlésienne,' 'American Art Tastes,' 'Tinted Art,' and 'Artistic Value of Myopia.'

His interest in the story of the 'Mad Roman-

tic,' Gérard de Nerval, lasted until the very close
of his life. We find repeated references to him in
his letters in Japan to Basil Hall Chamberlain.
One such passage may be quoted:

'Gérard de Nerval's "Voyage en Orient" (two
volumes, Lévy, f.3.50) seems to me the most
wonderful thing of the kind ever done. You
know he went to Africa, married a Mussulman
wife, who naturally hated him (because he was
mad) and ran away from him. He wrote the marvelous "Legend of Solomon" and "Queen Balkis" for that history — the work which inspired
Meyerbeer. It would have been put upon the
operatic stage, but the conception proved like
one of John Martin's pictures — too supernatural in depth and breadth for any stage. He
translated "Faust" very beautifully. Besides
the voyage, you might like his "Filles du Feu,"
beautiful, sober, sad, ghostly sketches, betraying
the incipient madness that was at last to drive
him to suicide. Doré, I think, made a picture of
that suicide; but the police broke up the litho-
graph stone and suppressed the work. Anything
of De Nerval's would please you. There is a marvelous mediæval story by him — "La Main de
Gloire" — worth anything in the narrative part
of Hugo's "Notre Dame." But I cannot now
remember what book it was in.'

Very strong indeed would one expect the personal note to be in the paper on 'Myopia,' and

only a little less so in that on 'Colors and Emotions'; and yet he writes, as it happens, on these themes with his usual impartial philosophic interest in the general bearings of his subject on art and human development. There was never any pose about Lafcadio Hearn.

In conclusion, it gives me pleasure to state that of the Editorials selected from the *Times-Democrat* there are a number, previously listed as undoubtedly Hearn's, which were later found in a scrapbook kept for some time by his friend, Dr. Rudolph Matas, and there marked as known by him to be Hearn's.

CHARLES WOODWARD HUTSON

EDITORIALS

EDITORIALS

∴

POMPEII [1]

THE announcement that the eighteen hundredth anniversary of the destruction of Pompeii, Herculaneum, and the other cities buried by Vesuvius under the reign of Titus, is to be observed at Pompeii next year, sounds a little odd; for modern usage lends a certain sense of jubilation to the word 'celebrate'; and the destruction of four cities modeled by graceful Greek art, and embellished with the refinements of a most exquisite and charming civilization — cities in which every article of furniture was a work of art — may perhaps be more fitly commemorated than celebrated. But the event will probably be commemorated by antiquarians specially, if not altogether; and these have indeed reason to thank Vesuvius for having preserved to them so many delicate works of art, and so faithful a picture of the domestic life of the ancients.

The celebration or commemoration (as you prefer) will probably be fraught with important consequences to art and to science. The greatest archæologists of Europe will perhaps gather at

[1] *Item*, June 24, 1878.

Pompeii, and plan the publication of a far more
exhaustive and attractive work on the curiosities
of the resurrected city than has appeared either
in the English, French, Italian, or German languages. Since the appearance of Gell's 'Pom-
peiiana,' the works of Overbeck, the German
antiquarian, and those of the learned French
archæologists, a vast number of fresh and important discoveries have been made. The great
classic scholars have been busied with half-
cindered manuscripts found in the ruins; and
archæological painters like Alma-Tadema and
Coomans have drawn fresh inspiration from late
discoveries of vases and bronzes. An antiquarian
assembly at Pompeii will have plenty of scientific work to do, and artistic visitors much to
study on the twenty-fourth of August, 1879. It
is also probable that measures will be taken to
procure a large fund for defraying the expense of
a more rapid excavation. The work has been
carried on so lazily that at the present rate of
proceeding there would be no chance of complet-
ing the disinterment of Pompeii within the next
half-century.

Pompeii may yet enable the learned to unravel
many curious problems in antique sociology, and
to fill some lamentable gaps in ancient history
and ancient literature. It is not impossible that
the lost works of Pindar, Menander, Sappho, and
other Greek poets — of whom we only possess

fragments — might be recovered in the débris of some Pompeiian library; for Greek was a familiar tongue to the cultivated classes of that Græco-Latin city. It is possible the missing books of various Latin historians might be unearthed, together with some of those fifteen hundred no longer extant authors quoted so curiously by Athenæus. Already several musical manuscripts have been found; and it is possible that we might yet learn the very airs played at Roman triumphs and religious processions, and perhaps those softer Greek melodies for the double flute, to which the Gaditanian dancing women danced in their *Coæ vestæ.*

FANTASTIC POSSIBILITIES OF INVENTION [1]

PERHAPS the next great electrical invention — after the telephone, microphone, and teleoscophone have been fully perfected — may be the utilization of electricity as a weapon. Bulwer Lytton in his 'Coming Race' seems to have dreamed of such a thing when he described the distinctive powers of the mystic Vril. There have been some curious scientific prophecies uttered in Europe of late years, predicting the invention of electrical locomotives and electrical engines of war; and in this age, when nothing seems impossible, it is not very difficult to believe that the armies and navies of the world may substitute lightning for gunpowder in the course of the next century. Who could have believed twenty years ago that we should be able to photograph sound and also color; that portraits of persons and places could be transmitted by telegraph; that two telegraphic messages could be sent in opposite directions upon one wire at the same time; and that a machine would be invented capable of enabling the user to hear distinctly a conversation carried on at the distance of miles? It may indeed come to pass that we shall find the inven-

[1] *Item*, June 25, 1878.

tion of a flying machine possible, and of many other extraordinary things now deemed beyond the reach of human science. If it be true that every impression received through the medium of the senses creates a tiny record in the plastic substance of the brain, perhaps we may yet have a microscope powerful enough to enable us to read a brain like a book. We might have a telescope which would reveal to us the minutest details of life in other planets, and discover some method of communicating with the nations of worlds belonging to other solar systems. The great newspapers of this world might some day be receiving daily messages from Mars or Venus; and strange secrets from astral continents, yet unnamed in the languages of the earth. Perhaps we may in future years discover that the magicians and alchemists of old were actually hovering on the verge of discoveries reserved for happier generations — discoveries too awful and vast for vulgar publicity! And last, but not least — if it be indeed a fact that the elements composing human flesh and blood, would crystallize into a living and intelligent being, were it possible to commingle them in the same chemical proportions as they exist in man — why may we not dare to fancy that some future student of the protoplasmic basis of life, might prove a more successful creator than Frankenstein?

MIGRATIONS OF THE HUMAN RACE [1]

SHOULD science, at some far future day, enable us
to follow the course of history upon other inhabited worlds, it will be a matter of curious importance to learn whether there is not a secret
law of force compelling all intelligent life to flow
in a vast current from East to West, upon all
habitable spheres revolving in the same plane
from West to East. The existence of such a
mysterious law upon our own world has long been
made evident; and yet speculation is at fault as
to its causes, of which the effects alone invite and
satisfy investigation. There are ample ethnological reasons for believing that mankind has
more than once begirdled the earth in its eternal
migration toward the setting Sun — whether we
acknowledge the primitive unity of the human
race, or prefer to grant, with some thinkers, that
the great first families of mankind were indige-
nous to the continents which they claim for
birthplaces. Whatever may be argued in regard
to climatic influences upon physical and mental
characteristics; whatever may be said in favor of
the common brotherhood of Man; whatever may
be believed as to the origin of nations — as to the
great Cradle of Humanity being somewhere in

[1] *Item*, June 27, 1878.

the shadow of the Himalayas — there can be no
question as to the existence of a mighty gulf
stream in the sea of human life, forever flowing
from lands of Sunrise to lands of Sunset — vigorous at the temperate and feebler in the torrid
zone.

The migrations of the great Aryan family have
been clearly traced from ancient India to the
Mediterranean; the early domestic religion of the
Greek and Roman nations has established its
kinship with antique faiths still prevalent in the
peninsula of Hindoostan, and the rites preserved
in the Sacred Sanscrit books. The mystic caste-
laws of India seem to have found a home in
ancient Egypt, and there are strange similarities
of art, of creed, and of regulations respecting the
preservation of animal life in both Indian and
Egyptian civilizations. Peruvian and Mexican
antiquities suggest with strange force the theory
of emigration across two oceans; and there are
interesting indications of a double kinship to
Asiatic and African nations in the characteristics
of the Pacific islanders. Of the events producing
such results we know nothing, and probably
never shall know; our information regarding the
ebb and flow of civilizations and of emigrations
belongs to periods far more recent. We are only
able to discover traces of a circuitous course
about the earth which the nations have always
followed and still follow; and to observe a *double*

action in the course of migration — a steady
progression westwardly, and a peculiar law of
recoil evidenced after any rapid and extensive
conquest, when the stronger nations drive the
weaker backward toward the East, and expand
their dominion toward all points of the compass.
The distinctive peculiarity of Western conquest
by a civilized nation is permanency, while Eastern conquests have seldom changed the face of
the world's map.

Advancing from the heart of Asia, the Aryans
have built up all the civilizations of Europe, and,
passing on their victorious way, extended their
dominion in every direction. In intervals of centuries, something is gained East, and lost; something is won West, and stoutly preserved. North
and South the great tides of emigration have
swept over the broad ocean-barrier and the
double continent of the Americas; the Northern
races of Europe conquering the North continent,
and the Southern races the South. From the
Pacific coast the hungry commerce of civilization
is reaching out mightily toward the palm-groves
and coral reefs of Oceanica, the vast sheep-
pastures of Australia, the ivory and diamond
riches of India, the tropical wealth of Java and
Malabar, the curiosities of Japan, the fragrant
products of China, and the furs of Siberia and
Kamchatka. Westwardly, ever westwardly, the
great migrations must continue, until the Ameri-

can Aryans leap the barrier of the Pacific and plant a firmer foothold in the Celestial Empire than the Tartar Khans — in the Indian Empire than the English colonists. So that at last, that same Aryan people, who left the shadow of the Himalayas in prehistoric centuries — with their horn bows at their backs as in the dream of Alton Locke — half naked, half starved, altogether savage — may return to the Cradle of Nations, wielding the lightning of heaven's artillery for their weapon, to plant the arts and sciences upon the very soil that gave birth to their race.

THE QUESTION IN GERMANY [1]

GERMANY now finds herself in the position of
Frankenstein. She has created for her own fame
a monster which has indeed accomplished the object of its creation; but which has also accomplished other things of a far less satisfactory kind.
Her military system has made her mightier than
all the nations in capacity to destroy, but weaker
than most of them in capacity to produce. If her
soldiers are numerous as locusts, they are hardly
less of a plague upon her natural wealth. She
has sown her dragons' teeth; and the harvest
of armed men is a terrible one. The land groans
under its iron weight, and the soil has almost
ceased to produce its proper quota. The people
ask for wheat, and the blades of the crop are
steel; they ask for fruit, and the fruit is iron. If
they murmur an iron gag enforces silence; if they
rebel an iron heel crushes them into dust; and
under the rule of iron and blood the fields lie
barren and the workshops idle. The people cannot destroy the monster which created the empire, but the monster is slowly destroying itself.

The Government is actually in a dilemma. It
finds the country impoverished and daily growing weaker under the strain of supporting this
huge armament; and yet to dismember its bat-

[1] *Item*, July 9, 1878.

teries of destruction would result in emasculation of its international power, and favor the great French scheme of revenge. It finds at home a smouldering volcano of dissatisfaction threatening a small eruption. Certainly it has no direct fear of Socialism. A universal outbreak of Red Republicanism would be instantly annihilated by those cyclone storms of steel and lead which the rulers can control at will. The French Revolution was only possible, as M. Taine points out clearly, when the Government troops had been rendered worthless by starvation, paucity of numbers, and an utter absence of funds in the treasury to supply their wants. Directly the Government has nothing to fear from Socialism, except assassination, which few rulers are afraid of. But indirectly Socialism has certainly alarmed the Government. Its very existence teaches the unfortunate condition of native industry, and the magnitude of the dissatisfaction born of poverty. It is the mirror in which the heart-sore of the nation reflects itself. It is the magnet which attracts all the iron of misery that enters men's souls. It is the legitimate and inevitable consequence of commercial prostration in Germany. It is very widespread, very vigorous, very desperate, and might be very formidable, but for that terrific overseer and chastiser, the Army.

Now comes the second Frankenstein phase of

the tragedy. Suppose the necessity for a reduction of the military power becomes imperative, as it must do sooner or later, and the army is disbanded in part. The disbanded soldiers are mechanics, artisans, laborers. They find a terrible prostration of business barring their first efforts to obtain employment. They become gloomy, dissatisfied, desperate. They listen to Communistic harangues and join Communistic clubs. The spectre of Socialism may then soar its head to a threatening height when supported by myriads fresh from the training of war. Do they want weapons? weapons are easily obtained. Do they need leaders? Yes; there are leaders enough in Germany who are not aristocrats, but are nevertheless capable generals. The prospect is unpleasant.

There is but one to-be-hoped-for solution of such difficulties in the future; — namely, the invention of labor-saving engines of destruction, the substitution of machinery for millions of men in warfare. Bulwer Lytton represents the Vril-ya, when declaring war, as disdaining to send any more than half a dozen children against the enemy's country. One child is sufficient to destroy an army with its vril-rod. What civilization wants is a vril-rod — a lightning machine to fight with — an electric battery capable of wiping out an army at a distance of a hundred miles, or pulverizing a city like London with a random flash.

THE ASIATIC HORIZON [1]

THE mere fact that it has been proposed to convene a European congress for the purpose of engaging the Powers to bind themselves not to place the science of modern warfare in the hands of the Asiatics is ominous, and may be recorded by historians as dismally prophetic. It is true that the proposal comes from Gortchakoff, whose motives are not always above suspicion; and who may have simply desired to evoke a great bugbear against the threat of England to turn India against Russia. But the bugbear is a gigantic one, and has made its impression on the European powers. The Mongolians, observed Gortchakoff, are most to be dreaded; and it is not the first time that Europe has gazed with apprehension in the direction of China.

The day is past in which valor and physical strength and patriotic ardor may be relied upon for the preservation of liberties and civilizations. It is now rather a question of numbers and weapons. In point of numbers China could certainly create an army as large as the combined military strength of all Europe, and probably larger. At all events her resources in this matter would endure far longer. Nor are the Chinese in-

[1] *Item*, July 10, 1878.

ferior in passive courage to any people on the face of the earth. Their characters have been moulded by a certain materialistic philosophy to that point of fatalistic endurance which fear cannot affect, and which is a far more dangerous sentiment to fight against than even the hottest fanaticism. A Chinese army might suffer innumerable disasters and bloody checks; but if once set in motion toward a given point, it would continue to move thither while strength remained to it. Chinese forces sent against English and French troops have repeatedly allowed themselves to be slaughtered to a man rather than seek safety in retreat or submission, although unable to make any impression upon their better-armed enemies.

Whatever the proposed congress might determine upon if convened, it does not seem in the range of rational probability that their efforts could result in anything more than postponement of what is most dreaded — the possession of the best modern appliances of warfare by the Asiatics. No government has ever succeeded, so far as history teaches, in keeping secret a discovery which would have secured it preëminence in war. The Greek fire was sold to the Saracens. The secret of gunpowder was purchased by the Turks. When Mahomet II was preparing to possess himself of Constantinople, it was a Danish or Swedish engineer who taught him how to cast cannon capable of hurling enormous masses of rock to the

distance of a mile, and battering down the strongest walls. Hardly had the English colonists fairly
established themselves in New Zealand, when the
Maoris declared war with the rifle; and taught
the astonished Englishmen that no civilized science could erect a fort so impregnable as the
native *prah*. The deadly revolving rifle was
scarcely invented in America before it was in the
hands of the Indians.

The very advances of Russia to China, however, are calculated to do more toward arming
Asia against Europe than anything which England has done. Naturally isolated, jealous of foreign commerce, unwilling even to hold communi-
cation with 'barbarians,' the ancient empire of
China gave no thought to Europe. Europe burst
open her gates by force, compelled her recognition, and extorted the commerce which she is
now regretting. Russia again is pouring her military to the Chinese frontier, as though to teach
the Chinese how to acquire the art of civilized
warfare. The situation suggests curious possibilities in the remote future. Gortchakoff's present policy might not find favor with his suc-
cessors. England might fulfill her threat of arming India against Russia with the terrific result of
prompting Russia to arm China against England,
and precipitate a war so colossal as to stagger the
imagination. But it is not very probable that
mutual jealousy would so blind civilization to her

own danger. The old Roman policy of self-preservation would prompt Europe to paralyze and crush the East so as to render her impotent to destroy; but while humanity forbids that policy, the short-sighted and selfish ambition of commercial speculation is paving a highway to the West for the innumerable armies of Asia.

INSECT POLITICS [1]

A LEADING New York daily has a delightful editorial upon 'Communism among Ants.' That
ants have a civilization has been known for a long
time; and naturalists never weary of studying the
government of their little communities. They
have an architecture, less mathematically beautiful, perhaps, than that of the bees, but more
varied, and more wonderful. Their builders con-
struct subterranean cities wonderful as the labyrinths of Egypt according to Herodotus; palaces
as fragile and delicate as the residences of the
Oriental Caliphs, and military fortifications
worthy of French engineers. The African white
ant erects domed structures sometimes eight and
ten feet in height and even higher, with minarets
like those of a Turkish mosque, and so strongly
built as to bear the weight of a heavy man on
their summits. The red and black ants make
fierce war, advancing to the attack in columns
and companies. They go on slaving expeditions,
and capture myriads of aphidæ — the beautiful
green parasites which love the juicy geranium.
These they feed and milk like cattle. But latterly
the discovery has been made that their political
system is occasionally disturbed by socialistic

[1] *Item,* July 11, 1878.

agitators. Certain ants who hoard too much golden honey, or other wealth, are occasionally the victims of communistic riots. The poor and starving ants strike against the tyranny of capital, slay the millionaires, and distribute their hoards throughout the community. So that there are more things to be learned from the ant than Solomon ever dreamed of.

IS THE SEA SERPENT AN EEL? [1]

THE sea serpent is writhing through the papers again. This time he lifted his head thirty feet above the waves, stared at a passing ship with emerald-flaming eyes, and departed, making 'the deep to boil as a pot.'

During the last year there has been a notable decrease of skepticism in regard to the sea serpent, notwithstanding the enormous joke perpetrated in the Glasgow *Herald*, and various humbug stories with which the public were deceived. In fact the attention of several prominent scientists, like Professor Proctor, has been given to the subject during the last twelve months, and the result has been to encourage the faith of those who love all that is marvellous and terrible. People remembered that the sixteenth and seventeenth century stories of gigantic cuttlefish who could twine their hideous arms about the main mast of a galleon, had been regarded as laughable fables, until the testimony of nineteenth-century witnesses — who produced in evidence fragments of prodigious tentacles — had set the matter at rest.

The most startling theory in regard to the recent visions of the sea monster was, we believe,

[1] *Item*, July 13, 1878.

that of Professor Proctor. Some naval officers
swore to having seen through telescopes a huge
whale attacked by an enormous serpent, who
coiled himself about the whale and finally
dragged his prey into the green depths of the
ocean. From the description given, Proctor —
notwithstanding the story of a school of whales
flying in terror from the spectacle — held that
the officers were probably mistaken by reason of
the great distance, and that what they had actually seen was not a whale wrapped in the folds of
a prodigious serpent, but a surviving member of
the antediluvian family of plesiosauri — a creature with a body like a whale, a long and flexible
neck — not devoid of swanlike grace — and a
head like an alligator.

It seems to us, however, that the serpents
which have been occasionally seen lately may be
nothing more than giant eels; and it is not unreasonable to suppose that the bed of the ocean
may be peopled with a writhing family which
might boast among its members a few eels of prodigious age, vast and formidable as Doré's leviathan. (Doré, with poetic license, represented the
leviathan as something very like a monster eel.)
When it is remembered that the eel lives to an
incalculable age — that in comparative vitality
and strength it is superior to almost any other inhabitant of the deep — that it has few known
enemies to fear after having attained a certain

size — that it loves to dwell in deep-ocean slime and seldom visits the surface, our theory seems not altogether unreasonable. Alison in his history of Europe, mentions that during the French revolution, the bodies flung into the river at Nantes, were carried back by a spring-tide, when there came with them the monsters of the deep. Among them were eels fifty feet in length.

If eels fifty feet in length could come up a French river, into the heart, as it were, of civilization, surely we may be justified in supposing that the ocean-deeps contain eels vaster than the famous serpent of Regulus. It would seem, however, that if the sea serpent be a gigantic eel, there is little hope of ever capturing him. In addition to the improbability of his approaching the neighborhood of a vessel, the colossal weight and frightful strength of an eel — say one hundred feet long — would render his capture not only highly dangerous, but almost impossible. What weapon, indeed, could produce any appreciable effect upon the awful vitality of such a creature? 'Behold leviathan which I have made. . . . Canst thou bind him for thy handmaidens? Canst thou cajole him with soft words?'

POOR MUMMIES![1]

IT has been proposed to the Khedive of Egypt to utilize all the mummy bandages contained in the hypogea and mortuary pits for the manufacture of paper. What sum the Khedive has been offered for these rags is not specified; but the iconoclasm of the suggestion is rather shocking. Modern civilization pays little respect to the graves of the ancients; and in no manner could its skeptical tendencies be more strikingly evidenced. What three thousand years had preserved intact, what long dynasties of conquerors had respected — what art and science had admired and wondered at, modern utilitarianism coolly proposes to convert into paper! Neither Turk nor Arab, with all their fierce hatred of idolatry and the idolaters of old, would have dared to dream of such tomb-violation until Frankish speculators had corrupted them with golden bribes. Only the skepticism of the Frank could have permitted mummies to be used as fuel in the furnaces of steamboats on the Nile. What was lawful in research for the archæologist and the historian seems hardly justifiable in the lucre-seeking speculator. Among most nations of antiquity to violate the rest of the dead was held a

[1] *Item*, July 14, 1878.

crime; but the fear of ghosts never affects the commercial enterprise of the nineteenth century, and the consideration that mummy bandages would make excellent paper, is stronger than any other consideration on the subject. In rational argument the paper manufacturers have the best of it. 'What is the use of allowing so many thousand tons of good material to be wasted on the dead? Of what interest are the red and black hieroglyphics commemorating the virtues of people who died three thousand years ago? What is there in the hypogea that antiquaries have not already described, copied, translated, and commented upon? What has science to regret? And if she has aught to regret, what reason is there to suppose that our practical researches might not result in discovering many things yet unknown to her?' Such are the questions to which the papermaker might vainly demand an answer. And still one cannot suppress a feeling of regret at this intelligence. Those poor Egyptians loved their dead so well! and it seems cruel to undo the kind labor which endured for thirty centuries, and robbed death of a complete victory. For the more we learn of the ancient Egyptians, the greater our sympathy with their system of ethics and their domestic habits. What is more pathetic than the discovery in their tombs of children's toys — pretty little toys worthy to rival the Swiss playthings of the nineteenth century — queer little toys, which must have had a peculiar effect upon the plastic imagination of Coptic babies. Little wooden crocodiles with flexible tails and movable underjaws (for the Egyptians never entertained the foolish notion that the crocodile moves its upper jaw); little manikins and monkeys, which kicked out their arms and legs at the pulling of a string; beautiful little sparrowhawks with women's faces; little sphinxes and cows and dogs and cats; little bats and balls and spades and bows and arrows; and little houses inhabited by little wooden men and women. And civilization must violate the sleep of these kind-hearted old Egyptians, and steal their grave-shrouds to convert them into paper!

ROMANTICISM IN MUSIC [1]

ONE of the most interesting features of modern musical study is the attention being given to the music of savage or barbaric nations. Exceedingly curious are the researches of travelers in this regard; and the compilations of Chinese, Indian, Japanese, South Pacific, Persian, Arabic, Mongolian, African and Finnish melodies which they have succeeded in gleaning deserve considerable ethnological attention. There are striking peculiarities in the music of peoples widely separated by ocean or desert barriers which seem to suggest important theories on the subject of primitive migration, and which may ultimately elucidate divers problems in regard to the wanderings of nations. Some attention is being given to this curious subject in the United States, and a few extraordinary musical collections have been recently made by musical critics and professors. It is an odd fact, for example, that the few ancient Greek melodies which have come down to us, are cast in a minor key strikingly similar to that of the melodies of various peoples of the East — whence beyond all question the Greek race originally came; and were we lucky enough to possess a few more specimens of their music, a

[1] *Item*, July 20, 1878.

comparative study of the modern Indian and the old Hellenic melodies might throw additional light on questions now agitated by Sanscrit scholars.

Among the most devoted and successful musical students in America, Mr. H. Edward Krehbiel, whose connection with the Cincinnati *Gazette* has rendered that journal one of the leading critical authorities in the United States, may be mentioned as likely to win peculiar distinction in this very interesting study. He possesses a very extraordinary collection of the music of all ages and nations, and has discovered some remarkable coincidences of system in the melodies of various races, which he is studying from an ethnological standpoint. He recently astonished Cincinnati musical circles by giving a Chinese concert, in connection with an essay on the history and growth of Chinese music; and the concert was especially interesting from the fact that the musicians were Chinamen, and the instruments — of a most grotesque description — were of Chinese manufacture. Subsequently he delighted a similar audience by the production of a Chinese play, translated from the fantastic hieroglyphics of that people, introducing a remarkable selection of queer Mongolian airs and ditties. These dainty little exhibitions, conceived in the romantic spirit of true art, were necessarily not less instructive than entertaining, and point

out a means of teaching an appreciative public
some highly important facts in musical history
which they could hardly obtain in any other way.
Some of the musician's recent views on musical
research are worthy of close attention. 'I feel
well assured,' he says, 'that ere long a study of
national music will be made that must compel
attention from ethnologists. There is a vast field
in this direction, which yet remains virgin soil.
I might instance as a feature of the subject
especially marked, the absence of the fourth and
seventh tones in the scales of the Chinese, old
Irish, Scotch, and of various people in the islands
of the Pacific, — a fact of so much significance
that a thorough investigation of the subject seems
to me worthy the study of a lifetime. Music
needs a Max Müller.'

The same gentleman not long ago at a private
musical party submitted some remarkable facts
in regard to savage music, showing that the most
enchanting of the arts is not without curiosities of
horror, and a horror not without fascination. He
submitted in example, among other fantastic
oddities of music, a cannibal song of the Mar-
quesas Islanders written in quarter-tones, and
producing an effect indescribably weird and
hideous, by a long concatenation of sounds unknown to any civilized or semi-barbaric scale.
It would seem that the Oriental tradition of
mystic hymns, whose tones were fraught with

invisible magic, might be founded upon the actual effect of certain wild melodies upon the mind of a savage people. As Mr. Krehbiel expresses it, music certainly needs a Max Müller, who might throw some startling light upon such fables as that of Orpheus, or those of the enchanted horns of Scandinavian legends; and who might trace out the vast history of musical evolution through all its infinite ramifications. There is no department of history so rich in legend, in romance, in poetic tradition, as the history of music, and it is rather curious that no modern writer has yet undertaken a good compilation of the myths and curiosities of musical literature.

WERE THERE COMMUNISTS IN ANTIQUITY?[1]

THE correspondent of a Lacrosse Republican paper, who evinces considerable ignorance in regard to antique society, attempts to prove the existence of the tramp nuisance in the Greek Republics. He actually endeavors to represent the Helots as tramps, and speaks of the *thetes* class in Attica as going about the country, from farm to farm, 'working for their bread'; committing thefts, inciting riots, and doing all that the tramp does in modern America.

In Attica and the Ionian and Æolian cities, there was an inferior class known under the name of *thetes* or *pelates*. This class, however, so far from being what our would-be philosopher represents it to have been, corresponded to the class of clients attached to the Roman *gentes* in the early days of the Republic. They were attached to the lands and person of their masters, and without exactly being slaves, they occupied a yet lower position. Under the aristocratic régime, as De Coulanges observes, the *thetes* was 'imprisoned in some family which he could not leave; he was under the hand of the Eupatrid (or Greek patrician), who possessed the same character and authority as the Roman patron.'

[1] *Item*, August 23, 1878.

Any writer who claims the existence of the tramp in the age of Cleon at Athens, or Archidamus at Sparta, betrays ignorance of the whole system of antique society. In those days communism could not have existed, neither could tramps have been known. Each city has its special religion, its *poliad* divinities, its prytaneum or public temple and altar, with the sacred fires; its social system, similar indeed to those of other cities, yet isolated and apart from them. Religion forbade intimate intercourse between cities, marriages were even prohibited. The stranger was never permitted to enter a city not his own, except by attaching himself to some Eupatrid or patrician, as a client. In that capacity he could own no property, acquire no rights, and contract no obligations, except through the protection and mercy of his patron. He could not become a citizen, could not marry, and was not permitted to worship the gods of the city which he entered as a stranger. The antique faith sought no converts; on the contrary it abhorred the idea of admitting any to its worship save those privileged by birth and race. When intermarriage was permitted between the inhabitants of neighboring cities, it was only after a solemn ceremony had been performed, in which each city agreed to adopt and adore the gods of the other, and the consent of the divinities themselves to the union had to be confirmed by favorable omens and auguries. People did not tramp about in those days; to be compelled to leave one's native place — except as the founder of a colony — was considered equivalent to capital punishment.

The day finally came when the inferior classes obtained their freedom, but freedom for these signified little more than freedom would be to the Hindoo Sudra. They demanded the right of independence from servitude, of acquiring property, of worshiping the gods, of governing themselves, or taking some little part in the government, or of becoming qualified citizens.

These were the revolutions of the early Greek and Roman Republics, of the *thetes* or the *pelates*, of the *clients* by birth or adoption. The revolt of the Helots was the revolt of the slave class against its masters. When the Helots almost succeeded in a revolution, it was when the inferior Spartan classes joined them in an endeavor to break the iron yoke of the aristocracy. The Spartan revolutions were in no instances analogous to anything in modern history.

The revolutions at Athens were not in any sense comparable to the labor-disturbances of to-day. The movements led by Cleon were movements which demanded privileges and changes of government — not movements socialistic or communistic — not disturbances provoked by ignorant ruffians and aided by tramps!

There came at last a time in antiquity when war broke out between the rich and poor — between capitalists and laborers in many Greek cities; this was a later era, when the old forms of society had been changed. It might be termed the dawn of the Age of the Tyrants, the word Tyrant not originally signifying in itself anything more than the civil ruler of an antique city. Communism then appeared in riot and murder. The rich were killed or exiled; their lands and goods shared among the poor. At Megara every wealthy man in the city was exiled — a punishment which antique society rendered almost equal to death — and their goods confiscated. . . . At Samos two hundred wealthy citizens were killed, four hundred exiled, and their wealth distributed among the poor. At Syracuse the same thing occurred. So also at Messina.

At Miletus, the children of the rich men, who had fled the city, were taken by the rioters and trampled to death by trained oxen. Subsequently the rich party, prevailing after a savage contest, revenged itself by seizing the children of the poor, plastering their bodies with pitch, and burning them alive. Yet in those days the hatred of the poor classes against the rich was hardly greater than it is to-day. At that era the war between the rich and poor invariably terminated in loss of liberty for the former. The efforts of communism had only a temporary success, and their ultimate result was the establishment of a despotism at once merciless and all-powerful. A violent outbreak of communism in this republic might lead to a change in government which would leave the riotous classes everything to regret.

FAIR WOMEN AND DARK WOMEN [1]

THE *Picayune* of Sunday contained a pretty translation (by 'Q') of some Spanish fancies in regard to blondes and brunettes — discussing the character of the fair woman as compared with the dark woman, rather than the respective physical charms of the contrasting types. The author, himself a Spaniard, ventures at last to express his preference for the darker style of beauty, and his decision is commendably loyal, and well supported by the opinions of poets and of artists.

Yet how much remains to be said in favor of the fair woman! The Greeks, who were surely master-judges of beauty, made fair the limbs and the locks of their marble divinities; and even in these years women have maddened in the presence of an antique Apollo, because the old gods could not or would not repeat the miracle of Pygmalion and transform polished marble to palpitating flesh. Was not Venus called 'the Golden'? The artists of antiquity gilded her hair. The locks of Phœbus were bright and flamboyant, as became the lord of the Sun. Aurora was fair-tressed and pink-fleshed, and twelve of the Horæ were as —

'Daughters of Sunrise, shaped of fire and snow.'

[1] *Item*, August 25, 1878.

Most of the glorious old gods were represented with golden hair; and the dainty flesh tints given to their statues are supposed to have been tints of exceeding fairness. For the fair beauty surely comes nearest to our ideal of divinity — a loveliness typical of light and life and immortality — a comeliness as of golden summer and golden suns. We can imagine a seraph only with tresses of waving light and radiant limbs! and fancy most readily realizes the Angel in the blonde woman. We might picture Lilith as a brunette; but Eve we dare not think of save as the loveliest of blondes — a blonde as 'blonde as wheat' — blonde as Rowena or Elfrida.

Semiramis, Cleopatra, Faustina, Zenobia, Esther, Messalina, were brunettes; yet fairness seems to us more queenly than olivaceous darkness. Phryne and Rhodope were fair; but were not Laïs and Thaïs and Archianassa and many others brunettes? Laïs was a model for Apelles; but Phryne alone dared in her own person to personify Venus Anadyomene before all Eleusis.

Perhaps we feel more reverence for blonde beauty, not only because it seems a reflection of celestial loveliness, but because it bears with it the suggestion of force and will and strength and royalty. It is the beauty of the Druidess and of the Viking's daughter — the glory of the North, cold, fresh, strong, and immortal. It may be cold as the beauty of an ice crystal; but it has the supernatural radiance of auroral lights.

White beauty inspires awe, like the calm beauty of the gods. Dark beauty — save in the purest Oriental types — inspires only love. Men might pray, like Kingsley's Viking, that a fair-haired beauty would honor them by trampling upon them. But unless the darker beauty own the falcon eyes and delicate aquiline nose of Balkis, Queen of Sheba, 'perfect love casteth out fear.'

The beauty of the North seldom inspires affection unmixed with awe. It is the charm of the priestess of Freya — the charm of the sorceresses of Scandinavia. When Venus appeared to Anchises as a Greek maiden, he feared not to embrace her; but his knees smote together with fear when the goddess became divinely fair, and her dark curls 'kindled into sunny rings.' The beauty of the North is a witchery.

When gazing into black eyes, one finds depth and softness and sweetness; but the depth is vague and lost in shadows of mystery. You can penetrate only so far and no further into the soul. But the northern blue or gray eye is more mysterious and unfathomable in the deeps of its transparency. Beyond the cool surface of amethyst or night-blue shines a deep of deeps, illimitable as Space, interminable as Time. The dark eye intoxicates like Cyprian wine; but the gray eye, like hasheesh, makes giddy the soul, as though leaning over the verge of Eternity, beyond the fields of stars and the courses of the comets.

The poets have spoken but timidly of blonde beauty; they have spoken with enthusiasm of that comeliness which blends Moresque grace with Gothic strength, the beauty which is Spanish. They have sung much of the Orient, and the flowers of the seraglio, and the bayadères of Hindoostan. Perhaps they might have sung more of the fair woman, but that they are overawed by her as by the splendor of a Statue of Snow. Had Godiva been a brunette we might have known more about her.

All the most famous canticles of love have been devoted to the darker types of beauty — the ebon hair and velvet eye and olive tint of the brunette — that tender brown tint which suggests the color-tone of antique marbles, mellowed by time. The greatest of love songs is Solomon's song of the Sulamitess — or the song of songs; and the Sulamitess was a brunette. 'I am black but beautiful, O ye daughters of Jerusalem, as the tents of Kedar — or as the curtains of Solomon.'

It is the beauty of the eyes of the Sulamitess which is praised by Solomon, above all her other charms — more even than 'the stature like unto a palm-tree' — 'the neck like unto a tower of ivory' — or the little white teeth, 'like a flock of sheep which cometh up from the shearing, whereof every one beareth twins, and none is barren among them.' For the dark eye is the eye of love itself — surely the eyes of Eros were dark. It is the eye of the gazelle, the fawn, the dove. 'Thou art all fair, my beloved, thou art all fair; thou hast dove's eyes. . . .'

'O my dove that art in the clefts of the rock, in the secret hiding-places of the stairs, let me see thy face, let me hear thy voice, for sweet is thy voice, and thy countenance is comely'! . . .

'Eyes like the eyes of doves by the river's waters, washed with milk.' So sang Solomon, even before any one knew the additional enchantment of a dark eye shining beneath a mantilla or flashing from behind a fan.

And our Spanish gentleman's gallant preference for the dark eye is half shared by ourselves. Cold Athena had golden hair and gray eyes; but Venus may have had eyes of golden hazel under her bright hair — that liquid, limpid, languishing Southern hazel, which always demands love and always obtains it.

CRIMSON MADNESS [1]

THE question of Poe's character as conflictingly described by various biographers is coming up again, in connection with the publication of a letter in some London paper from a schoolmaster at Natal, South Africa, who happened to be usher at the English school where Poe studied, and which he made the scene of his 'William Wilson.' It was at this same school that Eugene Aram was usher, and was then arrested for the crime made ever memorable by Hood's poem and by Bulwer's novel. The letter of the schoolmaster throws no very special light on the subject; and the littérateurs are again bemoaning the lack of a competent and satisfactory biography of Poe. There is no doubt, however, that such a biography will sooner or later make its appearance — perhaps from a French hand, for the French imagination best comprehends that eccentric genius. The only really interesting and scholarly study of Poe in the English language, is, perhaps, the analytical criticism of his works made by Francis Gerry Fairfield some years ago, and contributed to Scribner's under the title 'A Mad Man of Letters.' Fairfield's theory is certainly the most

[1] *Item*, November 20, 1878.

rational and plausible, in explaining not only the origins of such nightmare fantasies as 'Eleanore,' 'Monos and Daimonos,' 'Ligeia,' 'Morella,' the 'Fall of the House of Usher,' the 'Masque of the Red Death,' but likewise in pointing a rational cause for the peculiar eccentricities of the author in the latter days of his unfortunate career. Fairfield discovers in the very peculiarities of that amazing imagination the approach of madness; — and considered in their chronological succession, the fantastic poems and stories of Poe certainly bordered more and more upon the verge of the insane as this author approached his end. Like the astounding creations of Martin, the wonderful painter, who also died insane, and whose genius in its breadth and depth surpassed even the greatest conceptions of Doré, Poe's pictures, analytically considered, could be evolved by no healthy imagination; and they terrify even as madness terrifies.

It occurs to us in this connection that there is one evidence of Poe's unhealthy state of mind, which has not been considered by any critic — not even Francis Gerry Fairfield. As Turner's passion for the effect of a vertical yellow streak in his paintings is considered indicative of a certain mental defect, so, it seems to us, does Poe's strange passion for the hue of crimson indicate a peculiar and abnormal condition of the imagination. The lurid hue colors the majority of his pictures; and the faces of his eidolons and spectral ladies are tinged with it. It stains and colors everything described in his wildest stories as though the visionary's retina were gorged with blood. Crimson fires illuminate the vast mediæval hall, where appears the apparition of the Red Death; and the windows are paned with crimson glass. In the Venetian fantasy, wherein glimmers whitely, like a beautiful ghost, the figure of the Marchioness Aphrodite, the chamber of the victim of the Assignation is lighted by crimson windows. In one sketch Poe describes his ideal of a perfectly proportioned and properly furnished room: well, the window panes are crimson, the carpet is crimson and gold, and crimson is the wall-paper. In the parable of 'Shadow' the epidemic is characterized by crimson symptoms. The hideous but splendid bridal-chamber, pictured in the wild and crazy tale of Ligeia, is not without crimson tints of color. When curtains are not black and goblin-like in their suggestive folds, they are crimson and gold, or at best purple. When windows are not colorless and leaden-hued, they are either crimson or 'red-litten.' The moon in the fable of 'Silence' is described as 'crimson in color.' It is also crimson in the last scene of the 'House of Usher.' The ceiling of the Palace of Hell in the 'Duc de L' Omelette' is frescoed with crimson clouds. The fiendish images on the glowing walls of the furnace-prison in the 'Pit and the Pendulum' are crimson.

These remarks of course refer only to the most peculiar class of Poe's stories and poems; for his earlier sketches, such as the 'Manuscript Found in a Bottle,' and the analytical stories of the 'Purloined Letter,' the 'Gold Bug,' and the 'Murders of the Rue Morgue' indicate a healthier state of mind.

SPRING FEVER FANCIES

TOGETHER with the languor and dreaminess begotten by the spring's fragrance and its tepid winds, there comes to many, year after year, in whatever climate or country, but especially perhaps in our own, that vague longing for other lands and strange places — that thirst for the solitude of unfamiliar lands, so romantically termed by Curtis the Camel-Spirit.

Imagination, in this age, has developed this strange feeling to a remarkable degree; and the most imaginative are those most cursed, or blessed, perhaps, by its influence.

Yet it may seem curious that at no other period of the year is the feeling so potent as at this time. It is not winter that inspires dreams of brighter and deeper skies, of whiter moons and larger stars, of sunsets more golden and winds more witchingly fragrant, of feathery-crested palms and strange poisonous flowers that slumber by day and open their pale hearts only to the tropical moon.

In winter the fancy seems at least restrained by the local boundaries of familiar places. It hibernates in a species of psychological torpor. The call of daily duty, the strong necessity for

[1] *Item*, March 16, 1879.

active exertion, the hope inspired by present success, occupy the mind with material images and numb the fancy. The stream of Romance is bound up also in the rime of frost, however shadowy the frost-crystals.

Then the spring comes with its burst of roses, its magical perfumes, its genial warmth; — faint mists float up, like phantom Icari vainly struggling toward the sun; — and all the long-pent-up vapors of fancy float upward with them. The heart feels heavy with a vague and mysterious sadness, the walls of the city seem constraining barriers, the wild clouds seem pregnant with omens, and the winds, pure as the heaven of amethyst, seem to bear the dreamer ghostly kisses from lands 'where it is always afternoon.'

It is a homesickness, yet without memories of home; a thirst for freedom, yet there is no sense of imprisonment; a sort of world-weariness too vague for physical analysis. It is as though one might wish to wander through blue deeps of eternity to reach a rosy paradise in some far-sparkling world. Ideas of preëxistence, wild theories of metempsychoses and avatars throng upon one at such times.

Of what is this strange sickness born? Have philosophers written of such things or are such things unknown to the arid reasoner though familiar to the heart of the poet?

Darwinism does not teach us yet whether some

remote and antediluvian relationship may be found between man and the bird; yet one is almost tempted to fancy that man's spring fever of unrest might have had its origin in the palpitation of a bird's heart. The spring cometh; and the voice of the turtle is heard in the land. The wild birds fly north in the spring; southward in the autumn; happier than we, they may fearlessly gratify the Unspeakable Unrest.

Perhaps our Aryan ancestors, wandering in ages dimly prehistoric — traversing strange lands with their horn-bows at their backs — seeking softer climes and richer lands, may have bequeathed to us from forgotten years this feverish unrest of spring, this vague and undefinable longing for far-away lands.

DESERT OR SEA [1]

AFTER lying dormant for nearly ten years, the vast project of Mr. de Lesseps to convert the Sahara into an inland sea is again revived and discussed from a scientific standpoint of startling interest.

The great engineer has already plainly shown that the work can be accomplished. The cost is estimated at only 60,000,000 of dollars — a trifling amount when the enormity of the result is considered. At present the consequences of this prodigious change in African geography are exciting intense interest.

The Sahara converted into a sea would offer a water surface of some 20,000,000 of square miles, with a mean depth of 500 feet. The oases — at present highly elevated above the sandy level — would resume their ancient rôle of palm-crowned islands, made fertile by clear springs of sweet water.

There is no reasonable doubt that this huge desert was once a sea; but history gives no record of that era. Egyptian, Macedonian, Roman armies have striven against the desert storms in vain; kingly expeditions have been swallowed up by pillars of sand which advanced against them,

[1] *Item*, June 29, 1879.

terrible and mysterious as the genii of Arabian story-tellers; and hosts of pilgrims have whitened the waste with their bones. Ere the great civilization of Egypt commenced to write its chronicles of granite, the Desert already extended its ribbed and tawny pall to the edge of the solid land.

To convert this ocean of sand into an ocean of waters, would be a greater work than Egypt ever dreamed of — a mightier task than ever the ancient architects of India, who converted mountains of basalt into monolithic temples, ever conceived. The whole earth would feel the shock of such a deed, as though lifted at last by the lever which Archimedes longed for.

It has been estimated that the waters of all the oceans would sink appreciably. The rainless climate of Egypt would be changed; the furnace heat of Morocco cooled; the whole temperature of Europe affected.

As to the character of the climatic change there is a vast difference of opinion. De Lesseps and his followers claim that the effect would be beneficial to all Europe. His opponents hold that the north of Europe would suddenly find itself enveloped in an atmosphere of icy coolness; and that the Arctic circle, enlarging, would overlap the present temperate zone.

Such theories could hardly interfere, however, with the accomplishment of a work advocated by some of the greatest physicists of the century. The construction of the interoceanic canal was opposed as likely to result in turning the waters of the Gulf stream into the Pacific, and revolutionizing the climate of Europe. Yet the canal will be commenced in 1880.

A more terrible theory is that advanced by a New York engineer, who, writing to the *Sun*, declares that the transfer of so enormous a body of water as that necessary to fill the Sahara, would throw the world off its balance, and perhaps precipitate the Crack of Doom.

It might be equally well argued that the result would have a directly opposite effect — lightening the poles, and adding weight to the center of the globe; and thus delaying that change of axis which is predicted as certain to produce another era of cataclysm — a new glacial period and an age of deluge, in which the sea will devour the land, and the ice grind the mountain chains to powder.

But there are strong reasons to believe that the change would affect the duration of day and night, by accelerating the rotation of the earth.

It has been clearly shown that the works of the ancient Egyptians and Romans, together with the vast cities constructed by modern civilization, have actually increased the length of day. The building of the Pyramids delayed the rising of the sun.

Such constructions produce the same effect upon the earth as that produced upon a wheel by lightening the axis and adding the weight removed to the periphery. Rotation is retarded. The trillions of tons of matter removed from the entrails of the earth and placed upon the surface by man's hand alone has slackened the course of our world in its circling about the sun.

And would not a work of engineering, capable of decreasing by twenty-four inches the depth of water in all the ocean-beds of the globe, more than counteract the previous effect of the works of man — removing a vast weight from the surface nearer to the center? It is not improbable that the sun would rise earlier upon the flooded desert; and the seasons, and the fruits of the seasons, be strangely changed by a work vast enough to be observed even by the inhabitants of other worlds.

THE SECRETS OF THE INFINITE [1]

AN able writer in the *Bee* introduces an article in yesterday's issue of that paper with a startling comparison of the methods by which science seeks to discover secrets which at each new success seem further off than ever. This comparison between the labors of the astronomer and of the microscopist suggests fancies upon which our eloquent contemporary does not dwell, but which are well worthy of deep consideration. The scientists of to-day seem strangely like those neophytes of Egypt who sought to lift the veil of Isis. At each new discovery we seem about to seize the great secret; yet are soon startled to find that but one fold of the awful veil has been raised, and that the tissue beneath is more impenetrable than that already drawn aside. Each time a new fold is lifted with feelings half of terror, half of triumph, the Infinite mocks us with its interminable Enigma more fearfully than before. The astronomer vainly analyzes the cloudy nebulæ, which at first seemed but flakes of pale foam floating in the shoreless ocean of Eternity — vainly does he resolve them into systems of triple suns and galaxies of burning stars; beyond, in the Heaven of Heavens, in the im-

[1] *Item*, August 15, 1879.

mensity of everlasting Night, gleam other uni-
verses and other wandering worlds. The vaster
becomes the scope of human vision the vaster
and deeper the problems which defy its power;
the Infinite unfolding itself infinitely terrifies the
feeble human will which vainly seeks to comprehend it. Man may sweep the heavens with vision
strengthened by artificial cunning beyond aught
that the children of this generation may dream
of; but worlds shall be dissolved in flame and
suns fade out in darkness and new systems of
circling stars be born, and comets yet unborn
pursue their solitary course through centillions of
years, and the Infinite will keep its most awful
secret forever.

And yet it might have seemed that within the
narrow circle of self-existence the researches of
man in pursuit of the secrets of Nature should
prove more hopeful. Yet not so. Nature retains
her secret under the glowing eye of the solar
microscope with its magnifying power of some
hundred thousand diameters, not less securely
than beneath the naked eye of man. Again and
again the wise have fancied in their wild pursuit
of the unknown, that the secret of Life was
almost within human grasp. They fancied it
might be weighed and measured; for even a beam
of light had been weighed, and the spectroscope
had taught men to analyze the substance of other
worlds. The physical basis of life was discovered

and called protoplasm; but the secret law which formed that basis and crystallized unintelligent material into intelligent brain remained invisible as ever. Electricity might indeed be caught and imprisoned; but that Something which is subtler and mightier than lightning mocked at wise theory and eluded the grasp of chemistry and remained invisible beneath the microscope. A new school of bold and learned thinkers declared that the result of their researches had taught them that a human body is built by an infinite host of tiny beings, even as the rosy coral is formed in the bosom of the sea. Each complex organism was but a vast crystallization of innumerable simpler organisms; and human pleasure or pain represented the pleasure or pain not of one body, but of centillions of tiny bodies which composed it. Yet the mystery is even greater than before to those that accept the new dogma; who can explain the nature of the mysterious laws which rule the invisible builders of a human body, while we remain unable to discover even the secret rule by which the architect-bee constructs its many-chambered storehouse of honey? And who shall dare to say that should we discover the law which governs these living crystallizations of complex organisms that we shall have discovered all? — will that knowledge have taught us the deeper-lying laws which create the simpler organisms that build up all temples of life? Will the last folds of the Veil have been lifted; or, if lifted by some daring hand, may not the Vision of the Secret alone strike dead the neophyte who shall have penetrated into the Holy of Holies, even as that Egyptian who lifted the last awful veil of Isis, and seeking to behold the face of the Goddess, looked into the eyeless sockets of Death?

THE ONEIDA COMMUNITY'S ANNOUNCEMENT[1]

ONE of the most extraordinary events in the religious history of the century is the public abandonment a few days ago by the Oneida community of its peculiar practices. The aged president and founder of that community, the venerable Noyes, has issued a circular stating that in consequence of the violence of public sentiment against the practice of complex marriages and 'stirpiculture,' it would be abandoned; the communists, nevertheless, preserving their peculiar beliefs as to the moral nature of those peculiar sex-relations which they advocate. The children are still to be brought up in common, under a simple and healthy régime which brings to mind the old Spartan educational system; but the practice of monogamy is to be established in place of the system of stirpiculture formerly in vogue. Whether the branch communities will follow the example of the mother institution we are not as yet informed; but there can hardly be any doubt of it. It may be remembered that the efforts of the New York clergymen last spring to destroy the Oneida community, first evoked the hostile public sentiment referred to by the Apostle of Stirpiculture.

[1] *Item*, September 3, 1879.

Seldom indeed has it happened in the history
of religions that a society of believers in any
doctrine, however extraordinary, have voluntarily abandoned practices which they considered
divinely inspired. For the maintenance of religious independence, and liberty to act according to religious convictions, almost all faiths
have made their blood-offerings — pagans, early
Christians, Arians, Gnostics, Lutherans, Cal-
vinists, Jews, Mohammedans, Quakers — even
Mormons. The Oneida people have never been
persecuted. The denunciations of the New York
preachers did them no real harm. Their agricultural and other products were gladly purchased in Eastern markets where religious ideas
do not at all affect the demand for comestibles.
There was no existing law which could apply to
their peculiar practices, as the *Item* pointed out
upon a former occasion. There was no danger of
a crusade against them; and they were safe from
violence of any kind. They had also the sympathy of an intelligent class, who considered
the community and its practices from a purely
philosophical standpoint; and who, judging by
results instead of theories, found that the results
were by no means shocking. Not a single woman
in the community had died in childbirth or had
suffered from puerperal fever; not a single child
had been born which was not strong, healthy,
intelligent, and physically perfect. The worst

enemies of the Oneida Society could not deny the fact that, from a purely physical point of view, 'stirpiculture' was a fair success. It has been shown by the Oneida community that human beings may be subjected to the regulations of 'stock-breeding,' and produce 'thoroughbreds' under the same conditions.

It had been predicted repeatedly that the community would probably perish with the death of its founder; and several New York dailies, commenting upon the sensational war being waged upon the society by sensational preachers, openly declared that it was useless to attack conditions which must eventually destroy themselves, and which would only gain strength from persecution. The Oneida folk cannot have dreaded ordinary persecution; but it is possible that they beheld in the horizon of the future a vision of special laws forced through Congress for the purpose of annihilating 'stirpiculture.' At all events they have openly agreed to abandon the complex-marriage system so hotly denounced by the Eastern preachers.

. It may be asked whether this announcement, which effectually places the community beyond the reach of law or denunciation, is sincere — whether there may not lurk beneath this outward submission a secret purpose to continue 'stirpiculture' and other peculiar regulations of Oneida life. For it is certainly strange that those who believe a practice to be commanded by divine law, should abandon it, against precedent, because of an antagonistic public sentiment. It would be difficult to answer such questions definitely. But it may at least be remarked that whatever has hitherto been done by the society has been done in the frankest and most open manner possible. Nothing has been concealed from the public eye. A daily record has even been published in the little paper issued by the society of the most trivial events; and the doctrines of Noyes have been scattered broadcast throughout the land in book and pamphlet. It is probable that the recent circular has been sincere; but granting this fact, the destruction of the community is imminent.

Such a society could only have been held together by a religious idea, and a severe discipline; and it is hardly necessary to observe that all 'free-love' and 'free-thought' communities which affected to be controlled only by principles of philosophy fell to pieces within a few months after their establishment. If the practices of the Oneida 'religion' are abandoned because of public sentiment, there is no doubt that the religious idea itself will rapidly weaken, and the whole system crumble to pieces. A division of property will take place; the communists, dividing into families, will insist upon the right to educate their own children; and the great farming association will break up into little properties. The Oneida interpretation of Saint Paul's teachings will be preserved for years among these families and their descendants; but how long or under what modifications it is not for us to say. Neither can we predict what effect in after years such doctrines may not have upon other forms of belief which seem even now about to lose their integrity.

No religion has ever existed without a purpose; nor has there ever been a faith among men wholly unproductive of good. Whatever be the lot of the Oneida community, it has had a mission to fulfil, and a lesson to teach. It has clearly shown the good results consequent upon the observance of certain natural laws; and however unnatural or immoral have been some of its doctrines, the time may come when future lawgivers, sifting the good from the evil, shall so remodel our marriage laws, as to provide against the entrance into the world of children physically diseased or morally deformed.

THE DEVIL'S CATHEDRAL [1]

THE cathedral of Cologne, which is beyond all question the most magnificent specimen of Gothic architecture in the world, will be completed in a few months. It was begun in the middle ages, the foundation stone having been laid no less than six hundred and thirty-two years ago; and perhaps the most curious fact in its history is that the architect who designed it is unknown. His plans remain intact and will be followed out in the most minute details; but his name has been lost forever. A legend tells us that the Devil had something to do with the building of the cathedral. The forgotten architect was ambitious, according to tradition, of becoming the most famous temple-builder in the world. He desired to create an edifice which should surpass even all that Solomon realized. Visions of architecture more wonderful than the work of Genii nightly grew before him; but the ideas vanished with the dawn, and the airy creations of the night refused to realize into tangible form by day. Repeatedly the vision returned; and, awakening, the artist instantly sought to memorize the vast details upon paper. Under his pencil the fancy partly grew into form;

[1] *Item,* October 4, 1879.

columns and architraves, groins and buttresses, a forest of spires, and towers richly floriated, up-springing to pierce the clouds. But even as a paleontologist may vainly seek betimes to reconstruct some antediluvian monster from an imperfect skeleton, so the architect found himself vainly striving to complete the mighty design from the shadowy memories of the night. The plan seemed too huge for human realization — too large for the field of mental vision, like a disproportionate object in the field of a microscope. He could perceive distinctly the lower portion of the façade, and imperial arches soaring above the mighty columns within; but the towers soared up beyond his reach and lost themselves in darkness unfathomable. One day, a tall and swarthy stranger, whose eyes owned a strange light and whose brows seemed knit with ever-lasting pain, showed to the unhappy artist a complete plan — *his* plan, the dream realized by an infernal pencil. The artist became the victim of the Tempter, and that he might gain the precious design, signed a parchment with his blood. But years after, repenting, with the aid of a ghostly father he obtained the pardon of heaven as he lay on the bed of death. Again the dark and awful stranger stood before him. 'Thou hast well defrauded me,' he cried in a voice of thunder, 'but thou shalt not reap the benefit of thy crime. Thy name shall pass away forever, thy tomb shall remain unknown, and thy vain dreams shall never be accomplished. Unfinished as in thy vision, the building shall remain; nor ever shall the hand of man complete the work upon which my curse shall remain through the centuries.'

The architect passed away to an unknown grave; and the great work went on. Begun in 1247, the choir was completed and consecrated only in 1322; but two hundred years rolled slowly by before the north and south aisles were carried up to their full height, and roofed over with mighty beaming. And then there came a silence of three hundred years more. Generations upon generations of myriad workmen had toiled for centuries, in order to carry the building up to that point at which the artist had first dreamed of it — a maddening enigma of magnificent incompleteness. And for three hundred years the dark curse lay upon the unfinished towers and the great transept.

It was long believed that a terrible fate would befall the being who might dare attempt to complete the work; and the people of Cologne had built houses in the space between the choir and the unfinished towers — according to a writer in the New York *Times*—and nobody believed the cathedral could ever be completed. The powers of hell would pull down scaffoldings and dash workmen from the carven precipices of the towers! But in 1830 people became less super-

stitious than they had been in 1509; and in spite
of the devil an immense system of private subscription was set on foot with branches in all
European countries for the purpose of carrying
out the plan. The original designs have been
carefully followed out. We learn from the New
York *Times* that in 1848 the naves, aisles, and
transept were consecrated; and in 1863 the whole
structure was thrown open to the world. But
there was still an immense amount of ornamental
as well as colossal work to do. Now at last the
thousands of little pinnacles and the floriated
ornamentation on the outside of the main building have grown into shape; and before very many
weeks the great tower will have attained the
height (511 feet) and ultimate shape originally
designed, according to tradition, by the Architect of Pandemonium. Certainly the design is
worthy of a superhuman origin in its superlative
beauty. But perhaps the Powers of Darkness
may possibly even yet attempt a last effort to
prevent the completion of Cologne Cathedral,
unless their attention be wholly absorbed by
the condition of Louisiana politics during the
interim — which is not unlikely.

A FRENCH TRANSLATION OF
EDGAR POE [1]

SOME researches among the books on exhibition at an Exchange Alley antiquarian store inspired us with the idea of writing some hasty notes upon a well-known French translation of Poe.

Poe was a writer who understood the color-power of words and the most delicate subtleties of language as very few English or American writers have ever done; and much of the startling effect produced by his stories is due to a skillful use of words which have no equivalent in French. To translate Macaulay or Gibbon or Addison into French, preserving the spirit of the original, were much easier than to translate such a writer as Poe, who perhaps never had a superior in that literary mosaic-work which depends for success wholly upon a knowledge of the intrinsic properties of words in their effect upon the imagination. Writers like Macaulay or Gibbon, who founded their pure and resonant style upon Greek and Roman models, may be successfully treated by scholarly French writers who have studied the same antique masters; but an author who forms a style entirely original and peculiar, like that of Poe, for the purpose of artistically transferring

[1] *Item*, October 22, 1879.

the most fantastic ideas to paper, presents amazing difficulties to a French translator. Yet in
Baudelaire Poe really found a certain reflection
of himself — the same wild dreams, the same
strange despair, the same madness of melancholy, the same idiosyncracies of style marked
the literary character of both writers. We doubt
whether any other French author could have
succeeded in rendering Poe with one half the
success of Baudelaire. Yet no really capable
critic who compares the English of the Tales
with the French version can deny that they have
lost a great part of their literary value through the
process of transmutation. In order to show how
this may occur we choose at random a few examples of the Baudelaire translation, which will explain also some of the difficulties the translator
had to contend with.

It may be remembered that the word 'ghastly,'
which has no true French equivalent, was a
favorite one with Poe — who never abused it,
or availed himself of it ineffectively. It gives a
wild and strong tone to many of his sentences.
Baudelaire has frequently been obliged to grapple
with the dissyllable, and his attempts to render
it are very curious. The most successful one, we
think, is in his translation of 'Silence: A Fragment,' of which the English text, we believe, runs
as follows:

'On either side of the river's oozy bed . . .

extends a pale desert of gigantic water-lilies.
They sigh one unto the other in that solitude,
and stretch to heaven their *long and ghastly necks*,
and nod to and fro their everlasting heads; and
there is an indistinct murmur which cometh out
from among them, like the rushing of subterrene
water. And they sigh one unto the other.'

Here we find in the French edition the words
above italicized rendered by 'leurs longs cous
de spectres' (their long and spectral necks) a
powerful translation indeed, which almost pre-
serves the effect of the original. But further on
we have another treatment of the same word by
no means so successful:

'And the rock was gray and *ghastly* and tall,
— and the rock was gray.'

'Et le rocher était grisâtre, et *sinistre*, et très-
haut, — et le rocher était grisâtre.'

The word 'sinister' certainly does not give
the effect of 'ghastly'; but it comes as nearly to
it as the French is capable of. This word in
English has a very different effect when applied
to the water-lilies, and when applied to the rock;
and the translator has shown excellent judgment
in using another term in his own tongue to express it. 'Très-haut' means simply 'very high';
but Poe does not say the rock was very high;
he fancied it as a grim and fantastic object with
a suggestion of some goblin form in its outline —
it was 'gray and ghastly and tall'; but it was

not 'very high,' and here the translator has not succeeded well. Moreover, the alliterative force of the words is considerably weakened, though not destroyed as in the translation of the line— 'And the rock rocked to its foundation,'—which is feebly rendered by 'vacillait sur ses fonde-ments,'—as there is no French equivalent for that mighty northern verb 'to rock.'

Another word which Poe well knew how to use is 'hideous.' It is put to good effect in the closing sentence of 'The Telltale Heart':

'Villains, dissemble no longer—I confess all, —tear up the planks,—it is there, there,—it is the beating of his *hideous* heart.'

We find it hard to understand why the translator should have translated 'hideous heart' by 'affreux cœur,' instead of 'cœur hideux,' as the French equivalent is much stronger than the word actually used. Curiously enough, in the translation of the celebrated poem in 'The Fall of the House of Usher,' the word is preserved by the translator with good effect. The verse reads, if we recollect aright, as follows:

> 'And travelers now within that valley
> 　Through the red-litten windows see
> Vast forms that move fantastically
> 　To a discordant melody;
> While, like a rapid GHASTLY river,
> 　Through the pale door
> A HIDEOUS throng rush out forever,
> 　And laugh,—but smile no more.'

Here we have the words 'hideous throng' rendered 'hideuse multitude'; and the force of the original horror is preserved. But the word 'ghastly' has again given the translator trouble. This time he translates it by 'lugubre,' which is really very bad, and entirely unnecessary, as Baudelaire had the good taste to translate the poem literally instead of attempting to versify it. Let us give one more example from the Parable of 'Shadow':

'And the Shadow answered: "I am SHADOW; and my dwelling place is near the Catacombs of Ptolemais, and hard by those dim plains of Helusion which border on the foul Charonian Canal."

'And then did we, the Seven, start from our seats in horror, shuddering and aghast; for the tones of the voice of the Shadow were not the tones of any one being, but of a multitude of beings; and varying in their cadences from syllable to syllable, fell duskily upon our ears in the well-remembered and familiar accents of many thousands of departed friends!'

This fantasy was certainly a difficult thing to translate; but we should have expected from Baudelaire a better comprehension of the original idea than is evidenced by his version of it. Poe expressly refrained from using familiar terms expressive of familiar ideas in this fantasmagory. He did not say 'the canal of Charon,' as the translator makes him say, because that term would have evoked a familiar mythologic idea, and Poe sought after vagueness and the horror of vagueness. 'And hard by those dim plains of Helusion which border upon the foul Charonian Canal.' What could be more mysterious than the awful answer of the Shadow? But the translator says nothing of the 'dim plains of Helusion,' but plainly renders the sentence by 'ces sombres plaines infernales,' etc. The whole power of the phrase is completely destroyed. Further on, the word 'duskily,' so admirably used by Poe, is translated by 'confusément' — and this translation could hardly be improved; but the insertion of the words 'en imitant' in the last line of the story falls unpleasantly upon an English ear. Poe does not say that the tones of the voice *imitated* those of the dead; but implies in a very weird manner that they actually *were* those of the dead. The translator, not quite comprehending Poe, translates the last line in a way which would be equivalent to the following in English:

'... fell confusedly upon our ears, *imitating* (or mocking) the well remembered and familiar accents,' etc.

No doubt Baudelaire uses 'imiter' to convey the sense of a weird mockery or mimicry, which is a powerful fancy; but in attempting to supply this interpretation to the mysterious narrative he has exceeded the duties of a translator, and greatly weakened the power of the original fantasy.

We might quote many curious examples like the above from the work alluded to; but space forbids.

AMERICAN MAGAZINES [1]

WALT WHITMAN, being interviewed on literary matters some time ago, stated that 'there is a great underlying stratum of young men and women in America, who cannot speak, because the magazines are in the hands of old fogies like Holland or fops like Howells' — an observation which contains no little truth. There are not many magazines in the United States; and those that are successfully established and possess real influence are conducted with a rather narrow policy. Only a limited number of subjects are permitted to contributors. One magazine excludes any matter of a historical character. Another excludes antiquarianism in any shape. Others are entirely in the hands of literary rings or cliques — composed indeed of good writers, but rings for all that. *Harper's* is really better conducted in some respects than any other, articles being paid for as soon as accepted, and manuscripts examined no matter from whom they come. But *Harper's Magazine* is necessarily conducted in a lighter vein than what we should expect from a purely literary periodical. It owes its successful popularity to the fact that it is not purely literary, but largely

[1] *Item*, October 27, 1879.

instructive and historical. But there is no magazine in the country now to compare with the *Atlantic* of twenty years ago, when everything of real merit was gladly received from casual contributors. Its brilliancy at that period was really matchless. Latterly it has become a second-rate publication. To keep a periodical at the pitch of first class merit, it must be constantly refreshed with material from new contributors. As the literary medium of a small clique of writers it can never sustain itself above mediocrity; for the cleverest men will write heavily or uninterestingly at times, and the most imaginative minds weary of graceful invention. Perhaps it is rather a misfortune that such high prices are paid for magazine articles — as this enables a few men to live upon a periodical, and creates a system of literary office-holding which needs reformation. At all events, we know that the *Atlantic* was far superior in the days when the prices paid for contributions were far smaller, and that certain English magazines of remarkable merit pay very small prices. It were better, too, that noted authors should not be induced to seek pay from magazines, as it withdraws them from far more important fields of labor. It is the fire of youth, the first strong soaring of young imaginations, the first warmth of literary aspiration, which should nourish our magazines. For there is certainly a period in life in which young men can create such little glowing works of art as they could not in later years — when the style, indeed, becomes more correct, more precise, more polished, but when the heart has grown colder, and the beauty of things natural no longer excites that charming enthusiasm which, although never forgotten, in a maturer age can never be revived.

SELF-SUPPORTING WIVES [1]

'I THANK thee, O God, that I was not born a woman,' is said to be, or to have been part of an orthodox Jewish prayer; and after all the old-fashioned Jew had something to thank God for, when we consider the comparative dependence of the weaker sex upon the stronger in times past. The older the world grows, however, the larger the liberty allowed to women, and the more independent their existence. Indeed, if we except the trials of motherhood the women of the nineteenth century have really about as little suffering as men and perhaps almost as much pleasure in life. One sign of the times may be found in the discussion now being carried on through the columns of some prominent Western journals as to how wives might be made self-supporting. A certain correspondent declares that the present condition of affairs renders the keeping a wife quite a luxury, and is filling the country with old maids; — that the American girl tells her lover, 'You must house me luxuriously, clothe me magnificently, support me in absolute idleness, furnish me with all the money I may need, give me liberty to do as I please; and perhaps, then, I may consent to live with

[1] *Item*, November 17, 1879.

you.' This individual seems to have been soured against womankind by the misfortune of having an extravagant wife. Another retorts that the writer of such sentiments must be selfish, mean, and miserable; that it is the duty of every honest and honorable man to support his wife without permitting her to work for others; and that the man who does otherwise does not deserve to have a wife at all. Both of these gentlemen are certainly wrong. It would be of the greatest possible advantage to public morality, industry, and social happiness, if women could be taught to support themselves and allowed every opportunity of so doing — if, in educating girls, they could be taught something more solid and utilitarian than what they are taught to-day — and if all the trades and professions could be persuaded to accept members of the fairer sex into their ranks. Not that a wealthy or well-to-do man should require or even permit his wife to work for others; but that a woman, whatever her circumstances, need not feel helplessly dependent upon some drunken or immoral person to whom she has the misfortune to be united. It is not a question of economy, but a question of morality and public well-being. There would be much less ill-treatment of women were the brutes who are guilty of it convinced that their wives were not dependent upon them for support. And the American workman, whose

wages are gradually sinking to a European level,
and who finds it harder and harder to support a
family as the years pass by, might certainly feel
encouraged were he assured that his wife could
be a material aid to him in making a living for
the little ones instead of being perfectly dependent upon him. In France the condition of
women is certainly happier than in Germany,
England, or America. A bright, quick girl generally knows a trade, and knows it thoroughly,
and can earn good wages at it — especially if she
be a Parisian. When she is married to some
mechanic or tradesman, she does not cease to
work. Both unite their earnings; and if sobriety
and good sense exist in the household, they can
in time economize enough to start a little business of their own. That is the ambition of the
poor in Paris and all the principal cities of the
republic. Moreover, the French workman —
unless he be vicious — does not treat his wife as
an inferior being. In fact, as she is generally
quite as good a worker as himself he has nothing
to pride himself upon. He does not tell her that
it is her duty to stay at home and take care of
the children. He is not ashamed to be seen on
the street with her. . . . On the contrary, she
accompanies him wherever he goes, and as a
rule she looks well and is always dressed with
taste even if her whole attire costs only a few
francs. She is regarded by her husband as some-

thing more than a wife—she is a comrade, a companion, a trusted friend who is to be consulted about all his little troubles or hopes or aims. If they cannot get along together, she is not afraid of being thrown on her own resources, or of being unable to provide for her children. On the whole it may be said that the Frenchwoman is the most independent and the most able to care for herself in the world, just as she has earned the reputation of being the neatest and the most pleasing in her manners. This is largely the result of necessity; for were women in Paris as dependent upon men as they are in New York, Paris could not support its population. Republics first gave woman her rights in society; and with the growth of republican institutions the social condition of the fairer sex will probably improve. Perhaps the day may come in our own republic when the American woman may have good reason to remodel the old Jewish prayer, and to exclaim, 'I thank thee, O God, that I was not born a man!'

PENITENTIARIES AND PUNISHMENTS [1]

THE revelations resulting from investigations made into the condition of various public correctional establishments and penitentiaries in the United States have called forth much comment from the press in regard to the philosophy of punishment. It has been generally conceded that punishment as defined by law and dictated by morality does not justify the ill-treatment of convicts by unnecessary physical abuse, bad food, unwholesome air, uncleanly quarters, and, in short, aught that tends to destroy the system of a prisoner. Nevertheless it is astonishing how little effect the public exposure of cruelty in houses of correction produces; and how frequently new horrors are announced through the columns of some enterprising journal. The chief cause, we need hardly observe, lies in political corruption. The management of State penitentiaries is eagerly sought after by the most unscrupulous politicians, and directorships have become political offices; so that with every change of party success a change in the management of these institutions is apt to follow. How these abuses may be done away with we do

[1] *Item*, February 17, 1880.

not here intend to discuss; but any one at all familiar with the most ordinary phases of political corruption must be aware of the *modus operandi* which benefits the warden at the expense of the convict.

What is most interesting to us as observers of these current discussions on the subject is, however, the growing conviction of intelligent men that penitentiaries serve no correctional purpose. They are simply prisons in which dangerous characters are caged up like wild beasts; and which are chiefly beneficial in only the same sense that the cage of a tiger or a snake or a monkey is beneficial. The idea that a professional criminal can be transformed into a virtuous, honorable, intelligent man by incarceration in a frightful dungeon is not at all philosophic. It belongs in fact to a less enlightened age, which believed every human being in sound mind as capable of being honest and well-behaved if he wished to be so. We are more skeptical in modern days, however.

The nineteenth century respectfully discards much that the previous eighteen centuries believed in; and its learned men do not hesitate to declare that propensities to crime are simply forms of inherited mental disease, which no training can conquer and no punishment cure, and no intimidation prevent. Intelligent men no longer hate criminals, however they may pity such beings, or however earnestly they may advocate their elimination from a civilized community. Sociology considers the criminal as it considers the serpent or the panther — a dangerous creature naturally organized to destroy life or property. No civilized person would needlessly torture a captive lion or tiger; but neither could he persuade himself that any term of imprisonment would render such animals less dangerous than before. The records of all our prisons teach the same lesson. Professional criminals who serve one term seldom fail to serve another; and those who do not possess sufficient cunning to evade capture or sufficient money to cheat justice all their lives usually pass three quarters of their lives in prison.

They do little evil in the community while in prison — except that of entailing an immense expense upon the State; for there are very few correctional establishments in the world which can pay the cost of their erection and maintenance with the proceeds of convict labor. But during the brief terms they are set at liberty they inflict far more evil to the community than that involved merely by the exercise of their felonious callings. Numbers of these men have sons or daughters; and the children they bequeath to society, like curses, inherit too often all the evil nature of the parent, and the sins of the father are perpetuated for generations.

The real question as to how crime may be abolished has not yet been solved. It will not be solved in this generation. But when the remedy for crime is decided upon, we suspect it will be a realization of Lytton's romance regarding the laws of the Vril-ya. The criminal will be removed from society by death, death swift and painless, for his first infringement of any important ethical law — not as a punishment, not as a means of terrifying others, not because of anger, but simply as a part of the duty of society to protect itself by removing what is evil and preventing its perpetuation and propagation.

THE FRENCH IN LOUISIANA [1]

THE encouragement given by our Legislature
to the French language in Louisiana has been
ridiculed a great deal by persons apparently
incapable of reflection and clad in the impenetrable mail of prejudice. It has been said that
New Orleans is not a French city, but an
American city; and that the use of the English
language alone should be permitted in public
affairs and public schools. It has also been said
that the law was passed through Creole influence
and to satisfy the selfish ends of a small clique.
Finally it has been said that this maintenance
of a foreign tongue by legislative complaisance
is an ill-advised and ill-timed encouragement of
old fashions, old manners, and old prejudices
which should be abolished as soon as possible for
the sake of public prosperity.

It is needless to say that these statements are
wholly untrue. Even supposing that the law had
been passed for the benefit of a few newspaper
publishers, school teachers, and notaries, its
actual importance would not be lessened one jot
or tittle thereby. As far as the old-fashioned
French manners and customs go, we must say
that we admire and commend most of them, and

[1] *Item*, March 2, 1880.

are sorry to find that many are falling into disuse. The good old customs need encouragement; they ought to be maintained; and they make life in New Orleans more agreeable for strangers — especially Europeans — than may readily be described. It is really the old French population here which knows most of the philosophy of comfort and hygiene, and which lives most naturally and healthily. As to the remarks about old prejudices no sensible man can pretend for a moment that the use of any one language can keep the smouldering fire of old prejudices alive more than the use of any other language could do. In fact, we believed that the Legislature saw further than the prejudiced myopes who criticize them, and perceived that the encouragement of the French language in Louisiana was highly important from a purely commercial standpoint.

Let us explain ourselves more fully upon this subject. For years and years we have been conceiving and practicing and abandoning in despair all kinds of schemes for the encouragement of emigration. It would be a waste of time to record our failures. The old conditions are still extant; and the greater number of our real immigrants are from France and Italy. We believe that whatever may be said regarding other immigration, the French has been increasing of late years; and it is exceedingly important that we should do all in our power to encourage it. The French emigrant has almost always a good trade and is a first-class workman; he is remarkably industrious; he understands economy quite as well as the most thrifty German; and he always works with a fixed object in view. There are hundreds of thriving little businesses in this city which have been created out of nothing — one might almost say — by poor French emigrants who are now well-to-do citizens. It is true that the proportion of French immigration is not as large as we could wish, because the French — unlike the Germans — prefer to stay at home as long as any hope of comfort remains rather than go abroad to seek fortune. But there are regular periods in the life of every nation, however prosperous, which develop conditions that force emigration; and France cannot always remain exempt. We believe there will be a considerable increase in French immigration before many years; and we know that such immigrants will be only too glad to seek a French-speaking community in the United States. New Orleans, by proper management, might obtain at least four fifths of this foreign element, with immense advantage to herself, and might become the central point for America-seeking French emigrants. It is of great moment that the French language be encouraged in Louisiana in view of this fact, and the good effect of the new laws will be felt before many years.

PREVENTION OF CRUELTY TO WOMEN [1]

WE expressed our opinion some days ago in regard to the probable inefficacy of such laws against seduction as that which recently passed the Lower House of the Kentucky Legislature. The advocacy of the bill referred to nevertheless prompts us to the consideration of simpler and more efficacious laws to punish crimes against women — laws which we believe would have a positive and practical effect toward the improvement of public morals.

If there be any sentiment of true chivalry in these days it has not made itself manifest in the enactment of laws for the protection of women. Thousands of delicate women are yearly killed by brutal and cowardly abuse, and the husband is seldom punished. A sudden blow which kills on the instant is murder, but long years of ill-treatment and of cruelty which kills by inches, or, in other words, a systematized manner of torturing women to death, is not punished at all — unless, in the agony of despair, the unfortunate wife has the man arrested and has enough resolution to testify against him afterwards in court, which is seldom the case. Usually her affection forgives all — even the brutality which

[1] *Item*, April 6, 1880.

disfigures her permanently; and it has actually been claimed that some women find a strange pleasure in being beaten.

This is not true of one civilized country alone; but of nearly all; and it will perhaps be remembered that not long ago in London a man who stole a coat or some other article of small value, was transported for fourteen years; while a man who had thrown his wife out of a third-story window and killed her got off with six months' hard labor. Civilization cannot be considered very much advanced from a moral standpoint, while the primitive and savage idea of compelling woman to obedience by force continues to pervade the masses, and while the efforts of philanthropic organizations are directed rather to the prevention of cruelty to animals than to its prevention in the case of those delicate and sensitive beings whose only weapons of defense are beauty, affection, and gentleness. The old Norsemen, rough and fierce as they could be, were far more advanced in some moral respects than the people of modern times. They at least recognized in woman the divine Creator and worshiped her with a blind devotion and a noble idolatry which gave to another age the Spirit of Chivalry.

Perhaps it may sound chimerical; but we sincerely believe that a law declaring it a crime to strike or ill-treat a woman would have a most desirable effect upon present social conditions. The importance of protecting women from abuse may be best realized by considering how much of the moral and physical deformity of this generation has had its origin in the ill-treatment of women who were mothers.

As regards seduction, we have already observed that this evil is probably impossible to prevent by legislation. But, to a certain extent, judicious legislation might surely lessen it. In example, we may adduce an imaginary case, which represents the history of numbers of unfortunates.

A girl has been ruined, and lives with her seducer as his mistress — perhaps for a month, perhaps for a year. He tires of her, and feeling himself hindered by no legal obstacle, and knowing the helplessness of his victim, abandons her. After the first burst of grief, she is often compelled to listen to the advances of another who makes large promises. He treats her in the same manner. After a few more such bitter experiences, she becomes hardened, and abandons herself to degradation.

It is absurd to claim that so great a moral wrong as the above imaginary case presents, cannot be prevented by legislation. It is nonsense to claim that the law can afford women no adequate protection against such treatment as this. Let it be enacted simply that the man who lives with a woman for a certain length of time shall be legally considered, *ipso facto*, as the husband of that

woman, and bound by the law to support, protect, and honor her as well as though a marriage
ceremony had been performed with all ecclesiastical pomp and due formality of law.

HUMBLE FARE AND HIGH LIVING
IN ANCIENT ROME [1]

MR. CHARLES G. HEBERMANN, Professor of
Latin in the College of the City of New York, has
added a curious and instructive volume (just
published by Harper Brothers) to literature in his
'Business Life in Ancient Rome.' Several great
living scholars have made a more profound investigation into the social and domestic life of the
ancients than would have been deemed possible a
generation ago; and the results of their researches
have shown that the conditions of antique life
were in many things much akin to ours, or at
least resemble the social conditions of to-day
much more than those of the Middle Ages. A
classical scholar has already shown us that university life at Athens, in the age of the Antonines,
was not so different from university life in these
days at Oxford or Cambridge, as might have been
imagined; and now an American professor comes
to the front with a review of the business life
of ancient Rome, of so practically interesting
a character that a merchant of Chicago or St.
Louis, or any other busy American city, will read
it with pleasure and profit. We recommend this
tiny volume to our readers. It may be perused in

[1] *Item*, June 28, 1880.

half an hour; but it contains a mass of curious information which will not easily be forgotten. We cannot attempt to give a résumé of its contents in this article; but we must call attention to a few facts of more than special interest which will perhaps startle our readers.

As the luxury of the wealthy Romans was the most extravagant recorded in history, so the wants of the Italian poor in ancient times were the most simple and least expensive imaginable. According to the historian Polybius one day's board and lodging at a northern Italian inn during the second century cost only half a cent! In Rome itself, where the cost of living was high, in Cicero's day laborers lived at the rate of $44 a year. In the time of Augustus the cost of keeping a slave was reckoned at only ten cents per day. But these classes lived chiefly on corn, oil, and a little wine.

The condition of the free working classes was not proportionately low. Free artisans at Rome could earn from $95 to $125 and board per annum; and the shop rent might range from $60 to $75 per year. Considering the difference in the value of money in those days and the few wants of the laboring classes, the mechanic could do pretty well at Rome. His clothing cost him only about $15 per year. A felt hat cost $1; a pair of men's gaiters fifty cents; of women's gaiters, thirty cents; a pair of shoes, thirty-six cents; a pair of men's sandals, twenty-six cents; a pair of slippers, thirty cents; a tunic from $16 to $36; and a toga, from $20 to $48. The price of slaves varied from $50 to $30,000, according to the value in beauty or accomplishments of the slave. At least 900,000 of the population of Rome were slaves; but the free mechanics appear to have been able to hold their own, and they formed societies or guilds for mutual protection and assistance.

While these nourished themselves with such fare as a modern American mechanic would starve to death upon, many of the staples of modern provision markets were comparatively cheap, although beyond the reach of a working-man's purse.

The Romans did not care much for beef. Pork was the general meat diet. Beef or mutton sold at four cents per pound and fresh pork at six cents, nevertheless, while ham fetched ten cents. Eggs were six cents a dozen; milk four cents per quart; wheat sixteen cents a peck; vegetables fetched prices almost equivalent to those of modern times. Salt was very dear — twenty-five cents per pound. But fruit was delightfully cheap. From ten to twenty luscious pears could be bought for two cents; and about four pounds of rich and heavy Italian grapes for the same price. Honey, the sugar of the Roman world, was worth from four to twenty cents, according to grade; and oil was a little dearer. Chickens or quails were worth thirty cents per pair, but geese were worth $1 each. Ordinary fresh or salt-water fish were worth from two to six cents per pound; and salted fish — owing no doubt to the high price of salt — three cents per pound.

Those who kept slaves in the South in the old days will no doubt be astonished to learn that the monthly allowance of slaves in the city of Rome was one bushel of corn, one pint of oil, and a little wine.

In contrast with these facts illustrative of the simplicity of life among the lower classes, Mr. Hebermann contrasts the extravagance of the luxurious and wealthy, some of whom spent from $240,000 to $400,000 for a single meal. We can find space only to quote one example of these follies, however — that of Gravius Apicius, who, 'after spending $4,000,000 on the pleasures of the table took poison, because having only $400,000 left he saw starvation staring him in the face.'

THE ELECTRIC LIGHT [1]

WE are somewhat surprised at the editorial conclusion drawn by the *Democrat* from the exceedingly interesting facts and figures gathered by its energetic representatives and published in its Sunday edition. We refer to the rather dry observation that 'ten years hence, if not sooner,' a proposition to light a city by electricity will receive as much serious consideration as a railroad project.

Really we believed our good friends of the *Democrat* to be of a more sanguine temperament. They have already shown in the clearest possible way that at one of our public resorts the saving by the substitution of electricity for gas is more than enough in a single year to pay the cost of the machinery twice over. And yet they not only remark that the question of public illumination by electricity will be 'considered ten years hence, if not sooner,' but that, at the expiration of that tremendous lapse of time, it will only be considered as seriously as railroad projects are considered. This is not saying very much; for numbers of railroad projects which are seriously considered are never realized at all.

No: basing our own opinion upon the *Demo-*

[1] *Item*, July 20, 1880.

crat's own facts and figures, we believe that the proposal to light cities by electricity is already receiving more serious consideration than many concurrent railroad projects, and that in less than a year some American cities will have adopted the light for purposes of public illumination. Why not consider the question, and very seriously too, right at this time? Since the saving by the substitution of electricity for gas is already enough to pay for the cost of the machinery twice over in a single year, why continue to use an inferior and far more expensive light — especially in our present embarrassed condition?

It is true that there is a generally prevalent, and no doubt correct, opinion that electric illumination is as yet in its infancy, and that by waiting a few years a far more perfect and cheaper system of lighting than any at present in vogue will be ready to meet all public wants. But that is no reason why we should still continue to pay for gas while we can have a far better light at far less cost — even granting that our electric machinery is in a somewhat embryonic condition.

We shall not have to wait ten years or anything like it in order to see American cities illuminated by artificial lightning. Electricity is being rapidly introduced throughout the North; and has been very extensively used at Paris for a long time — where it will no doubt be universally substituted for gas at no distant day. The mere fact that the light, within six months after its invention, has been adopted in theaters, public halls, pleasure resorts, parks, and lighthouses is a certain guarantee that before another year it will be adopted for nearly all public purposes of illumination; and before two years have passed it will no doubt be used as a substitute for gas in private residences.

It occurs to us in this connection to make a little suggestion. The chief expense in the establishment of the electric light is the cost of engines, fuel, and attendance. Might not the enormous hydraulic power which we could draw from the Mississippi River be utilized for public illumination? If one or two engines can supply a whole city with water why could not the river itself supply the motive power necessary to illuminate a city? This is a matter for engineers and electricians to consider, and it seems to us to involve a question of economy eminently worthy of consideration.

MANUFACTURING INTERESTS AND ROWDYISM [1]

THE *Democrat* of yesterday had an article upon 'New Orleans as a Manufacturing City,' of which we consider the ultimate conclusions eminently just, but a portion of the premises defective.

The main point of the *Democrat's* article, briefly expressed, is that the paucity of our manufacturing interests accounts to a large degree for the increase of idleness and crime; that a mere commerce of exportation and importation alone does not afford sufficient employment to a population as large as ours; and that in order to accomplish a moral reform it is eminently important that New Orleans become a manufacturing city instead of remaining a mere market, and utilize for manufacturing purposes a large portion of the goods she now handles only as an exporter or importer.

All this we consider eminently just and true. We have ourselves repeatedly pointed out that the moral reforms so much needed can only be achieved by an immense increase of our commercial interests; and that increase we can only hope to find through the establishment of manufactures. It is true, as the *Democrat* observes, that

[1] *Item*, August 23, 1880.

the lack of manufacturing interests here accounts
for the large class of unemployed persons, for the
plague of pauperism, and the 'burden upon capital and the industry of the comparatively small
class who are employed in commerce and trade to
support the large number who are without employment and means of subsistence.'

We differ with our contemporary, however,
when it asserts that these conditions create the
'bummer class,' ... 'embracing many young
men who create disturbances in public places, en-
gage in desperate frays, and impose such severe
and dangerous duties upon our police.' And we
cannot believe that this class can be 'disposed of
by creating a demand for their industry by offering them employment.'

In our opinion no business man with an ounce
of brains would offer employment to such desperate ruffians, not only because they are dangerous
employees to have, but because they are absolutely useless. Whether we consider the lowest
class of rowdies and ward-bums, or the aristocratic young villains who consider that their
'social position' justifies them in a vicious idleness, which usually ends in some atrocious murder or other scandal, we find that our really
dangerous class are simon-pure drones by nature.
They are not producers. They can do nothing.
They have no trade or profession. They have
never learned how to make themselves useful in

society. Out of all the bummers and ruffians in New Orleans we do not believe there is one first-class mechanic or one person really the master of an honorable calling. Who would employ such men? Who would pay them enough to live upon when they are too worthless to produce anything useful? And how can anybody suppose that even if offered employment they would accept it? They have found out how to live without doing anything; and they will not work for a living as long as they can help it.

No; we believe that our bummer class is not the outgrowth of certain commercial wants. Every large city has its bummer element; its low ruffians and its aristocratic rascals — and perhaps manufacturing cities especially. Take Philadelphia, St. Louis, Cincinnati, Chicago; and you will find the same ruffianism as we have here. It is better suppressed; because those cities are strongly policed — far more strongly than New Orleans will be for years to come; and also because local politics are not quite so rotten perhaps. The manufacturers and merchants take an active part in the government of their city; and justice is more evenly distributed and less often intimidated and thwarted.

Nevertheless, we believe that the conversion of New Orleans into a manufacturing city would terminate the present saturnalia of vice and ruffianism — not, indeed, because there would be fewer rowdies, or because they could ever make themselves useful to a community (except in the workshop of a penitentiary); but because the manufacturers and merchants would have a far larger influence in city affairs and the administration of law than ever before. They would be obliged to take strong measures to protect their property and the lives and property of their employees; they would have to see to it that the city was well policed; — they would have to take such active part in politics as to modify the present condition of affairs at elections; and in return for the benefit they would confer by their enterprise and capital the community would be compelled to aid them in such a good work. The ruffians will always be ruffians, but they would cease to rule and bully the community as they do to-day.

FRENCH JOURNALISM [1]

WHILE Americans boast of possessing the most
enterprising press in the world, it must be acknowledged, nevertheless, that, outside of news-
gathering and rapid work, they have much to
learn yet from European journalism — especially
from that of France. The subject of French
journalism is too vast even to touch upon in its
various branches, though we devoted a whole
month to articles upon the subject; but our
readers will certainly be interested in a brief consideration of certain points of difference between
American dailies and the daily papers of Paris,
which undoubtedly rank before all others in the
world. Without mentioning any particular journal, we shall speak of the general model followed
by almost all of the Paris dailies.

The French newspaper has only four pages.
Once a week a four-page supplement is also
printed. But in no case is the reader ever afflicted
with a folded eight-page sheet. The supplement
is a distinct four-page paper; and the annoyance
of having to turn a newspaper inside out is never
experienced by Parisian readers. This, of course,
does not apply to illustrated dailies like the
Charivari, which are not strictly newspapers, but

[1] *Item*, September 16, 1880.

comic literary papers of such extraordinary merit
that they are able to put the price of subscription
at an immense figure. The subscription to one
of these journals is something like thirty-seven
dollars per annum in American money.

No minute type is used. All the French dailies
are printed in clear bold type. The leading articles are seldom printed in a type smaller than
long primer; and the long primer has a very large
face. The smallest type, even in advertisements,
is brevier.

In a four-page French paper there is usually
one page of advertising to three of reading matter. Advertisements are condensed in an extraordinary fashion, and are paid for at almost
incredible rates. What we style 'Wants' are
charged for at from four to five dollars per line.

Thus with one page, or even less, a French
daily of four pages can give more reading matter
than many of our large American dailies of eight
pages.

Small importance is attached to hasty news
gathering. The enterprise of the New York
Herald is regarded in Paris as something prodigious but nevertheless semi-barbaric. Telegraphic news is closely condensed in a French
paper. Comment upon a piece of important news
by telegraph is reserved until special correspondents have ascertained all particulars. Exception
to this rule is usually only made in cases where

news of the most important character is telegraphed under circumstances which allow of no possibility of mistake.

The enormous sums of money paid for telegraph news in this country by papers who have correspondents in every principal town of the United States, are not expended by the Paris dailies in the same direction. But they probably spend more in salaries. There are brilliant writers, among whom are many of the brightest minds of the country, attached to all great Paris dailies as traveling correspondents. When important news arrives by telegraph, one of these men usually visits the scene of action, and sends to his journal a letter which is worthy to rank as a literary *chef d'œuvre*. News, unless well written, unless written as the most fascinating writer of history would write it, is little cared for.

The articles of these correspondents are at once news letters and editorials. Otherwise a Parisian daily has no editorial whatever. The articles of its most brilliant contributors are printed in larger type than the rest; — that is all.

Writers are paid immense salaries. First-class reporters sometimes make upwards of five thousand dollars per annum. Such men are a combination of novelist, historian, critic, and artist. They have but little to do; but what they do must be perfect.

The name of every writer must be printed at

the end of his article. If a pseudonym is used, it must be known to the authorities. We can thus tell how often the regular attachés of a French daily write for their journal.

It is not every day as in the United States. Once, twice, and rarely thrice a week is all that is required of them. As the journal must be equally interesting every day from a literary point of view, it is necessary that many writers be employed. There are perhaps not less than forty contributors to a first-class daily. Moreover, whatever is really meritorious in a literary way is likely to be accepted by any great daily. Again, the writers are allowed the privilege of writing for as many papers as they please, unless a special contract has been made to the contrary.

But they do so at a risk. The moment a writer's articles cease to attract notice, his services are likely to be dispensed with, except in case of a contract. It is a recognized fact in French journalism that no man can write a really good article every day. If he attempts to do so he weakens his power. It is a pity that this fact is not recognized in America. The fact that it is not, accounts for the comparative mediocrity of American journalism.

As for the opinions of a French daily, we must remark that although it has no editorial, strictly speaking, its opinions are distinctly marked. The manager of the daily guides the policy of the paper. When a certain policy is determined upon, probably a hundred different writers, regular and irregular, will all direct their articles (no matter on what subject) to one point of view. Every department, every page, every line of the paper will reflect the same policy; correspondents, leader-writers, critics, feuilletonists, all alike will converge upon one point. The least dissonance is never perceptible.

In short, then, the first-rank French paper is not only a newspaper but a wonderful piece of literary work; a sheet in which every line is a work of art; a medium through which the most cultivated thought of the age finds expression; a journal whose representatives are deemed worthy to visit Kings and Emperors, and in which the privileges with which the journalist is honored are never abused; a power which does not attempt to impose upon the public by the mystic personality of one name, but which attacks evils overtly, Titan-like with a hundred hands, or praises like Mahomet's angels with myriad tongues; and which really reflects the opinions not only of a hundred writers over a hundred signatures, but indirectly those of all prominent persons with whom they are in daily association — for no brilliant thought shaped into words in the presence of a French journalist is ever allowed to waste its sweetness on the desert air. In America journalism is too often the business of

mere unlettered scribblers; — in France, it belongs to the highest department of literature; and
the most wonderful efforts of modern literary art
may be said to have made their first appearance
in the journals of Paris.

DEAD FOR A DUCAT — AND LESS THAN A DUCAT [1]

IT is curious that while there has been so much humanitarian discussion of late years regarding the most merciful method of executing criminals, none of those engaged in the discussion appear to have thought of the most simple and perhaps instantaneous of any. The guillotine is far more merciful than hanging; but there is the horror of the double gush of blood, and the agony of the delay while the victim is being securely fastened to the machine of death. Electricity has been warmly advocated; but the most expert electricians have declared that even in the hands of a scientist the galvanic battery cannot always be relied upon to do its work thoroughly. Poisons have been spoken of, but they vary strangely in their effects upon different constitutions; and in these times when many persons have become, by force of occupation or otherwise, almost Mithridatic in their ability to resist poison, the simple and merciful death-draught given by the ancient Greeks to the criminals could hardly serve the purpose of the law. To chloroform or etherize a criminal until the head or lungs cease to act would not be humane; — the awful interval of

[1] *Item*, October 25, 1880.

the sleep between life and death and the dreams
of that interval would render it almost as cruel as
hanging. The garrote is a hideous invention, and
the gibbet is really a disgrace to civilized nations.
Moreover the law does not even justify the practice of breaking the necks of criminals by a long
fall through a cunningly sprung trap. It simply
condemns the victim to hang by the neck until he
is dead — or in other words, to die of strangula-
tion. If the law has not been followed out in
England and America of late years it has been
because the humanity of the century revolted
against a method of killing not less barbarous
than the bowstring of the Orient.

Among the Choctaw nation the murderer is
simply shot dead. A mark is chalked on his
breast, and the executioner fires a ball from a
heavy rifle directly through his heart. He is not
disfigured or tortured, or made hideous by en-
forced contortions of agony before his death. It
is true that a poor shot might occasionally inflict
suffering were the custom adopted throughout
the United States. But such suffering would be
very brief, and infinitely less than that caused by
hanging, poisoning, guillotining, or garroting.
There is also an idea that to be shot is a soldier's
death, and too good for murderers, rapists, and
robbers. But this is mere romanticism. The
criminal in this enlightened age must be regarded
as a diseased creature, sent out of the world by

his fellow men, or caged in a prison, not for revenge or hope of reform; but for the protection of society. We do not hang horses or dogs or beasts of any kind that have become too injured or too much diseased to be serviceable. Humanity dictates that they be killed as speedily as possible; and they are shot. Why shoot an animal in mercy and hang a human being? Unless we must swallow the old theories about the perfect ease with which awfully wicked people should become saints and angels if they want to, we cannot perceive either common sense or humanity in treating morally diseased men worse than physically diseased animals.

PROLIFIC CRIME [1]

As the world becomes more philosophical and less superstitious more attention is being given to the origin of crime and the laws of its growth. Various means of checking crime which are more efficacious than imprisonment in a penitentiary from where one may be delivered by a pardon or a daring escape, and less austere than death have been recently projected. We have given considerable attention to one of them, proposing to subject criminals to a surgical operation which would render them incapable of becoming fathers and thus propagating not only their species but their crimes. However, it seems not improbable, in spite of all humanitarian dreams and moonshine, that in a more enlightened century — say the twentieth — civilized society will adopt laws like those of the Vril-ya, and condemn to a merciful death all persons with strong criminal tendencies, or with a depraved moral nature of any description. The ancients who slew weakly children were more sensible in some respects than we of to-day; and the time will come when people will seriously ask, 'Why build and maintain asylums for idiots and prisons for murderers, and perpetuate the frightful cruelty of isolating these

[1] *Item*, October 28, 1880.

wretched beings for a lifetime from the rest of the world?' But the old prejudices and superstitions must die out first.

Nevertheless even in the present stage of progress, it looks as though it would be found absolutely necessary before long to adopt some new iron legislation — laws without hate but without pity — to prevent the abnormal increase of vice and violence. Statistics are crying out for such legislation; they are irrefutable appeals to the common sense of mankind. A curious and shocking fact may illustrate the question better than any general observation. In Paris recently a family was tried and condemned for crimes so horrible that they cannot even be named, and that the trial was held secretly with locked doors. The chief criminal, a man still in the prime of life, was the father of *forty-seven children!* Forty-seven physically strong and healthy but morally diseased children! It is hardly possible to suppose that a single child of that multitude is not morally tainted with the father's sins, and if suffered to grow to manhood or womanhood will repeat the unutterable crimes of their progenitor. And as yet there is no legislation to prevent these things. The more we learn we find the less we know, and after one has read the particulars of that awful trial, he will naturally question the truth of the old-time idea that the Chinese custom of condemning all members of a family for the crime committed by one is wholly barbarous and brutal. There is generally a sound substratum of philosophy underlying the most eccentric of Oriental laws; and there are philosophical reasons in favor of the law above referred to. If nests of vipers be destroyed with all the young brood; if we kill young eagles and young wolves and young beasts and birds of prey of all descriptions, why not also destroy a brood of human beasts of prey? Such is the grim question philosophers are beginning to ask themselves, and perhaps the next century will answer it. And in the meantime one man has been suffered to create forty-seven of the wickedest children probably of which any human being ever was the father. In forty-seven years to what an infinite extent may not the sins of that father have spread!

A DREAM OF FUTURITY [1]

At a time when the wildest dreams of former centuries seem on the eve of practical realization, it is not surprising to hear that efforts are being made to discover the secret of life, nor would it astonish many even to learn within a few years that man had been able by chemistry to create living organisms. It is an old theory that could we effect a combination of the same elements which compose the human organism in the same proportion as they exist in the body of man, the result would be a living crystallization which would assume the human form. The chemistry that has become almost perfect in analysis is still sadly defective in synthesis; but who dare predict that it will always remain so?

It may seem doubtful whether the capacity to create life by scientific appliances could be of any immediate benefit to the human race, so far as the reproduction of complete living types is concerned. But it would be of incalculable benefit could the reproduction of lost limbs and faculties be effected. Should science be able to discover a means of replacing a lost leg by a fresh living one, or causing a new arm to sprout from a mangled stump, or a new eye to develop itself within an

[1] *Item*, November 18, 1880.

empty socket, of what incalculable advantage in civilization would such a discovery be! The lizard can reproduce his lost tail; but man cannot replace a lost member. There are faculties enjoyed by reptiles which man might well envy.

Indirectly the discovery we hint of might have far deeper consequences. The knowledge of the secret of life would assuredly involve a knowledge of the secret of death; and with these revelations might not man become capable of indefinitely prolonging the former and arresting the latter? This discovery again would have extraordinary results.

The capacity to prolong life indefinitely, if ever universally possessed by man, would involve at first an excessive increase of population such as would require a greater genius than Malthus to provide against. The struggle for life under such circumstances — especially a life of perpetual youth — would be something terrible beyond all that modern imagination can conceive, unless prevented by unfamiliar natural causes, or by certain philosophic previsions. One course might have to be adopted — the destruction of all inferior beings by the superior. The former, naturally incapable of comprehending the scientific force utilized in favor of the latter, might easily be prevented from realizing its benefits; but how prevent them from destroying those whom they would have a right to consider as foes, especially in the event of the establishment of laws against their very existence? Unless the secret should remain the exclusive possession of a powerful aristocracy, armed with force sufficient to maintain its ascendancy under all circumstances, there could be no question as to the result of such a discovery. Perhaps in any event the result would be dismal. Should man ever find the Elixir dreamed of by the alchemists and be able to prolong his youth and life indefinitely, sooner or later with the present natural rate of increase, the consequence would be unfortunate indeed; for the earth would be unable to support her population.

There is one theory, however, which offers a slight consolation. It is that the reproductive capacity of man diminishes as his mental capacity increases; and there have been men bold enough to assert that the human race would finally become extinct by the development of the mental at the expense of the reproductive powers. Should men become able to live for centuries there is no doubt that the mental faculties would develop to a degree of which we, poor short-lived creatures, can form no idea. But whether man would cease to propagate his own species in that event might again be considered doubtful. The triumph of science over nature in this difficulty would not after all be more wonderful than the previous triumph over old age and death.

Yet should man cease to become a father, science might then utilize the discovery of the secret of life in a new direction, and fabricate highly organized beings in her laboratories far superior intellectually and physically to aught now existing.

WOMAN'S INFLUENCE

A NUMBER of officials who recently resigned in France rather than aid in the execution of the government decrees against the religious orders, were sarcastically spoken of as having yielded to the influence of woman. There was an *odor di femina* about those resignations, it was said, and indeed it has been the influence of woman which the French republicans have found it most difficult to fight against, and which has done more to shape the policy of courts that are not republican than aught else. On the other hand the clergy, it is needless to say, have availed themselves of this powerful influence to oppose the legislation leveled against them, and there is no doubt that were the religious question left wholly to the decision of women in France, the decrees would never have been decreed, or if decreed would never have been executed.

Those who judge France by Paris, which does not represent her, are apt to imagine that free thought permeates a large majority of the French people. It certainly does not when we include the women. The Frenchwoman is religious, whatever else may be said of her; and even in the metropolis which is so faithless, and so heartless,

[1] *Item*, December 12, 1880.

the least pious mother attempts to inculcate piety into her children. The Revolution planted the seeds of skepticism very deeply in the French character; and to-day it must be confessed that a very large number indeed of the French people are men of little faith. But there was something the Revolution could not change, and which was destined to regenerate and redeem the country at a later day when the fury of the great and bloody upheaval had spent itself, when the old social conditions were destroyed, when faith was publicly mocked, when old ideas were broken up and the names of even the years and seasons were changed. That was woman's heart. There is something good in all women. Men may become wholly depraved; but there is something always good in the heart of the worst of women. Men may become wholly indifferent to ethical ideas; women never. Goodness is a part of their being, and faith, by which ethical principle is alone inculcated, a necessity for their existence. They have always believed in human nature, in right and wrong, in love and in a God; and will probably continue to do so in secret, even though faith should go out of fashion, and modern religion be spoken of as lightly as the gods of Rome or the mythology of Greece.

What the French Republic will have most to fear, after its strong leaders of to-day shall be in their graves, is the corruption of society which is making itself manifest. The Empire was not as corrupt as the Republic of to-day. There was corruption in office, but there was more virtue among the masses. No such extreme license was then possible in literature and journalism, and a moral corruption of society destroys the strength of a community. It is true there is now an attempt to force a reaction; but it is very feeble and its results have been unimportant. Against these evils the influence of woman may do a great deal; but she believes that faith is the conserving force which keeps society from dissolution, and perhaps she is right. There may be a reversal of the political tables in a few years, and the religious orders may regain more than they have lost. If they do, there will be an *odor di femina* in the transformation.

WHAT IS LIGHT? [1]

UNTIL very lately it was believed that light was a special substance, an element, a tangible reality — inasmuch as a beam of light could be weighed! It was believed that there were three different varieties of sun rays — the heat ray, the light ray, and the chemical ray. It was even stated in certain scientific works that the solar spectrum was made up of a heat spectrum, a light spectrum, and an actinic or chemical spectrum. But now it appears that this is all erroneous; and that, just as progress in chemistry has proven that elements are far less numerous than was formerly believed, so there is but one kind of ray instead of three; and that the different effects attributed to the special virtues of various light rays, are really caused only by the nature of the substance encountered by the ray, or in other words by the reflecting or absorbing capacity of that substance. It has also been proved that just as color does not really exist, being only the effect of what we have been accustomed to call 'light' upon the eye, so light itself has no real existence, being only the effect of what we ought to term *radiant energy*, or sun-force, upon the eye. An article in the *Scientific American* ably elucidates this fact;

[1] *Item*, December 21, 1880.

and shows that the retina of the eye is itself a photographic plate 'having a substance called purpurine secreted by appropriate glands spread over it, in place of the silver salts used in common photography.' The phenomenon of sight is explained by the fact that this purpurine is rapidly decomposed by the radiant energy or sun-force vibrations above referred to; and the molecular movement consequent upon the decomposition causes a vibration of the optic nerves, which vibration is the sensation we call light. When the purpurine is not normal in quality or quantity the result may be color blindness. But light is simply a physiological phenomenon; it has no objective existence independent of the eye; and it is incorrect to speak of the velocity of light. Light has no velocity, as it is only the effect of a disturbance of the optic mechanism. It is only the radiant energy of the sun that has the velocity of 186,000 miles per second.

In connection with these curious revelations it is worth while to consider how frequently man has mistaken his own sensations for objective facts; and effects for causes. We have found that there is no such thing in reality as weight; no such thing as sound; no such thing as color; no such thing as light. We have had false notions regarding the nature of the most familiar things. Sight, hearing, taste, and smell have no objective existence; they are simply impressions produced upon our nerves by influences very different from what we have imagined. We have found that cold is not the absence of heat; nor is heat the absence of cold. Light is not the absence of darkness; nor is darkness the absence of light. But it is also worth while to remember that all the science of the age is converging along innumerable paths of discovery toward one awful and startling fact. The more we penetrate the secrets of nature, the more we are astounded to find that millions of effects are not produced by myriads of varied forces, but by one force acting in innumerable and infinitely mysterious ways. As polytheism has been succeeded by monotheism in religion, in science also the theoretic polytheism of innumerable natural forces is yielding to the pantheism of one all-permeating and all-creating and all-destroying and all-remodeling force. Shall we ever learn what that mighty force is, of which our own lives are but faint sparks? — that force more truly recognized, perhaps, by the Brahmin than by the Christian, by the Oriental than by the Occidental mind?

CANADA *vs.* BERNHARDT [1]

RELIGIOUS and social prejudices and bigotries exist to a greater extent in Canada, perhaps, than in any other part of North America — a fact attributable in great part to the uncompromising religious character of the Scotch and other old-country elements of which the population is composed. Here in the United States, so long as a person does not publicly violate law, infringe morality, or violate social proprieties, he is not only free to think as he pleases but to express his opinions to his fellow citizens. If there be any exception to this rule it is only in remote country towns or villages where the old Puritanism of other days still lingers, or where the whole population are members of some one church, which dictates social as well as religious law for all. But in Canada it is otherwise. The infinite variety of religious or heterodox opinions to be found in any large American city do not exist; and those who would dare to enunciate in public any views contrary to those almost universally held, could not hope for sympathizers to support or defend them. The French element is not affected by this general spirit of intolerance; but

[1] *Item*, December 23, 1880.

the French element is not large enough to affect the social atmosphere appreciably, or thaw out its frigid spirit of intolerance.

That this intolerance does not seem to be confined to any one church in Canada, is inferable from the fact that the pastors of various churches at Montreal have warned their flocks against Sarah Bernhardt, and called upon their sheep not to visit her performances upon any consideration. Just why, the telegraph has not yet informed us. It certainly cannot be because Sarah's great rôles are indecent. It must be because Sarah herself is not a deeply religious person, or a strict observer of the moral code which governs fashionable society. It is useless to argue that the actress and the woman have always been considered separately in modern times; and that because society might not choose to welcome the former to her *salons*, there is no reason why she should refuse to admire the latter upon the boards. Nor is it any use to represent that Sarah was kindly considered by royal personages and honored in London and appreciated by the English public; for the English and Canadian publics are very different indeed. There is an effort to prevent Sarah from playing at all; and the effort is a serious and powerful one. Should she play in spite of all opposition, it would not even surprise us to hear that a mob had entered the theater, torn up the seats, and played havoc with the properties. There are mobs in Canada quite capable of such freaks.

All this will not personally hurt Sarah even financially, as her pecuniary harvest is already assured by contract. To the civilized world at large it will have the effect of rendering the Canadians rather ridiculous and behind the age. But it is certainly astonishing that those who fulminate against Sarah have not been shrewd enough to understand that they are simply giving her a gigantic advertisement the world over, and assuring more money to her manager than he had hoped to make. Denounce a book as immoral; it will reach a sixth or a sixtieth edition according to the amount of abuse or denunciation showered upon it; picture a woman to the world as wickedly graceful, dangerously seductive, unutterably depraved, and frightfully immoral, and she will draw better than a circus. They can prevent Sarah from playing in Canada, perhaps; but she will draw better than ever elsewhere.

THE FEROCITY OF THE SHOEMAKER [1]

THERE is no man who has greater power over the happiness of his fellow creatures than the shoemaker, as all who are afflicted with corns and bunions can bear witness. In this climate, where the feet swell with heat and where violent changes of temperature render it possible to easily wear a tight-fitting shoe one day which could not be borne the next, this is especially the case. Any experienced salesman in a wholesale or retail shoe store will tell you that a peculiar class of shoes are manufactured expressly for the New Orleans market, more on account of the climate than aught else. But we are not afflicted by the wholesale manufacturers or their wares, so much as by the local shoemaker who makes shoes to order by the pair. Neither do we propose to advocate an immediate reform in the style and shape of the modern shoe; partly because we feel such an advocacy would be useless, and partly because men far more learned and capable than we are have written excellent books to prove that the modern shoe is an abomination, in no way adapted to the wants of the human foot, and evidencing far less knowledge of anatomy on the part of the inventor than any

[1] *Item*, January 7, 1881.

footgear of ancient times, whether Greek, Roman, or Egyptian. We desire simply to commiserate the lot of those who suffer unspeakable tortures at the hands of the modern shoemaker who makes shoes by the pair.

Wholesale manufacturers have classified the human foot into a number of sizes adapted to all ages and sexes, and indicated by certain numbers. Wholesale clothing manufacturers have done likewise in regard to the human body. But there are numerous exceptions to all rules; and, as in some grammars, the exceptions to some rules are more numerous than the mis-styled general fact, 'which the rule covers.' There are men who can never get ready-made clothes to fit them, because a pair of pantaloons large enough at the hips for them would be too long in the legs, and a coat broad enough in the shoulders too long in the arms. So there are men who can never get ready-made shoes to fit them, because a ready-made shoe that would be long enough would be too narrow and one broad enough would be too long. Some have the instep abnormally high; others, toes unusually broad; many have one foot larger than the other, so that a shoe which would accommodate the left foot would create seven different kinds of bunions and corns on the right one. It is upon these unfortunates that the shoemaker exercises his diabolical skill and wreaks his insatiate fury.

The corn-sufferer is always recommended to the shoemaker by a particular friend who happens to have found satisfaction for the simple reason that his foot is perfectly normal. The corn-sufferer is therefore told that the shoes will cost him just double the price he has been in the habit of paying for shoes, but that durability of material and absence of suffering will more than compensate for the difference in price. He is then very carefully measured. Then the shoemaker tells him he will make the shoes upon a certain last and make due allowance for the corns. The sufferer indicates where the corns are, and thereupon the shoemaker glues or nails thick patches of leather on various parts of the last corresponding with the bunions and the corns. The shoes are made. The sufferer gets them on with less difficulty than he expected because they have been doctored with chalk-powder. He pays for them. They fit so exactly that he foolishly imagines it is all right. In less than a week he has several new corns and the old ones are worse than ever. He takes the shoes back to the shoemaker to get them stretched. They are well stretched, and when he puts them on again, he fondly imagines they are 'all right.' But the fact is that no amount of stretching ever cures the viciousness of a shoe. The leather shrinks back to its original position; and a shoe that binds the first week will hurt at the end of the year in

the very same place if it be strongly made. And
here the 'first-class shoemaker' shows his fiendish
spirit. His shoes are so strongly made that they
will almost endure forever, together with the
horrible corns which they create — they cannot
be worn out. And the victim may try a hundred
shoemakers and pay any price; and gather a new
crop of corns with each new pair of shoes. Nor
does the devilish malignity of the shoemaker
stop there. Often he only pretends to make you
a pair of shoes, and in reality tries to sell you an
old pair that have been lying in his window for
years, since the customer who promised to pay
for them never came back. Sometimes such a
shoe bursts in all directions shortly after being
put on. Sometimes the heel is so high that the
toes are pressed forward and crushed; sometimes
the shoe is too long, and yet crushes the instep;
sometimes it is too broad, and yet the upper has
been cut so low that the foot has no room in it;
sometimes the toes are so jammed together that
'soft corns' make their appearance between the
fourth and fifth toes; sometimes the big-toe nail
turns black and falls off; sometimes the sole of
the foot is squeezed into a wrinkle and an irradi-
cable corn grows on the wrinkle; sometimes the
toe joints are blistered; sometimes the heel is ex-
coriated; sometimes the instep is flayed; and
sometimes all these things are done at the same
time. No wonder that men madly seize pen-

knives and rip open new shoes with rage, lamenting that they could not also rip up the shoemaker, who inflicts injuries that are incurable. Yes: incurable. There is no cure for corns except to keep the feet constantly in water for six weeks; and then the corns will peal off, just as the hoofs of a horse would drop off under similar treatment. Is it any wonder that enraged victims should sometimes revenge themselves on the craft by ordering a hundred pairs of shoes from a hundred different shoemakers, and leaving the city next day?

AS IF PAINTED BY LIGHTNING [1]

NOT the least extraordinary result of recent progress in the magic of science is the new process of instantaneous photography, which is coming rapidly into general use, and threatens to supersede the older and more tedious method as electricity is superseding gas.

It was by this startling discovery that the long-sought mystery of the horse's movements in rapid trotting was first elucidated; and much to the surprise of artists and others it was found that the movements of a horse's limbs were altogether different from all preconceived theories and ideas upon the subject. Since that time curious investigations have been made by similar means in regard to the muscular movements of various animals in rapid motion. So instantaneous is the process that it renders the teeth of a circular saw in revolution plainly visible, and other things impossible for the naked eye to discern. Dancers have been splendidly portrayed in the whirl of a ball, every figure in motion being clearly outlined, and every attitude mirrored, as they could never be by sight alone.

Some results of this discovery will be very pretty and curious. In rapid motion, as in skat-

[1] *Item*, April 29, 1881.

ing, the body assumes positions which could never be preserved for any length of time except under the strong impulse of a forward movement; for in graceful skating the body of the skater is nearly all the time far out of the perpendicular, alternately bending to all points of the compass at such angles as the axis of a peg-top offers in its last circlings. In ballet dancing the same thing often occurs. Moreover there are moments when the body of the dancer does not touch the ground at all. All the marvelous grace displayed by some *premières danseuses* in their aerial gyrations and spinnings and *tours de force* may be reproduced exactly by instantaneous photography. In the theater the spectator only obtains a very vague idea of them; his eyes are dazzled by the rapid twinkling of feet and white crossing of limbs as if by a succession of flashes. He is often provoked by a momentary poise or attitude of inexpressible grace, which could only be taken during exceedingly rapid motion, and which remains visible but for a fraction of a second. But with the aid of instantaneous photography, these evanescent exhibitions of grace can be chemically crystallized into permanent pictures, upon which one may gaze as long as he pleases.

Imagine also what curious effects might be had by the application of instantaneous photography to athletic and gymnastic exhibitions. What a correct report might thus be made of a Græco-

Roman wrestling match, a pugilistic encounter, an exhibition of legerdemain, or a performance on the trapeze!

Suppose something still more fantastic. Were the camera properly adjusted by an electric apparatus to photograph a decapitation by guillotine or sword, a photograph might be taken just at the instant when the blade was but half-way through the neck of the condemned.

Another and very important application of the process could be made in the study of physiog-nomical expression. Some of you have, perhaps, seen Darwin's amusing little book on 'Emotional Expression in Man and Animals'; and you may remember how funny those photographs of chil-dren and others are, taken in the very act of laughing or crying or frowning. Interesting as these photographs are, however, those possible to make by the new process would be far more so. Fancy what delightful physiognomical studies might be made by instantaneously photographing several hundreds of school children at play, laughing, romping, crying, yelling, leaping, run-ning, watching, or quarreling; — the faces of several hundred guests in the dining-room of some great American hotel; the faces of an audience under the strong emotion of some powerfully acted tragedy; or the expression of actors or singers in the most impressive portion of a drama or an opera!

It has long been the custom in large cities to photograph important and dangerous criminals, who often resist by screwing their features into hideous grimaces. But with this process all such dodges would prove of no avail. The criminal may submit to the operation or not as he pleases; his photograph will be taken even before he has time to think of pulling ugly faces.

What a wonderfully interesting album might be made out of instantaneous photographs! We believe the innovation will have a very important influence upon the study of emotional expression in painting, of anatomy in sculpture, and of truth and grace in art generally.

SOME FANCIES ABOUT FANCY [1]

ANY one who has carefully watched for the productions of first-class writers of fiction during a course of years — we do not refer to the production of voluminous and worthless novels, but to really artistic creations of the prose and poetry of fiction — has probably noticed a certain periodicity in such work. An exquisite little story, or even a series of such, is produced; then comes a long interval of silence or commonplaceness. Then again some work of art appears from the same master pen; but of a different type, another subject occupies the writer's mind. Then another interval, during which it is often subsequently discovered that the writer has abandoned his early field, and betaken himself to what is usually termed in literature, serious work. There are authors who produce fiction continually, like machines; but they seldom rise above mediocrity, and even when they do, however great their masterpieces, many of their lesser works lack high merit of any kind, and bear the evidence of incipient mental sterility.

There is nothing really so difficult to produce, for example, as brief stories whose effect de-

[1] *Item*, March 28, 1881.

pends wholly upon uniqueness of conception —
sketches which although suggested by fact are
moulded and colored by imagination alone. Of
such, for example, are the sketches in Irving's
'Tales of a Traveler' and 'Wolfert's Roost';
Hawthorne's 'Twice-Told Tales' and 'Mosses
from an Old Manse'; the prose tales of Edgar
Poe; the short novelettes by French writers of
the same period — including such works as
Baudelaire's prose poems, Mérimée's intense
romances of the Dame de Pique sort, and Tour-
genieff's later and briefer tales. These of course
are only a few examples of many; but all present
illustrations of the rarest thing in literature, and
perhaps the most difficult to produce — short
stories of real power and originality, which
startle, charm, haunt the mind of the reader, and
inspire painters and musicians — tales which are
the offspring of a genius obliged to create without a thought of profit or fame, but only for
the pleasure of creating — art-children which are
after a sort the involuntary parturition of fancies
which can remain pregnant but for a certain
length of time, and which cannot avoid giving
birth to any beautiful conception once conceived.

Like certain Venetian glasses wrought with such
beautiful fragility as to forbid their practical
use, the works of pure imagination seem to have
little practical value. A French writer dared to
say that it is so with most productions of painting

and sculpture and music: the most beautiful things have no real utility. In one sense they have not: in another their importance is vast. Poets and novelists enrich language; everything in art which cultivates the sense of the beautiful has a nourishing influence upon thought and consequently upon action — upon spiritual and indirectly upon social freedom. The stories of Hoffmann in themselves would seem to be of little worth; but the flowers of fancy they contain have been borrowed by numberless writers to adorn and render attractive works of a more serious character. A volume of history or science written with ornate grace will find far more readers and accomplish far more good than a work of equal learning written in a dry and bony manner. The collections of traditions, super-stitions, legends, fairy tales, goblin stories, im-possible anecdotes, supernatural romances to which so much attention has been given in this century, have a prodigious influence upon the use of language and the formation of style. The purely imaginative stories of real merit produced of late years have a real value besides that curi-ous value which the rarity of their creation lends them. We make these few remarks in order to impress upon the reader the difference we de-sire to establish between historical fiction or fiction based upon established fact, and fiction which is the offspring of fancy alone, or of fancies suggested by involuntary theories upon fact.

No man who ever lived has produced a very large quantity of this fine rare work — either in prose or poetry; and the less the volume of production, the greater appears to be the merit. Quality is sacrificed to quantity if an attempt be made to force production by the hothouse nutrition of pecuniary inducement. Take two examples in recent times. Murger made a great reputation by his 'Scènes de la vie de Bohème,' in which he fairly exhausted himself; and although he produced a great deal subsequently with profit to himself, he produced nothing so worthy to survive. To come nearer home, Bret Harte, having made a reputation by the spontaneous products of a fancy enriched by experience in California, was offered a fortune to continue such work for a Boston firm. Unfortunately he accepted the contract and failed, and has never since produced anything of sterling value, nor is it likely that he ever will do again in the same line.

The fairy soil of fancy is rapidly exhausted, and when its first crop has been garnered, another similar one can never be raised. This is a fact which will be more generally recognized by publishers at some future time. The ground of imagination may be enriched by new experience, new sights and sounds and perfumes, unfamiliar colors and forms and music; but the thing must produce a new crop wholly different from the old. And with imaginative artists of this kind, the misfortune generally is that they are too poor to afford the expense of such fancy cultivation.

RAINBOW BIRDS [1]

ANY lover of the beautiful who has not read the admirable article upon 'Hummingbirds' in *Harper's Magazine* for May, has missed a rare treat — unless, indeed, he happens to have made special studies in the same direction himself. We cannot, for our part, resist the temptation to attempt to present to our readers the impression produced by the article in question.

It is supposed by learned ornithologists that the hummingbird originated in the slopes of the equatorial Andes, and existed even at that inconceivably remote period when the greater portion of the American Continent was submerged; dwelling in the valleys and forests of the mountain chains which first arose above the surface. In other words, the hummingbird is, perhaps, the oldest species of the feathered tribe in existence; having been able — through some strange capacity of adapting itself to climatic changes and atmospheric revolutions — to survive the vast mutations which swept away so many varieties of monstrous animals and reptiles.

Then, through the laws of natural selection, operating through perhaps many millions of years, were developed those marvelous jewel

[1] *Item*, June 5, 1881.

tints which render the plumage of the hummingbird the most beautiful thing in regard to color
known to human eyes; the incomprehensible
loveliness whereof proves in itself the enormous
period of time through which the hummingbird
must have existed. No human art can convey
any idea of the wizard colors which make the
little creature so bewitching — its throat and
breast often present tints which are only equaled
by certain passionate tones of tropical sunset.
The emerald of the Orient and the blood-crystal
ruby; the magic opal and the chrysolite glowing
like the eyes of a leopard in the night; the blue
of the lapis-lazuli that seems borrowed from a
Southern midsummer sky, and the rainbow tints
of the pearl — are cold and dull compared with
the colored fires of the hummingbird's feathers
— well chosen by Aztec kings for the mantle of
royalty. The glow of burning coals and the colors
of the sunset are the only things to which their
colors can be compared — they are not only
colors, but colored fires that flicker with every
motion of the bird.

And here is a strange and pleasing fact concerning one species, the smallest, or nearly the
smallest of all. It inhabits only the crater of the
extinct volcano of Chiriqui, in New Granada;
and as if the dying lava-fires had bequeathed
their splendors to the tiny inhabitants of the
crater, the breast of each bird is lurid with a

drop of blazing crimson — one flaming spark — one radiant ember of color. So that this hummingbird is well called the 'Flamebearer.'

And there are more than four hundred distinct species of hummingbirds — one of which, the Ruby-throat, is hardy enough to migrate during summer far north into the British possessions in Canada, even to the fifth degree of latitude. Moreover, the hummingbird is altogether confined to the New World. Nothing better evidences the extraordinary manner in which the bird has adapted itself to varying circumstances, and the inconceivable length of time required for the modifications to which it has been subjected, than the variations in the beaks of the species. They actually seem to vary in length according to the character of the blossoms from which the creature extracts its food of honey and insects. In some, it is no less than six inches long, or six times the length of the bird; in others, only a third of an inch; in some, it is curved downward so that the bird can without difficulty extract its fruit from the cups of flowers whose petals point skywards; in other hummingbirds, the beak turns up in a curve, so that it can readily be used in probing certain trumpet-shaped blossoms which hang from tropical shrubs and trees. Two eggs are usually laid at a time by the mother-bird; and the nest is frequently lashed with spider webs to the chosen branch.

Hummingbirds have scarcely any enemy to fear except man. They are absolutely fearless of hawks and other birds of prey, and never hesitate to attack when they even suspect danger. Falcons and other fierce princes of the air have no adequate means of defense against hummingbirds, and are frequently severely whipped, as the little warriors always strike at the eyes of the enemy, and can fly round him like a swarm of gnats. They are as cunning as brave; and will feign death or affect docility in the hands of a captor in order to find an opportunity to escape.

It appears now, however, that these beautiful creatures, which survived the cataclysms and changes of millions of years, threaten to become extinct owing to the savage war made upon them by man. Commerce is always absolutely heartless in these matters; and there is a tremendous commercial demand for the skins of hummingbirds. The skins are stuffed and used to decorate women's hats; and probably the fashionable beauties thus adorned with borrowed plumage, never even think of regretting the sunny little lives sacrificed for the ornamentation of their headgear.

THE SEXUAL IDEA IN FRENCH LITERATURE [1]

IT would be impossible in the brief space allowed to an article intended only to interest readers during a few moments' leisure in the afternoon, to give the least idea of the relative merits of contemporary French literature — nor is an evening paper the proper medium for such an expression of critical opinion; but in view of the general interest which modern Parisian literature is exciting the world over, and the enormous production of contradictory criticism provoked by it, we may certainly hazard a few remarks about one general and striking characteristic of the Parisian school of modern fiction which does not appear to have been much touched upon by Anglo-Saxon critics.

If this literature be the most dainty and beautiful in the world, the most artistic in conception and execution, in outline and shading, in form and color, in realism or idealism — it is owing in no small degree to the fact that all of such art, whether of literature or painting, of sculpture or decoration, is influenced by a sexual idea little comprehended by those not of the Latin race. *L'éternel féminin* appears in the idea of a novel

[1] *Item*, June 17, 1881.

as well as in the shapeliness of a bronze; the *odor di femina* impregnates everything artistic produced by the magic of Paris. The idea of love, not spiritual or vague, but love as warmly material, as sharply defined as the old Hellenic idea of passion, is there omnipresent as an atmosphere tinting all it touches and penetrates. Such passion seeks a real object unveiled — it tears away any drapery that does not antique-wise reveal as through a mist or by a suggestive falling of folds, the charms concealed; the old Greek love of physical nudity being partly revived in the modern French love of what might be termed psychical nudity — the nakedness of passion seeking passion without concealment, and as if it were the most natural thing in the world. No winner of a Pythian or Isthmian prize ever exhibited his unclad body with more pride than the modern French writer lays bare the physical electric mechanism of passion. Nay, he goes further, lifting up fiber after fiber of the heart, as though working at a dissecting table: impulses of imagination, influences of circumstances upon passional excitement, philosophy of cause and effect, action of violent sentiment upon character — all these are studied with a certain terrible precision which suggests the steely nerve of a surgeon gained by long familiarity with what others fear to touch. Passion is the mighty electricity which vibrates through all human life and causes all

grand vibrations in its flood; it is again the power
which creates the music of the instrument, which
guides the chisel and the brush, which directs
the witchery of the pen. This is to some extent
the modern Latin idea: it is the old Greek idea
also in a modern garb — Aphrodite *à la Pari-
sienne!* We Northern races still adore Odin and
Thor. In Anglo-Saxon, or German, or Scandinavian, or American life, passional feeling is
merely an incident — a tiny spark hardly distinguishable in its surroundings; it is rather a
consequence than a motive. But with the warm-
blooded Latins it is the motive rather than the
consequence; — to them the relation of passion
to life is that of the spark placed in a vase of
alabaster all illuminated by its presence. Read
an English or American novel of the best class;
it is a mere report of facts and fancies in which
love only appears as a drop of flavor sprinkled
upon an otherwise vapid dish. It is even then
a very weak flavor — hardly perceptible to the
palate. But in a fine French romance, passion is
the motive and its consequence, the effect as well
as the cause, the dish as well as the flavor — the
beginning and end of all; and the least drop of that
flavor has the intoxicating sweetness of Persian
rose-essence. Paris has been called atheistic; but
it is rather pantheistic. *L'éternel féminin* is there
the all in all — a veritable Alpha and Omega
— a feminine Brahma. Such eyes behold all

Nature languid with passion; even inanimate objects create amorous fancies, the clouds suggest aerial love, the trees have a feminine grace, the hills own voluptuous curves 'like the hips of a woman.'

It was such a feeling among the ancient Greeks that produced all their most splendid virtues and talents; and the French art sentiment is to the modern world what that of the Greeks was to the ancient. All that is most tender, most graceful, most lovable; all that is most bewitching, sympathetic, exquisite in modern art has sprung from this source. It would be almost enough to make one believe in the worship of Venus, were we not only too well assured that the source of this art is as dangerous among the moderns as among the ancients; it produces fruit indeed as fair as those of the gardens of the Hesperides, but as foul also as those borne by that mythic Oriental tree whose roots reach into the deeps of hell and the fruit of whose branches are the heads of devils.

One grand result of this passional feeling is visible, however, in another branch of French literature altogether, whereof we can in this brief article cite only one divine example — Michelet, the historian. We doubt if any man, unfettered by prejudice and superstition, could read Michelet without feeling nobler and purer and better afterwards. Michelet is the Historian of Sexual Affection. He has analyzed history with the chemicals of human love. He has shown the result of repression upon legitimate passion through periods of centuries; — and perhaps the great secret of the Middle Ages has never been so fully and boldly, certainly not so skillfully told as in 'La Sorcière.' We might cite hundreds of examples from his 'History of Rome,' his 'Women of the Revolution,' his 'Bible de l'Humanité' — in which there is a wonderful paper upon Solomon's Canticle — his 'History of France,' to illustrate the peculiar value of his extraordinary application of sex philosophy to historical enigmas. Almost wherever the English language is spoken, translations of his 'Love' and 'Woman' are read with the best results. But Michelet felt the spirit of passion impregnating all Nature like the 'Soul of the World'; he studied its results even microscopically; he looked at the life of birds and fishes and insects with new eyes. After perusing his works, 'La Mer,' 'L'Oiseau,' 'L'Insecte' — especially perhaps the last, in which we read so wonderful a history of the republican ants and monarchical bees, one feels the great tenderness of the man to all living creatures entering into himself. A friend told us not very long ago that, after reading that book, he could never find courage to kill either an ant or a spider.

RECENT AMERICAN NOVELS [1]

THERE has been what we might call a literary spurt lately among the younger school of American writers to catch up with the trans-Atlantic English literature of fiction. We refer especially to society fiction — to novels illustrating American society as British novels portray various phases of English society. We are represented, not largely, but well, in historical romance not American, but written by Americans, and European romances written by natives of the United States. But as regards novels illustrating American life proper we have had few productions of late years. At the same time there is a quantity of light American literature produced with this very aim, never attained though incessantly pursued. Some publishers have taken a good step in this direction by issuing series of anonymous novels intended to be peculiarly American. The intention was excellent, but its fulfillment has been found very difficult indeed. No fine American romance has been called into life by this new phase of enterprise. The creations it has begotten are imitations mostly of English or French novels, with nothing American about them except here and there a bit of scene painting from New England or Virginia. There

[1] *Item*, June 18, 1881.

is a curious similarity about all these romances;
they are all the production of one particular
school. Those who write have all breathed the
same educational atmosphere, been guided by
similar social influences, read the same literature,
studied the same philosophy, traveled in the
same countries, and studied art-ideas from the
same standpoint. And all this study and thought
and feeling and experience, is not only confined
within the narrow circle of a certain preconceived
Boston sentiment; but under the influence of that
sentiment to such an extent everything is pedan-
tically colored. There is much fine writing, much
elegance of expression, much evidence of scholarship; but no idea whatever of studying American life from a standpoint not New English.
The idea of seeking for the beautiful and the
picturesque in the lower strata of society as well
as in the upper, of studying agricultural home life
as well as Fifth Avenue drawing-room personages, of portraying distinctly national and local
characteristics, of picturing phases of existence
to be found in the United States only, does not
seem to enter into the mind of these novelists.
And this is the reason that in spite of style and
scholarship and fine taste, the finest of those productions will find no readers within a few years.
They teach nothing new, reproduce nothing of
striking interest, contain nothing which may not
be found in European contemporary novels in a
far more acceptable shape.

The characteristics of the upper class of society are similar in all highly civilized countries; and even the tone of cultured thought has a universal resemblance. Differences of nationality create only the faintest tints of variation. For strong and characteristic color and sentiment, we must study not this hothouse growth of fashionable intellectuality, which resembles a flower that may be found in the private conservatories of all climates and countries; but rather the wild plants, the natural blossoms of human life. Bret Harte did this. Elizabeth Stuart Phelps did it. Oliver Wendell Holmes did it; and Hawthorne and Irving before him. What is wanted now is something distinct and unique and truthful, which cannot be found in the factitious life of drawing-rooms, but in the workshops and factories, among the toilers on river and rail, in villages fringing the sea line or hidden among the wrinkles of the hills, in mining districts and frontier towns, in the suburbs of vast industrial centers, in old-fashioned communities about which quaint traditions cling, among men who, without culture, have made themselves representatives of an enormous financial force, and among those who, in spite of culture, have remained unable to rise above the condition of want, in the office of the merchant, and the residence of the clerk, and the home of the servant, and the rented rooms of the laborer.

A GLANCE AT GYPSY LITERATURE [1]

FROM Seville there comes to us a queer little book in a red paper cover, whose author masks his identity under the pseudonym, 'Demofilo'; but who certainly deserves to be better known. The book is nothing less than a most curious collection of Spanish gypsy ballads, not written in Romany, but in the country dialect of Andalusia, and resembling pure Spanish about as closely as our Creole patois resembles the language of educated Paris. 'Cantos Flamencos' is the book entitled; for the Andalusians have long been in the habit of calling the gypsies 'Flemings,' owing, it is said, to the fact that with the Flemings who entered Spain in the time of Carlos I there came also a great multitude of the Romany or gypsy people. These songs are those to which the gypsy girls so admirably sketched by Doré, dance naked-footed, while the singer with one leg crossed over the other thrums his guitar, and the audience forms a wreath of cigarette smoke about the scene.

These gypsy songs form an entirely new collection, written down probably from dictation by Silverlo, La Lola, El Muerto, Miguel Brava, and others whose picturesque names are given in an

[1] *Item*, July 20, 1881.

index at the end of the work. The songs themselves are evidently of much more recent composition than the gypsy ballads collected by Barrow
and others; for there are very modern ideas in
them. A lover tells his mistress that his love has
the impetuosity of a railroad train:

> 'Yo t'estoy queriondo a ti
> Con la mesma violensia
> Que yeba er ferro-carril.'

Another compares the beating of his heart to
the agony of the engines of an ocean-steamer in a
tempest. Mention of steamers is frequent. One
gypsy tells his gitanella that he sees all the
steamers come into port; but her steamer he
never sees — a poetical lamentation for ships
that never return. Mention of trips to Havana
and South America is frequent, just as in our
own Creole ballads we find the phrase so often
recurring —

> 'M' allé à la Havane
> Fou gagnin larzan.'

The gypsy also sings, 'Yo me voy a la Havana
pa ganar dinero' — but adds that he was robbed
on the way home.

These are all love ditties; but such love! —
furious, Oriental, full of frenzied passion and
tortured symbolism. 'I can brave the madness
of a bull,' cries one; 'I can tear trees up by the
roots; but with thee I can do nothing.' Besides

love, there is little else in them — only a smoth-
ered cry for vengeance here and there. 'The
brother of my heart, they have killed him; they
have killed the little sister who sucked the milk
of my mother: I shall kill them.' And these
strange vows of vengeance often contain a terrific
force. The singer warns his enemy:

> 'If I cannot reach thee in life
> I shall come to thee in death;
> I shall go to all the tombs
> Until I find thee.'

Knives and knife-wounds are frequently mentioned in connection with great singers. 'Do not
go to La Lola; La Lola carries a knife to defend
her person.' Or again — 'Beware of La Sena; —
La Sena carries a knife for the man who would
put himself with her.'

But this fierceness is rare; it is generally only
the fierceness of love we hear, mingled with
strange tenderness. 'I dare not go out,' whispers
one gacho, 'because I have not seen thee to-day;
and when I cannot see thee, I go along the streets
weeping and talking to myself, so that the people
hear me.' Then he breaks out into these reproaches, mingled with gushes of affection:

> 'Thou sayst thou canst not see me;
> There will come to thee in the day
> Moments when thou canst not dance.

> 'Thou sayst thou canst not see me:
> Thy little face is yellow
> With the force of love.

'Thou sayst thou canst not see me!
  Thou still yet remember that saying,
By the milk thou hast sucked!'

We translate the verses line for line. 'By the milk thou hast sucked,' signifying mother's milk, is a strong oath among gypsies. When reproaches seem to have no effect the lover pretends to forget that his sweetheart still lives. 'When I pass before thy door,' he exclaims, 'I say an Ave Maria for thee, even as if thou wert dead.' But he bursts out suddenly in a flood of passion which sweeps away all this effort at self-restraint:

'I love thee more than God —
  Jesus! What have I said! —
I deserve the Inquisition.

'If I thought
  Thou didst not love me,
I would deny God
  And go to live among the Moors.

'I go out of my house,
  I go out of my house cursing —
Cursing even the saints that are in the pictures,
  On Earth and in Heaven.

'My gypsy-girl, when thou diest,
  They shall paint thee on the tombstone
With the blood of my veins.

'I see all the rest,
  Only thee I do not see,
Madre, my heart is striving
  To leap from my lips.

> 'For a year no shirt
>   I have vowed to put on
> Until I find myself again
>   United to my "compañera."'

Then he adopts yet another tone. He attempts to point out to her all the evil she has done him: he says he will enlist in the army, but stays awhile to reiterate his love for her again:

> 'I have more power than God;
>   For God cannot forgive thee
> That which I can forgive thee, sweetheart.

> 'I am going to serve the King;
>   And the winds that shake thy door,
> Are the sighs that I give.

> 'See if I have love for thee;
>   The poison thou wilt give me,
> That poison I will drink.'

But at last she appears to be softened:

> 'By the milk I sucked!
>   It giveth me a shame to look at thee,
> And to thee too when I gaze upon thee.'

Then there is a pretty allusion to the gypsy marriage when the camisa of the bride is exhibited in the morning, 'bearing three little roses' — three little drops of blood.

But to give our readers anything like a fair idea of the spirit of these strange little songs, we must devote another article to the subject on some

future occasion. Probably our readers will not
fail to find some new beauties of fancy and feeling
even in the few verses we have already translated
at random.

A NOVEL LITERARY ENTERPRISE [1]

AMONG notable enterprises in the literature of instruction, we may signal a French work, which, although yet only begun, is already attracting much attention, and will probably be translated into many European languages before long. If not so translated, it will in any event serve as the foundation for a wholly new plan in the construction of historical works.

The work referred to is neither more nor less than a Universal History, compressed into the comparatively small space of sixteen volumes — running about five hundred pages to the volume. History is at once treated from an ethnological, climatological, and geological standpoint; it is rather a history of races than of nations, and deals largely in that peculiar philosophy which considers natural characteristics the result of various local and climatic influences — that philosophy upon which Taine based his studies of ancient and modern art, and of which he was one of the earliest and most successful expounders. First of all the historian presents us with two maps of a country — one ancient and geological, the other modern and ordinary, serving rather as an index to the former than aught else. Then he

[1] *Item*, June 28, 1881.

describes the formation of the mountains; draws out the whole osseous structure of the land; tells us its elementary substance, whether gneiss, basalt, granite, or other rock; recites the hollowing-out of valleys or the filling-up of chasms by glacial revolutions; finally treats of the modern soil and climate, their productiveness and comparative geniality, the vegetable and animal life of the continent; the fauna and flora. Then the influences of that climate and soil upon the character of the human race are shown; startling analogies are drawn between the calmness or tempestuousness, the steadiness or variableness, the harshness or tenderness of the human character and the character of Nature in those regions. Following this we have a summary of all known facts regarding the origin of races and their languages; their migrations, the development of their religion and society, laws and government. Finally comes the great record of the history itself — written from a purely scientific and positive standpoint — not a mere record of facts, but a vast analysis of their causes and consequences — not as regards one people only, but as regards all others brought into close relationship with it.

In short, this 'Histoire Universelle' is a condensation of all acknowledged modern historical science into a wonderfully brief space. The tendency of modern historians and writers on scientific subjects is to compactness; and the editor of this history, Marius Fontaine, has the art of compactness coupled with brilliancy — a style solidly splendid as a ruby-jewel. Every word is chosen; there are no discussions, no theories. The idea of this history has been to create something which will not only always charm, but always endure, and can never be pushed aside by new discoveries. Nothing has been admitted into this history but what is scientifically certain, and the statement of which no future discoveries can prove false. The nature of such a history, containing a summary of all modern scientific discovery relating to history — German, English, Italian, Spanish, Swedish, French, or Russian — is enormous! But one volume has already appeared — 'L'Inde Vedique' — Vedic India. After one has read it he has learned all that is known of ancient India, Indian literature, and early Aryan history — not to speak of positive information regarding the geology and botany and climatology of the Hindoo peninsula.

It is only of recent years, indeed, that the application of science to history has been successfully made; and in the coming century history will only be studied from this point of view. The appearance of works like that above described shows that the time is not far off when the testimony of writers and witnesses, of books and parchments and archives, will be less considered as intrinsically trustworthy than as mere clues to general facts to be perfectly elucidated by a positive science, inaccessible to prejudice and enthusiastic only in the pursuit of truth and the worship of beauty in Nature.

A JOURNALISTIC OUTLOOK [1]

A CURIOUS feature of journalism has been developed in the United States within comparatively recent years, which has certainly no parallel in the literature of any other civilized country — the humorous sketch. The humorous paragraph existed long before the special humorous features which we refer to as of recent growth — the paragraph sprung into existence spontaneously with the development of the natural American character — sharp, strong, vivid, with something satanic in its flash. But the paragraph is not a labored production when good. It is simply the utterance of a really witty mind, which amuses itself by presenting the most absurd image created by some announcement, incident, contrast, or discordance. The American paragraph is the supreme expression of satirical wit. Nothing rivals it. English fun is heavy and grotesque compared with it; the brilliancy of French fun becomes a very feeble light in its blaze. The American paragrapher does not waste words; he assails the imagination directly with irresistible suggestions of colossal absurdity, instead of actually drawing the absurdity for us to look at. It is really to be regretted that the

[1] *Item*, September 2, 1881.

majority of immensely funny paragraphs which have been read and laughed at all over the country, were never collected and united into a volume — a volume which would be valuable as showing the development of a peculiar national humor, and the spirit of the steam-and-lightning period to which it belongs.

The development of this paragraphic humor into ridiculous pictures of large size and perfect framing belongs, however, to a much more recent epoch in journalism — the period of the *Free Press*, *Burlington Hawkeye*, *Oil City Derrick*, and numerous other papers whereof everybody reads something occasionally, whether he ever sees those particular papers or not, for they furnish the entire press of the country with comicality. The young journalists who developed this peculiar literature had at first no idea of becoming noted. Many were reporters, who dressed up their reports of small incidents in a humorous dress for the mere pleasure of giving their friends a good laugh. But the public became interested to such an extent that the young writers obtained a national reputation, and in all parts of the country efforts were made to imitate their humor. Among the would-be imitators those who possessed real wit themselves, soon abandoned all attempts to follow their models' system of sketching; but by applying the same principle of humor to their own work, succeeded in creating distinct and powerful originalities. There is hardly a city of importance in the country now, where one humorous journalist may not be found. Competition is intensifying and heightening the quality of this humor year after year, and will certainly develop something very extraordinary before very long.

But the success of several young journalists in this way offers indications also of a still more important era in American journalism. It is highly probable that a taste will yet be created for literature of a higher order in the daily press — such literature as is now to be found only in magazines or periodicals of a purely literary character. This would give us in the course of time newspapers with all that brilliancy and art which mark French journalism and that unrivaled enterprise in the obtaining of news which is purely American. This age in the future of our newspapers is yet remote; but we may feel assured that it will come even from present indications in the great centers of American journalism.

AMERICAN ART TASTES [1]

A FEW years ago, except in the matter of literature, it was truly said of America, that she possessed no native art taste. The East, which led in matters of literary taste, chiseled sternly according to New England standards, gave to national thought in such matters a somber tone, a peculiar gray tint of puritanism. This puritanism has not yet wholly disappeared; it is visible in a thousand shapes. Even at a very late period when Eastern publishers reproduced the publications of European dilettanti, there was a great deal of ridiculous emasculation done, and much fig-leaf nonsense displayed. Even to-day there is much of the spirit visible among the people — the nudity of true art shocks them, the antique spirit horrifies them. Only under such conditions could an American 'artist,' who actually ridiculed the antique art, and spoke of the Venus di Medici as 'misshapen,' have imposed such an absurdity as the Greek Slave upon the public as a true work of art. The same spirit has manifested itself in the reproduction of foreign literature; nearly all American translations from the various Latin tongues being shamefully emasculated.

With the present generation, however, much

[1] *Item*, September 30, 1881.

has been changed. The students of art now trained in the schools of Rome, Paris, Munich, and Florence, have shaken off the conventionalities which the old-fashioned home spirit imposed upon them. They inundate their canvases with life and light and warmth; they model their plastic work unfettered by puritanical ideas. While it is true that they must first succeed in Europe — as a general rule — in order to be appreciated at home; still, it is encouraging to know that thereafter their pictures and statues do not lack generous American purchasers. Not long ago, the *Protectionist*, a very able paper, was lamenting the absence of art taste in New York, and mourning that our metropolis should not be an art center, like London, like Paris, like Rome, like Madrid. But the fact is that New York will certainly become before another half-century the art center of the Western world and well worthy to vie with any European capital. In fact the treasures of European art are gradually but surely flowing there; the capitalists of the United States are doing all that wealth can do to establish a correct standard of American art tastes. And they will assuredly succeed. Art flourishes only in those centers of civilization where wealth and leisure combine to create a class of dilettanti. The West is rich; but the West is too busy, and will be for generations to come, to produce such a class as is now forming in the East. We shall probably live to see the result; and we may dare to predict that the development of correct art taste in America will be as rapid as her industrial progress during the past century.

ENGLISH THE UNIVERSAL TONGUE OF THE FUTURE [1]

PROFESSOR JOHN FISKE, in a recent number of the *Atlantic Monthly*, utters a curious prediction regarding the future of language. He computes that by the close of the twentieth century, eight hundred millions of the human race will have learned to speak the English language, and the strong Anglo-Saxon tongue, having once acquired such a preponderance, the entire civilized world will be obliged to learn it, and learning it will gradually force its use even among barbaric races.

The progress of the present century clearly indicates that the commerce of the future will entirely abolish Old World state lines and boundaries between nations, and will assuredly compel such a brotherhood of races as never existed there before. The growth of telegraphs and railroads, the enormous improvements in steam merchant marine, and the universality of the postal system, all tend to confirm Professor Fiske's idea. But there is also another side to the question. The growth of a language is in proportion to the growth of the commercial wealth of the nation which speaks it, and the political strength and in-

[1] *Item*, October 23, 1881.

fluence of that nation abroad. Thus Rome forced her language at one time upon a vast portion of the world; thus the Arabs imposed their tongue at a later day upon millions of Asiatics, Africans, and Europeans; thus Spain made a Latin tongue the mother-speech of the new Western world; thus France, at one period, made the knowledge of French an indispensable polite accomplishment for all civilization. At the present day English influence is paramount in commerce and in foreign lands; and the English-speaking Americans will certainly force their tongue sooner or later as far south as Cape Horn, slaying the weaker dialects opposed to it, but always incorporating a something from each local idiom. The English are making it the natural language of Australia, New Zealand, and innumerable colonies; the Americans will make it the speech of all the West Indies. Should the political status of England remain the same until the end of the twentieth century, Professor Fiske's prediction would certainly be in a fair way of realization. As for our own commercial ascendancy, we have no reason to doubt of it until then; the Nation is too youthfully vigorous and of a creative power too prodigious to fear competition. But it is not so certain that British power will remain what it is. Had it not been for the victory of Charles Martel, some great historian observed that Arabic might be taught to-day at Oxford and Cambridge; and we might surely say that but for a possibility of Russian conquests in the East and rival struggles with German and French commercial competitors, English might yet become the language of Asia. The Germans will yet become formidable competitors for the commerce of the East; the French are creating a navy equal to the English. There will be such a struggle for commercial supremacy during the next two centuries as never before; and it is not at all certain because England has the ascendancy to-day that she will keep it. Nevertheless the dream of an universal language is quite delightful!

SOME GROTESQUE THEORIZING [1]

WHEN we leave this world — as some of the noted nineteenth-century astronomers have done — to travel theoretically in the limitless domain of stars, there can be no limit to hypothesis, and no restraint to imagination. After having perused some literature produced within the last generation by writers upon the subject of life in other planets, everything previously conceived by romance writers seems pallid and pitiful. We have been told of worlds where suns never set, and where there is no sleep, so that people must work, presumably, all their lives without ceasing. Life in such worlds might resemble an eternal factory-day — or, symbolically, a perpetual-motion machine, with self-renewing parts.

We have been told of worlds illuminated by blue, green, scarlet, pink, yellow, and purple suns; and even of some where a green sun rises while a blue sun sets, with a red sun all the while in the zenith. We have been taught to dream of planetary nights illuminated by seven moons.

We have been told of spheres so much more advanced in knowledge than our own, that a brief interview with one of their philosophers

[1] *Times-Democrat*, May 24, 1882.

would result in advancing our own knowledge by thousands of years.

We have been informed of worlds where the senses of sight, hearing, and touch must be developed to the perception of colors, forms, sounds, and taste and feeling of which we have no more idea than we have of those octaves of color whose existence, although betrayed in a ghostly manner by the spectroscope, remain imperceptible to our sense of sight.

We have heard also of worlds where men, organized as we are, could leap in one bound across oceans, like the apes of the Ramayana, or skip lightly over the mountains like the Beloved in Solomon's Song of Songs. We have also been told about worlds where it is always summer, and worlds where it is always winter; — but without further recapitulation, it is enough to observe that the tendency of these teachers is to inculcate a belief that our own earth is a very poor concern indeed, illuminated by a small white vulgar sun, and not at all to compare with those other worlds illuminated by royal purple suns or by suns of cardinal red. It is true there are several hundred small planets which circle between Mars and Jupiter like a swarm of luminous bees, some of which are only a few miles in diameter; but the inhabitants of these tiny worlds, supposed to have been formed by the fragments of some vaster destroyed planet, or perhaps one of Jupiter's vanished rings, are better off than we; for they are giants, and can jump half-way round one of their little planets at a single jump. You might imagine that the small worlds would have small inhabitants, and the large worlds big ones; but the astronomical theorists assure us that such is not the case. On the contrary, the big worlds must have very small inhabitants, and the very small ones enormous inhabitants — just as some of the largest mammalia are tormented by very small parasites, and some of the very smallest by large ones!

And this reminds us of another theory that worlds are living creatures, huge animals, of which we are only parasites; and that these huge animals circulate and propagate themselves in space — not like the planets and stars of the Grand Inquisitor's dream in Balzac's 'Succubus,' but rather like those spherical animalculæ whose revolutions Loewenhock and other microscopists describe. Such a theorist laughs to scorn the ideas of attraction of gravitation and cohesion; the worlds are simply gregarious creatures, brought together by mutual affection. We are only their fleas!

We do not recollect, however, a single instance of this fine scientific theorizing in which there is not a tendency to imagine the inhabitants of other worlds as being shaped somewhat like ourselves — anthropoid creatures more or less highly developed. But as the theory of evolution — of 'descent through modifications' is now being applied to so many branches of human research, we do not see why it should be overlooked in hypothetical astronomy. We have certainly a right to theorize a little in our own private way; and therefore propose to consider the inhabitability of other worlds according to the Darwinian theory.

Assuming the truth of the hypothesis that we are but highly developed *mesopitheci* or Miocene apes, it does not at all follow that the most intelligent beings of other worlds should belong to a corresponding species of planetary quadrumana. Such accidental modifications of the earth's surface which developed those necessities which developed the intelligence of apes beyond that of any other form of intelligence, might in other worlds have developed the intelligence of birds or insects so as to make them the ruling powers. There might be planets inhabited by birds capable of building cities, writing books, conversing in many languages like the birds of Arabian tales, and subjecting all other animated life to their control. There might be in some planet a realization of Swift's fable of the Yahoos and Houyhnhnms; there might be worlds ruled by insects small as our ants, but more learned by far than we are, although having their brains in the neighborhood of their stomachs.

Still, it must be confessed that at this point

we are nearing a world of fable so much wilder than the stories of Scheherazade that Talking Fishes and Golden Birds become uninteresting — that Phantasmion itself is a commonplace sojourn — that one is ready to believe in the existence of beautiful women with sky-blue skins and sea-green hair. After going so far, we must acknowledge that the country where the soil is all breakfast chocolate and the mountains all rock-candy capped with ice-cream, ceases to seem altogether unattainable.

THE ALEXANDRIAN LIBRARY [1]

A CONTEMPORARY, in a recent issue, declared that the traditions current respecting the famous Alexandrian library were more or less untrustworthy; and that the statements regarding the size of the collection were probably exaggerated.

Some of the best modern scholars, however, think differently. The famous library founded by Ptolemy Soter and mentioned by his son, Ptolemy Philadelphus, would not indeed compare with that of the British Museum of to-day, nor with the great national libraries of other European capitals, nor even with the public library of Boston; but when we consider that its foundation antedated the discovery of printing, and was accomplished at a period when knowledge was but little diffused, its existence seems a more wonderful fact than that of the greatest libraries of the nineteenth century. We must also recollect that the manuscripts which composed it occupied a far larger volume than the same literary material could occupy to-day, if printed in large type upon thick paper. But the number and value of these manuscripts were certainly prodigious; and modern scholarship has never ceased, with the best of reasons, to regret their destruction. It is possible

[1] *Times-Democrat*, July 23, 1882.

that further researches in Pompeii may restore us something of that ancient learning and literature we so justly mourn for; yet it certainly can never supply the vast void left by the incineration of the Alexandrian museum.

For, like the greatest of English libraries, the Alexandrian library formed but one of the attractions of a prodigious museum. That museum was situated in the Bruchion, which was the 'West End,' or fashionable quarter of the city. It was built of marble; and the choicest statues, mosaics, and paintings of antiquity were exhibited within its vast halls. The library itself eventually comprised four hundred thousand volumes. The librarians were selected from among the most learned of the ancients; and were given almost unlimited powers of purchase for the securing of rare books. Under their orders were an immense corps of copyists and translators. When a work was purchased, the original was placed in the library, and the original owner received a copy, together with a large pecuniary indemnity. Draper states that the indemnity thus paid by Ptolemy Euergetes to certain Athenians for the manuscripts of Sophocles, Æschylus, and Euripides amounted to something like $15,000. It was in this library that the famous Septuagint translation of the Bible was made.

It is not to our purpose to speak of the schools (attended by fourteen thousand students) — of mathematics, geometry, philosophy, astronomy, literature, medicine, and natural history — nor of the botanical and zoölogical gardens connected with the museum — nor of the invention there of the first steam engine — nor the famous laboratory in which the first alchemists, perhaps, sought to discover the Elixir of Life. The library was the glory of the institution. We have said it reached 400,000 volumes. This collection was consumed by fire during the siege of Alexandria by Julius Cæsar. But there was still another Alexandrian library. When the museum could not accommodate the ocean of literature poured into it, another library, called the Daughter Library, was established in the Serapion, or Temple of Serapis, in which 300,000 volumes were finally collected. Even before the siege of the city by Julius Cæsar, the two Alexandrian libraries contained the grand total of 700,000 volumes.

In order to console Cleopatra for the loss of the chief library, Mark Antony presented her with a splendid collection made by Eumenes, King of Pergamus, and this, added to the collection in the Serapion, elevated the Alexandrian library to half a million volumes. This collection was not destroyed by the Arabs, but by order of the Christian Emperor Theodosius, during the last struggle of Paganism against Christianity.

It was a thousand years after the time of

Ptolemy Soter, that Amrou, lieutenant of Khalif Omar, captured Alexandria, and there found a library of immense extent, containing perhaps many works which had escaped the fury of fanatics and fires of war. But the main portion thereof cannot have belonged to the older libraries. It is needless to report here the story of the Khalif's order for their destruction, on the ground that the Koran contained all that men should know. But the last remnant of the antique literature that had been struggling for existence during ten long centuries was then finally destroyed.

It has been said that the library of Tripoli, burnt by the crusaders, consisted of three million volumes; but we may well doubt whether it could ever have compared in value or extent with the libraries of the Ptolemies.

PRESENT STATUS OF THE GERM THEORY [1]

'IF,' says Pasteur, 'the doctrine of spontaneous generation be what I am convinced it is — a chimera, it is in the power of man to make all parasitic maladies disappear from the surface of the globe.' This is, perhaps, the most startling utterance made by that most extraordinary man.

It has been imagined by thousands having only a very superficial knowledge of the vast questions involved in the discussion, that the opposition made to Dr. Bastian and his fellow champions of spontaneous generation, was largely inspired by orthodox sentiment and anti-materialism. On the contrary the most positive scientists have battled the theory with most purely scientific purpose. If the doctrine of spontaneous generation be established beyond doubt, it will be futile to attempt the extirpation of epidemic diseases; and the most important hope of the future of medicine will be extinguished beyond resurrection. If the doctrine be erroneous, as Pasteur holds, then, indeed, we may trust that it will be yet in the power of man to destroy all known sources of contagious disorders, and to provide

[1] *Times-Democrat*, August 8, 1882.

against the development of sources yet to be discovered.

Professor John Tyndall has taken up the scientific cudgels for Pasteur with admirable skill. In his recent work upon 'Floating Matter of the Air,' he presents the results of an enormous and varied system of experimentation which he has pursued with singular success. The inferences perfectly coincide with Pasteur's views; — they offer convincing proof that we have as yet no grounds whatever for belief in spontaneous generation. In no single instance of several thousand experiments with sealed tubes containing infusions of all descriptions did life appear when the tubes were so constructed as to exclude the exterior air. The least crack, the most imperceptible orifice, was, however, sufficient to produce an opposite result. Many of the experiments which occupy the bulk of his work are of the most curious and interesting sort; and the astonishing vitality of certain germs is amply proven by their resistance to eight hours of boiling.

The theory of spontaneous generation, as offered by the Bastianites, is indeed even contrary to the now generally received notion of evolution. While the most advanced school of recognized science does not discountenance the theory that at some period infinitely remote, the formation of the first organisms may have been in a certain sense spontaneous; nevertheless all that it has discovered tends to prove that all existing forms, even microscopic, were gradually developed from simpler forms by influences continually acting through incalculable periods of time. Much of the microscopic life recently discovered is highly complex — far too complex to admit of spontaneous generation according to present notions of evolution.

There is certainly nothing more wonderful than the generative methods of certain varieties of microscopic life. There are tiny rodlike creatures which multiply by breaking off in the middle, each half subsequently developing a head and a tail, and rapidly maturing only to part again. The frightful result of this system of compound multiplication within the blood will be readily understood by any one who has ever worked out the blacksmith's problem of charging a cent for the first of thirty horse-shoe nails, the price to be doubled upon the second nail, quadrupled upon the third, and so on!

Huxley has told us of another creature which possesses a triple system of propagation. The individual is bi-sexual, and two propagate. But occasionally a number form themselves into a globe. The globe gradually solidifies; the bodies composing it become a shell; the shell bursts and gives birth to countless myriads. And what is not less extraordinary, a single individual will propagate if left in solitude.

Yet these are innocent compared to the germ of splenic fever discovered by Pasteur. A transparent jelly-like rod appears in the blood. It lengthens with inconceivable rapidity. In a brief period it has grown to a hundred times its original length. Then dots appear all through it, side by side, like peas in a pod. The rod suddenly falls into innumerable pieces. Each piece, with its dots, lengthens into a rod. Centuple compound multiplication! The complexity of such magical organisms does not harmonize with spontaneous generation — unless we are ready to swallow the notion of alchemy, that were the elements of a human body united by chemistry in just proportions they would crystallize of themselves into human form.

It is a curious fact that there is no record of these creatures being found in the atmosphere in developed condition. Bacteria, for example, appear to develop only upon finding a center or medium favorable for propagation. They have undoubtedly a preëxistent stage; but what it is we do not precisely know. The air is full of their germs. When the air with which the tubes of Tyndall were filled, before the tubes were sealed, had been purified by flame, no trace of them subsequently appeared. An hydrogen flame which emits no smoke, shows above it masses of blackness resembling smoke nevertheless. Experiments by Tyndall show these masses of blackness to be only clear space, in which heat has consumed and destroyed all organisms. The air is full of them; the most carefully polished surface is shown to be covered with them by the microscope! Only by heat and certain chemical means can they be destroyed.

But the revelation of these facts has saved innumerable lives. The antiseptic system of surgery has been revolutionized by them. The hygienic philosophy of the future will be based upon them. It is even possible that later discoveries will give us the means of destroying beyond possibility of reproduction some of the deadliest forms of microscopic life. For the present we may hope that the theory of spontaneous generation will prove a fallacy. Pasteur positively asserts as much. Tyndall is more cautious, even while supporting Pasteur. It is perilous to be positive regarding such matters. But the evidence is certainly in favor of the opponents of Bastian; and the views of Pasteur in thorough harmony with the vast discoveries of Darwin regarding the genesis of forms.

FOR THE SUM OF $25 [1]

A PHILADELPHIA paper has recently supplemented our endeavors toward the suppression of execrable translations from foreign tongues, by publishing an eloquent exposition of the method in which these translations are made. Written at random moments, upon bar-room tables, these mangled versions of great French and German masterpieces are paid for at the magnificent rate of from $25 to $100 per volume. Yet no phase of literary toil is so laborious, even while so ill paid. The translator may be a charlatan, but he receives a remuneration inferior to that of the commonest physical labor, when the comparative physical strain is considered. One translator, we are told (a lady), has to write 75 foolscap pages a day; and under pressure may have to turn out two translations in one week — representing, at the very least, 600 pages of printed matter. Remuneration: $25 to $100!

No wonder that the works of French writers are murdered — no wonder that the translators of real ability can find no employment. Imagine the agreeable task of translating two volumes of Zola in one week for the glorious sum of $50! Needless to say that no person of talent would

[1] *Times-Democrat*, September 24, 1882.

dream of working for such employers, or of stultifying himself by attempting to perform in days what ought to be the laborious work of twice as many months.

When we attempt to make anything like a fair estimate of the labor needed to effect a faithful and meritorious translation of the great masters of the French language, we cannot imagine it possible to translate more than five or six pages a day (long primer, leaded, 16mo). For it is by no means sufficient to reproduce the general meaning of a sentence — it is equally necessary to obtain a just equivalent for each word, in regard to force, color, and form — and to preserve, as far as possible, the original construction of the phrase, the peculiarity of the rhetoric, the music of the style. And there is a music in every master style — a measured flow of words in every sentence; — there are alliterations and rhythms; — there are onomatopœias; there are tints, sonorities, luminosities, resonances. Each word in a phrase is a study in itself, and a study in its relation to other words in the phrase; and the phrase in its relation to the sentence, and the sentence in its relation to the paragraph, and the paragraph in its relation to other paragraphs. Then besides precise shades of meaning, must be studied harmonies of tones and their relation to other tones, and their general interrelation with the music of the entire idea. A most laborious, cautious, in-

genious, delicate, supple work — a work demand-
ing perhaps even a greater knowledge of one's
own tongue than of the French tongue — a work
to be aided, not by French dictionaries, but
by English dictionaries of synonyms and deri-
vations and antonyms and technicalities and
idioms and rhymes. A work requiring intense
application, wearisome research, and varied linguistic powers. A work of giants indeed —
easily flowing as its result may seem to careless
eyes thereafter — eyes unable to analyze the
secret of the art that pleases them. There is no
more difficult and scholarly task than to translate perfectly a masterpiece from one tongue
into another. Wherefore the proverbs — French,
Spanish, and Italian — *traduire c'est trahire, tra-
ductor, traidor;* and *traduttore, traditore* — syn-
onymizing 'translator' and 'traitor.' Faithless
indeed must be the translator who imagines that
he can produce in one week or one month a fair
translation of some work which cost its author
years of literary labor.

And this very new school of French literature
— the school of Daudet, Goncourt, Zola, and
Flaubert — so ruthlessly treated by persons who
produce these bogus translations, is that which of
all others demands the most careful labor. The
sense, forms, force, sonority, color of every word
must be studied; the shape of every phrase chiseled out; the beauty of every naked sentence

polished like statuary marble. Men have killed themselves at this terrible literary labor, so utterly ignored by American translators. One of the brothers Goncourt perished from the nervous exhaustion entailed by intense application. And it is such work as this, the labor of years — work produced in nervous tortures, prostrating fatigues, brain agonies unspeakable — a work of blood and tears — a work in whose every line quivers the vitality of the creator — that some vulgar scribbler sits down to translate at a bar-room table under a contract to complete the task in one week, for the sum of $25!

THE FATE OF THE COMET [1]

THE prediction by certain eminent astronomers of the fiery fate of the comet now visible, cannot fail to awaken in thoughtful minds some ideas regarding the birth and death of all stars and planets, all suns and worlds, throughout that awful Infinite whose apparent stability is illusion — where all is changing in the external flux of forms, slowly according to our human conceptions, but rapidly enough in fact, forasmuch as a million years are but as a second on the dial of Immensity.

The fate of all comets is probably the same. Like luminous moths circling round and round an attracting flame until their scorched wings cease to bear them and they fall headlong into consuming light, so these swift and brilliant circlers about the sun must at last be devoured by his fires.

When a celestial body circles continually about another, always following the same curve, the centripetal force or force of attraction, must be continually counterbalanced evenly, along all the points of that curve, by the centrifugal force. But if the centrifugal force be persistently weakened by some other, the centripetal preponder-

[1] *Times-Democrat*, September 25, 1882.

ating, results in the ultimate absorption of the satellite by its center, of the planet by the sun.

Ponderously solid as our planets are, steady as are their orbits, it is scarcely possible that the centrifugal force could be weakened in their regard by any common accident. They could withstand the shock of innumerable comets — mere ghosts of fire, which do not possess weight enough to shake the mighty framework of any inhabited world in our solar system. And the planets voyage through shoals of nebulous matter as easily as a trading vessel through the phosphorescent waters of some tropical sea by night. But the comets, frail as dreams, lighter than gas-flame, impalpable as phantoms (except, indeed, the few which possess a small nucleus of solid matter) cannot do so. They travel not through empty space but through vast regions in which omnipresent and omnipotent Force is ever active — through shoals of embryonic nebulæ floating in immensity like fish-spawn — through shoals of cosmic dust, the ashes of burnt-out suns — through films of matter half-formed, partly ether, partly gas. All this checks the course of the spectral comets, their plumes of light drag heavily through these obstacles; their swiftness is each time thus diminished, the centrifugal force is weakened, the prodigious enchantment of the sun draws them nearer to the furnace each time they return.

The more comets devoured by the sun, however, the more advantageous for us. They will augment his heat, replenish his energy, increase his volume and his attractive power — and by augmenting the swiftness of our own movements shorten the years. But it would require an infinite number of comets to produce any marked effect upon that ocean of fire. For were the whole world flung into the sun like a coal, it would only furnish him fuel for ninety-five years.

And he needs fuel. The sun is dying. The spots upon his face are like the dark spaces obscured in a heap of burning coals, when their carbon is on the point of exhaustion. He was once far warmer and brighter; his disk vaster. He now belongs to the class of variable yellow stars; — he burns unsteadily with a maximum and minimum period, extending over about eleven years. We see other suns now in the condition he will yet be. Some are blood-red like fading embers, some deep blue, like dying alcohol flames. The sun will yet appear as in the prophecies of the Hebrews, 'red as blood,' and that lurid light will herald the end of man. Perhaps, however, even after that epoch, the red corpse of the central star will emit heat enough to sustain life upon Mercury, or upon that extraordinary little world Vulcan, still nearer to him, if we are to believe certain astronomers. But before the sun gives up his flame-ghost to God, strange things will be seen. His light will die down for long periods and suddenly flame up again — as a coal-fire long unpoked, sends out a flicker at intervals.

Let us feel small when we remember how poor a sphere is this sun we call glorious. He would make a dark spot against the face of Sirius; and were the latter mighty star to take his place in the center of our system, every planet would be instantly withered by the terrific heat, would pass away like vapor. The sun himself would be easily consumed by Sirius.

But how long will the sun last? Two calculations have been made upon this subject. The sun loses one tenth of a degree of heat every 2000 years; or one degree in 20,000 years; or 100 degrees in 2,000,000 years. His present heat is calculated at 8,000,000 degrees. Therefore it will require 100,000,000,000 years to exhaust it. We have time to become as gods ere that!

Again the geometrician Fourier has shown that the rapidity of cooling of two unequal spheres is in inverse ratio to the square of their diameters. It has been estimated that our own earth (once a star) cooled at the rate of one degree in 33,000 years; and the diameter of the sun is just 110 times greater than that of the earth. Therefore the sun would cool off 12,100 times more slowly, or at the rate of one degree in 400,000,000 years. This would place the time of his total extinction at the remote future of

3,200,000,000,000,000 of years. Time enough to improve in!

But the dream of Byron will yet indeed be realized, when the icy earth shall 'swing blind and blackening in the moonless air.' Its realization seems far off; but our notions of time and space are meager — we are only ephemerides.

Yet, when we know that the stars die in their courses, that the worlds do indeed pass away as smoke and the heavens do melt as wax, wither up as a scroll — how strange that thoughts of death should ever cast a shadow upon our lives! Shall not the force that throbs in our hearts be reborn under a myriad million forms? Shall we not aid to form the light of other suns, to think the thoughts of other worlds yet unformed? There was no beginning save of Shape; there shall be no end, save of Form. How grandly has the telescope of astronomy magnified the pantheism of the East, and the strange thought of the Hebrew psalm:

'The heavens are the work of Thy hands. They shall perish; yea, all of them shall grow old like a garment. And as a vesture Thou shalt change them, and they shall be changed.'

SUBMARINE GOSSIP [1]

THE annual meeting of the Cinq Académies has been rendered unusually interesting this year by the address of Professor Milne Edwards, regarding the deep-sea life recently discovered — including a variety of unknown flora and a number of extraordinarily organized creatures never before heard of.

Solar light penetrates the most transparent water with difficulty; and when we descend in the diving bell of our imagination to those abysses of ocean, whose depth must be measured by miles, it is, indeed, awful to consider the blackness of that liquid night. Here dwell multitudes of sentient beings absolutely blind, guiding their Cimmerian wanderings by the sense of touch alone — a sense in their regard marvelously developed, as their antennæ extend to a length unknown in the insect world. Theirs must be a strange life! In those abysses there is no sound; there are no undulations; there are no odors. Feeling alone remains; — millions of blind lives are born to crawl and quiver through those salty darknesses without seeing, hearing or smelling — using the lengthened nerves of their antennæ as a blind man uses his stick.

[1] *Times-Democrat*, December 10, 1882.

But side by side with them swarm billions of radiant beings — the fireflies and glow-worms of the deep — the stars of the sea-night. These have enormous eyes, like the fantastic insects Doré always represents crawling about the doors of his mediæval witches. Their entire bodies glow with luminosity of different tints — lilac, green, pink, crimson, violet; they make their own light; they see by the radiance of their own eyes. They are to zoölogy what are to astronomy the thousands of brilliant suns — blue, scarlet, sapphire, emerald, lapis-lazuli, orange, crimson — single and double, whereof the mere varieties of color as indicated in astronomical catalogues daze the imagination of the student.

Such is the radiance of these zoöphytes that small print may be read by it; and some possess the singular faculty of extinguishing it at will — as when a vessel, pursued by pirates, masks all her lights, and changes her course in the dark.

It has long been supposed that color was inseparable from light; that in regions never reached by the sun all life must be white and colorless as grave-worms or as those pallid parasites that are born in the intestines of the creatures upon whose being they live. But this has been found to be erroneous. Carmine, purple, cochineal-red, amethystine and ruby beings live in the very blackest depths of the ocean. One deep-sea starfish has rightfully been called *Brisinga* by the

Norwegian discoverer — for it flames like a topaz, and *Brisinga* was the name of the jewel-necklace of the Goddess Freya.

These beings belong to a special fauna not resembling existing species, but strangely similar to species preserved in petrified form from geologic ages — from the period of the plesiosaurus and ichthyosaurus when the leviathans of the primitive world made the deep sea 'to boil as a pot of ointment.' Nature, so active in remodeling forms under the sun, seems to have forgotten these most ancient children of hers — dwelling in the chaos of abysses, beyond the reach of solar chemistry.

We have spoken of fauna and flora; but the flora mentioned do not exist in the deepest portions of the ocean-bed where dwell the creatures above described.

The *fucus giganticus* which grows to the length of eight hundred feet can find no root in gulfs where the wrecks of shells are being steadily converted into marble by the mere hydraulic pressure of the sea. There are no plants at this depth whatever. The tiny creatures must be fed, as if by manna from above. The carrion of upper-ocean life must be buried in the stomachs of these zoöphytes — all débris, fragments of sea-weed, limbs of dead jellyfish, scales and fins lost in piscatory battles near the surface, everything which at last sinks to feed this wonderful life at the bottom. At such a depth the ocean holds rich material in solution. The zoöphytes need not actually eat; they absorb the thick fluid as we inhale air — but with more nutritious consequences.

Since something of the antediluvian world has been thus found alive, might it not be hoped that science will yet secure living specimens of the monsters of the early geologic periods? Some hold this to be less probable than the discovery of a herd of mastodons in Central Africa, or a flock of pterodactyls at the North Pole. But others, arguing by analogy, declare that we may yet find monstrous creatures in those parts of the ocean where marine vegetation attains most enormous luxuriance — in those jungles of Ocean which are its Javas and Malabars — its Indian and Brazilian forests. Where sea-plants grow to the length of eight hundred feet, what anacondas and pythons might not be found! There the Leviathan himself might lie coiled up, dreaming of that lurid day when he must rise to the surface at the call of the Trumpets of the Last Judgment. And who knows that the sea-serpents have not made to themselves a lair in some silent temple of Atlantis, even as the cobras haunt the long-deserted fanes of Ellora and the shrines of the Indian Christ?

SUN–SPASMS [1]

DURING the past week several extraordinary changes have been taking place in the sun — changes so tremendous as to be visible through a common opera-glass, remarks the New York *Sun*. We are told that on Tuesday four huge spots united, bridged themselves, and finally changed themselves into a host of small spots — dividing and subdividing like the yolk of an egg in process of segmentation. Eruptions inconceivably violent accompanied these phenomena. All we can imagine of volcanic energy is surpassed by the mention of craters, large enough to swallow half the planets in the universe, casting up columns of fire to a height of 200,000 miles and more. Such explosions have been recorded at various times by observers of the sun.

What these sun-spots positively are, no one yet knows; and although — as one astronomer observes — the sun seems to be 'the plainest thing in the universe,' none have been able to read the mysteries of his face. Sun-spots are not always accompanied by solar explosions, and these may take place independently of sunspots. Whether a portion of the glowing photosphere is blown aside — whether the flame of one burning gas be temporarily extinguished by the

[1] *Times-Democrat*, June 26, 1883.

uprising of other and heavier elements, cannot always be decided. An easy explanation is that afforded by writers like Richard of Paris, who compare the dark spots upon the sun to those visible in a bed of blazing coal. It is true that portions of the coal alternately flame up or die down, so that the dark spots in the coal fire appear to shift like those upon the face of the sun — none of which last more than six weeks in one shape. It is also true that other suns of far brighter luster show no spots; — their light is electrically white and terribly pure; our sun would look coffee-colored beside them. Lastly it is reasonable to view the existence of sun-spots as indicating the vast antiquity of our solar center, and heralding its period of extinction — now fixed at 3,200,000,000,000,000 of years more. But the periodicity of solar agitation has been thus far an inexplicable enigma. Every eleven years or thereabouts, the solar outbreaks wax and wane. The last maximum of solar disturbance was strangely coincident with the Franco-Prussian War. The last minimum was in 1878. We are now approaching another maximum which will be reached in 1885.

The latest theories regarding this periodicity attribute it, not to interior solar changes, but to external astral or planetary influences. Still, the theorists frankly confess their doubts. We only know that the sun's power and heat and magnetism wax and wane regularly as to period though irregularly as to violence; and as he grows older we may suppose the intervals will become longer. When half of his face becomes dark, the phenomena will assume an aspect as terrible as the prophecies of Isaiah; and, still later, in millions of years, when his light shall have died down, and he will appear at his minimum like a monstrous blood drop, the last inhabitant of the earth might well watch with anguish for those spasmodic maximum-periods at which the crimson globe would partly burst into yellow flame, and create a flickering daylight for a few months, or a season.

So intimately connected is the life of the world with that of the sun, that our globe throbs to every movement of solar energy. It is not now necessary to watch the sun in order to ascertain the number of eruptions; — a magnetic instrument sensitively records every single one of them. As many as 3200 have been chronicled in a year of maximum solar activity; the number may sink below 500 at the minimum period.

Telegraph instruments are seriously affected by solar outbreaks, and all terrestrial energies act sympathetically. There are strange atmospheric disturbances, auroral phenomena of weirdest aspect — sometimes earthquakes. Eruptions of terrestrial volcanoes often follow upon solar explosions; and it is worth while to note that during the recent changes in the sun both Cotopaxi and Vesuvius began to threaten the lands below them. This, however, may be only indirectly the result of solar power. It is important to remember that a fall of two inches in the mercury indicates the removal of a weight of two millions of tons from each square mile of the earth's surface; and such variations are not so uncommon as might be supposed. The statement seems startling, but when we remember that the total weight of the atmosphere is 5,825,000,-000,000,000 tons — or 2125 pounds to each square foot when the mercury stands at thirty inches — the fact does not appear so wonderful. Now the increase or diminution of air-pressure upon the crust of the earth depends on solar influences, and recently that influence has been prodigiously exerted. A sudden decrease of air-pressure almost invariably precedes an eruption in volcanic centers.

The last maximum of solar energy was coincident with perhaps the greatest war of modern history, and our American Civil War was coincident with the previous maximum. What will the next bring? There are theorists who believe that the lives of nations are affected by the great Eye of the sun; — and this new astrology is based upon facts — not upon fancies. Is the world about to be shaken by a war greater than any of modern times?

Assuredly we are more intimately subject to the sun-god than those early Aryans who called him *Surya*, 'the Begetter,' 'the Producer,' ever imagined. Science has taught us, not only that the life which quivers in a gnat's wings, or which in heart-throbs marks the seconds of our lives, is sun-given, but that our world and our moon are sun-born, sun-created. Knowledge now compels us to give unto the sun those attributes of old accorded to the androgynous gods of the East, with phallic emblems and symbolic skeletons — typifying not only two-fold creative power, but also the might of destruction; — all-producing, all-dissolving — animating and corrupting, vivifying and putrefying.

THE DESTINY OF SOLAR SYSTEMS [1]

READERS will recollect our comment on various mathematical calculations of the time at which the sun must die. The calculations of Laplace would give the sun upward of 160,000,000,000 more years to burn; — this estimate being based upon the supposition that the sun loses one tenth of a degree of heat in ten thousand years or thereabouts. But the calculations of later mathematicians allow a period of some three quadrillions two hundred trillions of years to elapse before the extinction of our central star. His final agony will nevertheless be comparatively short, according to what astronomers like Hevelius and Herschel have learned from witnessing the death of more distant and mightier suns. The great light, No. 50 Hercules, expired precisely on the night of the 24th of March, 1791 — at least his last radiant gasp reached the earth on the night of that date. Ten years before it the star had ceased to flame steadily, and turned red — flickering at intervals like an exhausted lamp. Its crimson death-struggle endured therefore little more than a decade.

It now remains for us to gossip about the period and character of the death of the planets —

[1] *Times-Democrat*, July 22, 1883.

all of which will doubtless become mummified corpse worlds millions of years before their giant creator shall have yielded up his awful spirit. First of all, let us chat about some theories regarding the period of existence allotted to the human race.

Man can already endure variations of temperature of 100 degrees and more; and it would therefore require a diminution in solar power of more than 100 degrees to cause the extinction of the human species. Allowing the sun to lose one tenth of a degree of heat in 2000 years, he could not lose 100 degrees before the lapse of 2,000,000 of years. The calculations based upon the maximum period allowed for solar extinction would, however, prolong the chances of the human race to 40,000,000,000 years. When the sun shall have lost 100 degrees of heat, the ice-caps of the poles will have whitened out over the breadth of both temperate zones; and all terrestrial life will have rallied about the equator. There the final struggle must take place — according to this view of planetary destinies — a struggle to be grandly prolonged by the vastly augmented powers of man, who will summon to his aid a magic mightier than any sung of in the runes of the *Kalewala* — the magic of science!

This, however, is an idea of human destiny in support of which few sound facts can be adduced. It is indeed a sublime fancy that man might be capable, by increase of knowledge, to prolong his existence through numberless future geological changes and cataclysms, and still battle against death even when the face of the great sun should be paling into ghostliness above him. But there is equal reason to fear that the period allotted to him upon earth is not so long. There have been many gigantic renovations of the earth's surface already; and there will certainly be many more which may not easily be survived. Some predict another glacial epoch at the expiration of another six thousand years — a sudden wrenching of the earth from its present axis — an upheaval of mountain-ranges — a sinking of continents — a rush of oceans from their beds, covering the globe's surface with prodigious ruin. Man would thus disappear, to be succeeded by some other species of dominant and intelligent beings in some other great geological period.

It is now pretty generally conceded that we can only hope to guess the future of the human race through the revelations of the telescope, as we have already more than guessed the destinies of the sun. At distances of dizzy enormity we behold the dying-down of sun-fires, the palpitating agony of stars; we watch new systems being formed within the fiery matrices of nebulæ; we see likewise the fragments of dead worlds raining down in meteoric dust upon our globe in its incalculable voyage through the wastes of night.

But so ephemeral are human lives, and so huge the existences of worlds and suns, that only through the labors of thousands of astronomers studying the heavens for thousands of years, can we ever hope to know positively the whole great story of a system's dissolution. Not even thus may we expect to learn the entire history of any one system; but by observing a catastrophe here, a sun-birth there, a satellite begotten somewhere else — by simultaneous watching of new things beginning and of ancient things disintegrating, it may be given us at last to divine all the mysterious laws of star-life and planet-growth. It is not absurd to believe that some optical intercommunication between sister-worlds in our own solar system will be ultimately established to aid these researches; yet, for the time being, the fate of our nearest neighbor, the Moon, must continue to be the most important key to the enigma of planetary death.

The moon appears to be dead, or dying; but her corpse has not become disintegrated; and throughout the infinities and eternities the law of universal death is the same; — dissolution of the being. A faint spectral atmosphere is now said to have been perceived clinging about the satellite during recent occultations, as the breath of a traveler in icy lands hangs about him in a cloud — the ghost of the moon, perchance, hovering above its dead volcanic mouths. But the true pulse-life of a world seems to be connected with volcanic force — that force whose precise nature and origin are still ignored even upon earth. We have reason to believe, in spite of this ignorance, that while a world lives, its lava-veins never cease to throb; and the moon's heart is chill, her arteries are dried up; her body is mummified and yellow as any corpse in any necropolis of Egypt; and its approaching dissolution is indicated by huge cracks in the dry skin. These, it is believed, will stretch and widen until the satellite shall split open, and fall apart, and the fragments would circle around the earth in the form of many smaller moons. The core of the lunar body might at first form a spherical center about which the remnants of the broken crust would whirl in a ring; but the core itself must crumble at last, and the entire remains of the satellite fall away by degrees into volcanic dust. Should the human race survive a few millions of years, it is probable that the disintegration of the moon will be actually witnessed; and, again, the first cleavage might occur in a less remote time. That the disruption of the moon will be gradual, rather than sudden, is almost certain. By the time its last fragments shall have been dispersed, the world may have lost its oceans, and the tides have shrunk into their graves as in Byron's dream.

This spectacle of a satellite's disruption and

dissolution would certainly settle for us all doubts as to the fate of the earth itself. The moon, once a blazing star, cooled before the cooling of the world, and died before its parent-globe had arrived at middle age — simply the moon is far smaller. Its present fantastic testimony leads us to believe that when the African, Asiatic, and American deserts shall have overspread and devoured terrestrial vegetation, and the oceans have shrunk up, and the rivers have ceased to flow — then will the earth also split in all directions. Volcanic energy will cease, and the cooling of the globe's heart will be followed by further contractions of the crust, and total absorption of the atmosphere.

The planets may all thus crumble away before the sun shall have wholly burned out; and there may be no such spectacle in the universe as that of a dead black sun with the corpses of his crew of planets shadowing around him in the night. Astronomy gives little reason to believe that suns ever exist in the condition of 'ships that are drifting with the dead to shores where all is dumb.' The sun has yet to become inhabited, in which case he could not be burdened with a family of dead worlds, as he would himself be obliged to wed his destiny with the fortunes of some other system, and circle around some vast star like Sirius or Vega.

The bulk of evidence so far gathered leads us

to believe that such is the most probable fate of solar systems. The central sun will gradually cool down. The planets will die with their moons, will crumble away, and their dust be scattered like seed through the limitless fields of space. Then the burnt-out sun would become a great world, in need of the light and warmth of a vast and vigorous star. The center of a system would survive only to become a planet in some other system; and the further planets of our own, which are known to differ materially from Jupiter, Saturn, and the rest, may be old suns of other systems adopted into our family circle. As for the crumbling of planets, we need hardly refer to the astronomical belief that the swarms of asteroids between Mars and Jupiter are the fragments of a broken globe. ·

For systems thus destroyed there can be no resurrection. But as matter and force are eternal, the work of formation and disintegration will continue forever as it has always been. And as a certain number of units are susceptible only of a certain number of combinations, the substance of suns and worlds may have already passed numberless times through all combinations, all forms, all metamorphoses of which it is capable. If that substance have limit, its utmost capacities of form and change have been exhausted and repeated from all eternity, and will be repeated in endless iteration throughout endless eternities to come. This system might thus have been formed and dissolved an infinite number of times in the past, and would in such case be refashioned and redissolved at intervals throughout eternal cycles to come — so that in one sense all which is hath always been, and all which hath been will always be, and forms only vanish to reappear. But who may surely say there is or there is not a limit to substance and to life; who may even say that the hundred millions of suns revealed by the telescope are not to the Unknown only as the quivering of animalculæ in a speck of putrid water?

CHEAP FRENCH LITERATURE[1]

IF novels afford — as the German chancellor says they do — fair indication of the moral condition of the people who read them, one might carry the inference a little further with safety, and aver that the opinions of society may be justly judged according to the manner in which they are depicted — not by one romance-writer, but by the majority of romance-writers. A curious book might be produced at this time upon the manner in which the modern aristocrats of France have been painted by popular contemporary novelists of that country. While some English authors of fiction have, indeed, pictured a few detestable personages of title, the bulk of modern English fiction bears testimony quite favorable to the British nobility. It is altogether otherwise in contemporary French literature. Out of many thousand titled characters who appear annually upon the immense stage of Parisian fiction, nine hundred and ninety-nine are either villains or idiots. The barons and counts have remarkably black reputations; they are nearly all debauchees, hypocrites, gamblers, or worse. As for the marquises and the duchesses, these are almost invariably represented as mar-

[1] *Times-Democrat*, October 31, 1883.

vels of vice or folly, whose least crime is conjugal
infidelity. Concerning the connubial relation
among this imaginary aristocracy, it is generally
referred to as a mere sham; the husband and the
wife respecting each other in public and hating
each other in private; Daudet and Edmond
Goncourt — the novelists *par excellence* of
middle-class life — do not harmonize in this
respect with the great host of second-class novelists; but the Naturalists have created a veritable
gallery of odious counts and barons and dukes.
A peculiarly morbid class of writers also, like
Mendes, who always confine their theme to
vices and villainies of the most abnormal and
surprising kind, have chosen to bestow titles
upon their worst characters. The *feuilletonistes*
of the daily papers, and the infinite swarm of
smaller novelists, seem utterly unable to conceive a plot without a wicked duchess or an
orgiastic count. Their bad characters always
wear a title, just as the ordinary stage villain
wears false eyebrows. If there be some worthy
and intelligent personage in the *dramatis per-
sonæ* it is always a plain 'Monsieur' or 'Madame'
— a *bourgeois*, or *bourgeoise*.

All this proves nothing, however, regarding
the classes thus portrayed or defamed; but it is
significant as depicting the real political sentiment of the French reading public. A vast
majority of the twenty-five or thirty thousand

novels and novelettes published under the present Republic were written in the popular journals and to be read by the middle classes. Among these middle classes still survives that antique hatred of the aristocracy which found tragical expression in the last century; and the success of this class of literature — poor as the bulk of it may be — has been so great, that even professedly monarchical or royalist journals do not scruple to make profit of it. Speaking of royalist papers, it is amusing to notice that one of the leading journals of Paris, which is forever officially mourning over the decadence of morality under the Republic, recently printed on its outer page one of the most obscene novelettes ever published, in which the invariable Count and Countess make their appearance; and the subject of which is founded upon the catastrophe of Ischia! That morbid and revolting tendency to bring death and obscenity into nightmarish union is making itself more manifest in a certain class of foreign literature. Were it not for that small but brilliant galaxy of grand master-writers whom the reading world honors, such a tendency would justify the prediction that before another generation the real art of fiction would be a lost art in France.

THE TWO ARNOLDS[1]

THE interview between Matthew Arnold and a reporter of the New York *Tribune*, as published October 23, reveals some curious traits on the part of Mr. Arnold. He expressed himself astonished that any one should ever have supposed Edwin Arnold to be his brother, and clinched his point of astonishment by observing: — 'He is no relation whatever. His book, "The Light of Asia" seems to have taken a great hold here, it seems to me quite unintelligible, and not to be compared with the great work of Saint-Hilaire, "Le Buddha." It is like the character of Christ written by a Jew. One prefers to go to more authentic sources.'

There was something petty in this observation; — betraying a peculiar vanity — much ruffled at finding that Edwin Arnold was better known and loved in the United States than Matthew Arnold. The unintelligibility of 'The Light of Asia' has been discovered by none but the 'distinguished essayist,' and its immense popularity wherever English readers are numerous — whether in America, India, New Zealand, Australia or Great Britain — affords a very large denial to the green-eyed observation of

[1] *Times-Democrat*, November 4, 1883.

Mr. Matthew Arnold. The comparison of 'The Light of Asia' to Barthélemy Saint-Hilaire's work is simply absurd. 'Le Buddha et Sa Religion' is no more a poem than is Max Müller's essay upon the 'Stratification of Language'; — it is a very exhaustive and valuable review of Buddhism ancient and modern, based upon Oriental authorities; and it comprises a curious and trustworthy biography of Siddhartha. But Saint-Hilaire never attempted to do what Edwin Arnold has done so nobly and so touchingly — to make us feel the spirit of all that is grand and pure and unselfish in a faith confessed to-day by unknown hundreds of millions of worshipers in the remoter East. Interesting as are the works of men like Spence Hardy and Saint-Hilaire, they were written more with the view of proving the inferiority of Buddhism as compared with Christianity, than for the purpose of teaching the Occident to appreciate those marvelous ethical beauties which the religion of Gotama certainly possesses for any unbiased thinker. Says Saint-Hilaire: 'I have only one purpose in publishing this book — to bring out in relief by strong contrast, the grandeur and the beneficent truth of our own spiritual beliefs'; — Spence Hardy tells us that he only wrote 'for the messengers of the cross.' These biographical sketches of Buddha are in consequence far more worthy of the criticism about 'a life of Christ written by a Jew,' than

Edwin Arnold's master-work of verse. Had no
books upon Buddhism been written but those of
Burnouf, Saint-Hilaire, Beal, and other scholars,
the great majority of European and American
readers would never have known, or cared to
know, the story of the Indian Christ — although
the great scholar Fansboll well said: 'The sooner
all mankind shall have been made acquainted
with his doctrines, the better it will be; for he is
one of the heroes of humanity.' Edwin Arnold first
taught the vast reading public of Great Britain
and of this country — the English-speaking races
of the nineteenth century — what Buddha's life
was, and what his doctrines were. He presented
this strange and beautiful jewelry of Eastern
thought in a setting of verse richer and stronger
than anything poetical Matthew Arnold has ever
written, or could write. The author of 'The Light
of Asia' has even enhanced the original beauty
and pathos of the story in his treatment of it; —
let any one compare the story of the Flight as
told in the Singalese 'Nidanakatha,' in Beal's
'Romantic Legend,' in Saint-Hilaire, in any other
translation from original manuscript, or compilations based upon such authorities, with the
stanzas of Edwin Arnold, and decide for himself
which narrative is best calculated to elevate the
thoughts of the reader. Perhaps the luminous
interpretation of *Nirvana*, with which that
superb composition closes, might excite scholarly

criticism or positivist doubt; but the interpretation is in truest harmony with that universal yearning of the human heart for many a thousand years, and will surely inspire noble thoughts to all who read it.

'Going to more authentic sources' than Edwin Arnold is something Matthew Arnold would certainly prefer in view of his belief in his own immense superiority; but those who desire to go to the most authentic sources for information upon the very subjects of Matthew Arnold's lecture and colorless poems would scarcely care to pay for the sound of his voice. Whether 'authentic' enough for his jealous namesake, Edwin Arnold is certainly authentic enough for the American public; and thousands would gladly flock to hear the author of 'The Light of Asia,' were he to visit the United States.

FORGERY IN ART[1]

IT would be well if a little book, just published in Paris, by Paul Eudel — upon the extraordinary and countless varieties of fraud by which collectors of paintings, engravings, curiosities, antiquities of all descriptions are duped — were translated and printed in this country for the benefit of American visitors to Paris. After reading this little book, it is more than doubtful whether any intelligent stranger would venture to purchase any *bibelot* except upon the advice of a recognized expert; we say *recognized* because there are counterfeits of experts as there are of everything else. There are imitations of everything — of thirteenth-century furniture and tenth-century armor; of mediæval swords and Louis XIV tapestries; of Elzevirian and Manutian print; of Venetian glasses and Japanese pottery; of monkish chronicles on vellum; of Chinese vases and Indian ivory-carving; of Moorish leather and Fiji javelins; of New Zealand woodwork and Mexican figurines; of sixteenth-century carving in ivory and Persian decorations *in niello;* of Buddhist manuscripts and Arabian Korans; of Pompeiian statuettes and Corinthian bronzes; of Cashmere shawls and

[1] *Times-Democrat*, November 8, 1883.

Alhambraic tiles; of Etruscan vases and Trojan antiquities. It is not as generally well known as it ought to be that a great majority of the Chinese and Japanese curiosities purchased in Europe are manufactured in Belgium, Amsterdam, Paris; and that the 'imported idols' of Buddha or statues of Confucius which decorate so many mantelpieces were made to order in London. England has been shipping idols as well as missionaries to multitudinous parts of the world.

But the most dangerous things to purchase are certainly paintings and engravings. So superbly are masterpieces imitated, that the talent of the counterfeiter sometimes approaches the sublime! It is not long since Count Raousset-Boulbon only prevented the purchase — by a veritable connoisseur — of a magnificent 'original,' by crying out in the middle of the auction: 'Don't buy David Teniers' *Card-Players;* the original is in my possession!' He was much luckier than Gavarni, the famous caricaturist. Gavarni was present when an auctioneer offered for sale a selection of 'rare drawings by Gavarni.' He protested, announced himself, declaimed all to no purpose; the assembly believed him to be an impostor; and after he had been flung out of doors, the 'original Gavarnis' were bought up at high prices.

Old canvases are imitated by covering the fresh painting with a paste, and subsequently baking the whole scientifically in an oven until the proper ancient tinge appears, and the cracks of the varnish are sufficiently multiplied. Mellow tones are produced with liquorice juice, and somber tints with lampblack. Fly-specks are counterfeited by filliping the end of a camel's-hair brush dipped in a mixture of gum and sepia — so that a shower of infinitesimal black drops are flung upon the canvas. Signatures are counterfeited by very learned experts in the history and literature of painting; — men thoroughly acquainted with all the monomanias of celebrated masters, and able to imitate any painted signature with 'stupefying exactitude.' These are called *monogrammistes*. Old ink-stains are imitated by rubbing the canvas with a damp cloth, so as to produce a peculiar mold upon the varnish. This trick is called a *chanci*. Imitating the afterstrokes or corrections of contours, made by certain famous painters, is styled 'making a *repentir*.'

As for etchings, engravings, etc., the fraud practiced in their imitation is quite as versatile. Paper is scorched to make it look old; old copper or steel plates are worked over, and the prints sold as 'first impressions.' Very old engravings are imitated by first forging the engraving, and then dipping the paper into a solution of copper! Eighteenth-century engravings in the *rococo* style are counterfeited by simply smoking the paper. At the sale of a famous artist's effects, an unfinished sketch will often fetch more at auction than a complete one: — for the reason that it is bought by a speculator in fraud. A few days later there will be an advertisement in all the Paris papers to the effect that another work by the late lamented artist X—— has been discovered; and the outlines filled in by expert forgery, will find purchasers at a fabulous price.

It is now seriously proposed in France to establish a law against the counterfeiting of works or objects of art — and to organize a detective force of experts to track up and denounce all who either fabricate or sell forged masterpieces. Such a law is certainly much needed.

A MAD ROMANTIC [1]

THE curious legend regarding the supernatural ancestry of the Queen of Sheba, elsewhere printed, may recall to lovers of the French Romantic school some extraordinary facts connected with the history of perhaps the most remarkable of Oriental romances ever written by a European — 'Histoire de Balkis et Salomon,' which may be found in that portion of Gérard de Nerval's 'Voyage en Orient,' bearing the alluring title 'Les Nuits du Ramazan.' This writer was certainly the most singular personage of the Romantic school; and at the time when the history of that grand galaxy of writers is being compiled, and given to the world in a series of valuable memoirs, some few remarks about De Nerval will certainly interest those who have thus far pleasurably perused our notes upon distinguished French novelists and poets.

'Gérard de Nerval' was only a *nom-de-plume*, although it was destined to become ineffaceably graven among the names of the Romantic movement; — Gérard's real name was Labrunie. Nor was 'De Nerval' his only pseudonym; for in the early part of his career he successively

[1] *Times-Democrat*, February 24, 1884.

adopted and abandoned as many different *noms-de-plume* as he wrote articles; but he finally became so celebrated as De Nerval that his real name was forgotten save by a few intimate friends. The history of his earliest literary ventures which have not been preserved, is partly narrated in the pages of Gautier's 'Histoire du Romantisme'; but for present purposes it will only be necessary to mention those of his writings by which he is best known, and which are destined to endure by reason of their eccentricity of conception and elfish beauty of style. The impression produced by his works is totally different from that created by the perusal of other Romantic authors; — yet this intrinsic peculiarity is not easily analyzed. It is not wholly due to the spiritual delicacy of his writing, nor altogether to the character of the subjects which inspired him; although partly traceable to both causes. Like Edgar Poe he possessed the very remarkable power of expressing in words the feelings and fancies of dreams; but, unlike Poe, he gave to such expression a sense of gentle happiness or of drowsy melancholy which communicates itself to the reader. There is a sleepy beauty in his thought, an unconscious charm in his style, that lulls the fancy like an opiate. But there is also something more — something not of the living world. He who reads Poe's 'Ligeia,' 'Eleanore,' the 'House of Usher,' or 'Monos and

Daimonos' for the first time knows that he is
reading of specters, of nightmares — (the phantoms of a disordered brain, if we are to accept the
well-grounded theory of Francis Gerry Fairfield). But the women of De Nerval deceive and
charm — disguising their true character like the
spirits of folk-lore who only reveal their kinship
to the invisible world when menaced by mortal
love or hate. One must spy their every action and
gesture more closely than did the Count of Lu-
signan watch Melusine, to discover a hint of
their unearthly origin. They are very lovable, very
real in aspect, yet by close observation we find
they are bodiless as the women of dreams; —
they cast no sharp shadows; — they are beings
of mist, daughters of air or fire, as De Nerval
himself styles them in 'Les Filles du Feu.' It is
not easy, indeed, to discover their ghostliness
unless we are placed upon our guard. Madmen
have painted wonderful pictures of which the
madness is not at first perceptible save to a
master-eye. Gérard was such a painter among
word-artists. He was insane! It is even doubtful
whether he ever had any prolonged 'lucid intervals.' All that he wrote (except, perhaps, his
translation of 'Faust,' which Goethe pronounced
the best of its kind) was more or less affected by
his mental affection. It has been said that the
wakeful state of the mildly insane may be compared to the state of dreaming in normal minds.

This is the secret of the impression made by De Nerval's pages, which have the strange interest and the semi-diaphanous unreality of dreams. Another peculiarity of his books is a certain incoherency, at once provoking and charming — the incoherency of high cerebral exaltation. He interrupts the most fascinating of recitals with curious interludes, with astonishing digressions at brief intervals. Imagine the most accomplished of scholars and *raconteurs* flushed with wine! — he is telling a delightful story, and from time to time breaks the narrative with digressions of a character totally foreign to it. This feature is discernible in most of Gérard's stories, with two notable exceptions; and in the creation of these he was assisted by some writers of uncommon talent. One is 'La Main Enchantée'; the other the 'Histoire de Balkis.'

It is seldom indeed that an insane man is capable of producing literary work of the very best quality; and Gérard de Nerval must be considered one of the most extraordinary instances of this ability ever known. He was doubtless insane when he translated the first and second parts of Goethe's 'Faust,' whose immortal author exclaimed on reading De Nerval's version: 'Never before was I so well comprehended!' He was certainly insane when he wrote 'La Bohème Galante' — an exquisite medley of folk-lore, antiquarianism, and fantastic narration. This volume contains among other things some very dainty chapters upon the French ballads of the sixteenth century, and two marvelous stories — 'Le Monstre Vert' and 'La Main Enchantée.' The first is curiously brief; but no one who reads it will forget the soldier's experience at the Dance of the Wines in the haunted cellar, when the chosen bottle falls and breaks, to change into the nude body of a blonde woman lying in a pool of blood. The other tale, of considerable length, is superior perhaps to anything Hoffmann wrote; it is a masterpiece of mediævalism. How weirdly vivid is the scene of the execution, when, after the bewitched Hand has been severed from the felon's body, it runs like a crab through the narrow streets, and like a spider up the walls of a certain quaint building even to the window at which the wizard stands awaiting it! An equally odd medley is 'Les Filles du Feu.' The names of fair women which form its division-titles would seem to promise a collection of character-studies, and a general uniformity of purpose. The reader will find himself deceived, but not disappointed; for this intermingling of philosophical treatises, romances, and dramas is so pleasingly original that its incongruity is readily forgotten. 'Les Filles du Feu' contains the prettiest thing De Nerval wrote, 'Sylvie,' the sweetest imaginable episode of modern country-life — a delicate idyl which Théophile

Gautier ranked with 'Paul and Virginia.' It also contains a totally unique creation, 'Angélique' — supposed to be the history and results of an antiquarian research among curious manuscripts of the sixteenth century; — the touching story of a knight's daughter who fled from her home with a common varlet, and well paid the penalty incident to such amorous follies.

Gérard's mild insanity occasionally aggravated into violence, exciting the alarm of his friends; and it was once found necessary to confine him in an asylum. He utilized the experience in a singular manner; being one of those madmen *who know that they are mad*. 'Aurélie; ou La Rêve et La Vie' is a romance in which the phenomena of insanity are scientifically treated by a madman! Something of the same morbid tendency to study mental hallucinations may also be found even in Gérard's Oriental story, 'L'histoire du Calife Hakem,' in the second volume of his 'Voyage en Orient.' By those two admirable volumes of Eastern travel, De Nerval is best known; and the origin of the work belongs to the most extraordinary incident of his life — his wanderings in Egypt.

Perhaps only a madman could have successfully carried out such a project of travel; for the Orientals, fiercely as they detest the Frank and the Christian, treat the insane with something of superstitious tolerance and even kindness. Gérard was permitted to sleep in the caravansaries, to smoke his narguilah in the cafés, to listen to the Arabian story-tellers reciting the legends of Islam in a tongue which he did not understand, to attend marriage-feasts and Moslem rites of various kinds — possibly to enter the holy mosques, for he did not fail to adopt the dress of the people in whose picturesque life he sought to mingle. Every incident described in his 'Femmes de Caire' ('Women of Cairo') is fact; nor has any doubt been thrown upon the narrative of his marriage. At some slave-mart or other he bought an Abyssinian girl, 'yellow as gold'; he rented a queer Arabesque house in some obscure quarter of the city, and began housekeeping in Oriental fashion. The ménage was not a happy one; — a change came over the spirit of Gérard's Oriental dream. His African wife was young, passionate, and petulant — little fitted to be the companion of a dreamer of dreams, who loved to sit speechless for hours meditating upon the magic of Hermes Trismegistus or the mysteries of the Kabbala. She desired the things that are of this world — much petting and caressing, many comfits, pretty robes shot with silver and gold — the poetry of love rather than ecstasies about the chant of the muezzin and the tinkling of camel bells. She knew also that her sale to

Gérard was illegitimate; — (was he not a 'Christian dog?') and De Nerval acknowledges that he was continually beaten by her. Whether he really repudiated her, as Maxime du Camp tells us, or whether she simply ran away from him, as recorded in the 'Voyage en Orient,' is not positively known; but it is certain the twain lived together but a short time, and that the comely Abyssinian subsequently found a Turkish husband who suited her better, and by whom she had many children.

There is only one characteristic of insanity in these exquisite volumes wherein De Nerval has recorded his Oriental experiences — and this is visible in the 'Story of Balkis, Queen of the Morning.' It is the same characteristic which is observable in the wonderful pictures of the wonderful John Martin, who also died mad — *enormity of conception!* Meyerbeer at one time thought of utilizing Gérard's romance for an opera; but he found it too superhumanly large for any stage. Martin's picture of the Israelites leaving Egypt is a puny fancy compared with that scene of the Oriental narrative entitled 'The Brazen Sea,' or that other scene in which the artificer Adoniram assembles by a mystical sign his nations of workmen, his legions of smiths, and armies of carpenters. There are dreams of mountains wrought into statues so awful that God Himself dare not animate them — of huge valleys converted into reservoirs supported by flying buttresses under whose curved shadows innumerable battalions might find shelter from the sun; — there are lightnings and voices as of an Apocalypse; — there are exaggerations even of the enormous exaggerations of Arabian fancy.

... But this very prodigiousness has its fascination; — one reads the story with such wonder as a volume written by the inhabitant of some other and larger planet might inspire.

Gérard returned from the East much madder than before — really believing that the ruins of Egypt were fragments of the palaces of the Preadamite kings — that the Pyramids were the anvils upon which was wrought the magical buckler of Gian-ben-Gian — and that Solomon really sate upon them to review his armies of *Djinns* and *Afrits*. Whatever means he had left was soon squandered in eccentricity. He wrote, but wrote less lucidly than before; — he composed poems strangely obscure, with only a few gleams of lucidity here and there — gleams which Gautier has prettily compared to the flashes emitted by some barbaric idol, covered with carbuncles and emeralds, in the darkness of a crypt. He could still readily procure a market for a certain class of articles; but the money thus earned he wasted in the purchase of artistic luxuries. Once he bought a magnificent bed, in which some queen had slept; — he had dreamed that an actress whom he secretly and silently loved — Jenny Colon — might one day slumber in it. The bed was so immense that he had to rent a costly apartment to place it in; when he became still more destitute he had it conveyed to a garret. His superstitious dread of parting with this expensive and cumbersome article served one good purpose — it secured him a place of repose. He clung to it as long as he was able to earn or borrow the price of rent. Finally it went the way of many other curious things. Gérard's brain was too much affected to enable him to make fresh successes in literature, and he became dependent upon the charity of Théophile Gautier and others who loved him for the ruined beauty of his mind and the exceeding goodness of his heart. But this condition must have been a torture to one who found Reality so false and Phantasy so real. Sometimes he starved rather than confess his hunger; sometimes he lied to save pain or expense to his friends. Like a shadow he walked the icy streets of wintry Paris, dreaming of the Impossible that he sought in vain — also, doubtless, of the Orient that he had seen — of azure skies that never weep rain — of the tinkling of far caravan bells — of the fantastic streets of Cairo — of the musical chant of the muezzin — of those veiled women whose raiment perfumed the air with odors of musk and frankincense — of his Abyssinian bride, dark but comely as the curtains of Solomon. . . . One icy day (January 27, 1855) his lifeless body was found hanging from the bar of an iron grating in the 'Rue de la Vieille Lanterne.' Weary of the world's harsh realism, the Dreamer of beautiful dreams had voluntarily sought that eternal slumber that knoweth no dream whether of good or evil.

THE BURNING OF THE DEAD[1]

THE strong feeling in favor of cremation both at home and abroad is a sign of the times. It is true that this feeling is by no means that of the great majority as yet; but it is the feeling of a very intelligent and imposing minority which has the power to make converts rapidly in multitude. The mind of the nineteenth century is undergoing a reaction in favor of ancient funeral rites and pagan common sense. Is this because we are growing skeptical — because the old superstitions and the Folklore of the Dead are rapidly passing away? Certainly the feeling against cremation is most strong where superstitions do most survive. But the vanishing away of certain dark forms of belief, and the tendency of the times to abandon old customs and old ideas, are themselves due to those vast economical changes which have already modified the face of the world, and broken down barriers between nations. The skepticism of the period is a cause, perhaps — but only a subordinate cause, for the open advocacy of cremation. The great primal cause is the enormous industrial progress of the period, enabling countries to maintain populations ten times larger than could have found support some centuries ago. The world's markets

[1] *Times-Democrat*, March 30, 1884.

are becoming more colossal than was ever Babylon or Egyptian Thebes; cities of a hundred thousand people spring up every few decades in the midst of what were previously wildernesses; and towns of insignificant size receive sudden nourishment from railroads and swell to metropolitan proportions. In many American cities population doubles itself at astonishingly brief intervals; and the intervening lands are cultivated to their utmost extent by a rapidly increasing race of sturdy farmers. In Europe the increase of population is slower by far, but it is nevertheless astounding when compared with the populousness of the sixteenth and seventeenth centuries. A generation ago London had barely three millions of inhabitants; she has now almost five millions. All the great capitals are becoming more populous. Science and invention have enabled the human race to multiply extraordinarily. But with the increase of life there is the inevitable increase of disease; and the work of Death is becoming so gigantic that the living can scarcely find place for his harvests. Cemeteries are too quickly filled; — the city grows out to them and around them and beyond them; the expenses of extramural burial increase continuously; the earth is overfed with corpses until she can no longer digest them, and the air of each metropolis becomes heavy with odors of dissolution. Inhumation can no longer meet the demands of hygiene; — Science has taken the alarm, and seeks to summon Fire to the assistance of earth. Fire, the All-Producer, as personified in the sun — (*Surya*, 'The Begetter') — is also the All-Purifier. Fire, not earth, shall devour the dead in centuries to come as in centuries that have passed away. Cremation will become at last, not a choice, but a necessity. It may first be established as optional; it will then become obligatory. These are the declarations and predictions of its advocates.

Elsewhere we publish extracts from an excellent article upon that subject, which appeared in the Paris *Figaro*. The author, who is a devout Roman Catholic, admirably points out the absence of any potent religious argument against the incineration of the dead, while he also dwells upon the horrors of slow decomposition and the involuntary yet inevitable condemnation of thousands to a *living burial*. But there is also a poetical side to the sinister question, which might be dilated upon — the swift restoration of the substances of being to their primal source of light and air — the remelting of the body into the pure and luminous elements which formed them. The body soars with the rising of the flame which enwraps it, soars toward that blue to which all eyes turn at times with an indefinite longing — as though there were something of the bird in every human heart.

'The earth,' poetically sang a Vedic poet, 'receives the dead even as a mother wraps the fold of her robe about the weary child who sinks to slumber in her arms.' The thought seems beautiful, but the words are untrue. For the earth is a cannibal; — she devours her children as hideously but infinitely more slowly than the python devours his prey — so hideously that only the bravest soldiers of Science have ever dared to peer into the processes of her digestion — as did Orfila. Perhaps it would be well if certain sentimental opponents of cremation should behold that indescribable treatise of his upon Juridical Exhumation with its frightful colored plates, whose horrors surpass the most loathsome conceptions of madness and the most appalling monstrosities of nightmare. One glance at these secrets of the tomb were enough to convert the bitterest anti-cremationist! And how slow the decay! Sometimes in five years the earth has not consumed its food. Poets may write touching pantheistic madrigals concerning the ultimate blending of all flesh with that 'Universal Paste formed of the shapes that God melts down'; but has the poet ever dared to raise the coffin-lid and observe the ghastly transmutation for an instant? Could even the philosopher dare so much; — for the breath of the tomb is fatal. Death permits only the high-priests of science to study that ghastly chemistry and live! Surely the noblest works of God are wrought in fire; — in flame were born all the hosts of heaven, and of flame is the visible soul of stars; — fire is the creative force of Nature; and to fire alone rightfully belongs the task of redissolving that which it first warmed and shaped into life. Modern respect for the dead is really superficial: it stops at the surface of graves and at the entrances of vaults. To abandon the body of a friend, a child, a woman beloved, to worms and to all the frightful fermentations of the tomb, seems, when we reflect upon it, barbarous — hideous! Even the Parsee Towers of Silence, with their vultures and birds of carrion hovering in spiral flight, contain naught so frightful as do our fairest sepulchres; — better surely abandon the dead unto the birds of heaven than to the worms of earth. Death was not a nightmare to antique civilizations; it became so only when the funeral pyres had ceased to flame, and the funeral urns had ceased to be. There was nothing sinister, nothing awful about the tombs of the Greek or Roman dead — only the graceful vases containing the 'pinch of scentless and delicate dust' gathered from the pyre — 'the dust of the soul's own butterfly-wings,' as it has been so daintily termed.

The crematories of the future will do the work better than the pyres of the ancients — much more perfectly, and much more cheaply. Incin-

eration, if not complete, also has its horrors; —
excepting a corpse in decomposition, there is
nothing so goblin-like and appalling as a half-
burned body. The antique process was slow, and
in the intervals of feeding the fire there must have
been ghastly sights. But in the strong, clear
flame of the crematory-retort horror cannot
endure an instant. There will be no room for such
a spectacle as that described by one witness of
the burning of Shelley's remains.

The desire for cremation is a sign of progress, a
token of a healthier tendency of mind. Yet, it
must be confessed, even cremation, as now advocated in its most scientific form, does not
wholly satisfy human feeling in regard to the
disposal of the dead. There are strange doubts
— obscure as any Egyptian prayer — anxieties
and fears. . . . If it be true that one person in
every 5000 is buried alive, might not one in every
5000 also be burned alive? Where is the guarantee, since there is no assurance of death before
visible decomposition sets in? Again, who knows
precisely when all thought and sensation dies
within the most secret chambers of the brain?
When must the last spark of being fade out into
utter darkness? Only a ghost might know; but
the dead have no voice — even in dreams. The
assurances of science do not wholly reassure; for
science has scarcely yet begun to comprehend
the deeper secrets of physiology and the mys-

teries of life. Some day revelations might be made too terrible to think of — revelations of consciousness resurrected momentarily in the midst of the material dissolution — strange flaring-up of sensations, of fancies and memories long forgotten — weird vitality of remembrances rekindled by the touch of destruction, by the combustion of death — just as characters of invisible ink are made visible by the approach of flame. Electricity alone — that holiest form of fire — may furnish ultimately some satisfactory means of answering all fearful doubt, when it shall become possible to dissolve a body instantaneously — as water is decomposed by the galvanic battery.

TINTED ART [1]

Mrs. Langtry's departure from the traditional 'make-up' in 'Pygmalion and Galatea,' has been variously commented upon by many American and transatlantic journals. Her own reasons for refusing to disguise her skin with ghastly white were that she had seen a 'tinted Venus' in the London exhibition of 1862, and that one 'could scarcely imagine Pygmalion loving pure white marble.' The veritable Greek legend, to be artistically carried out, would probably demand less drapery by far than Mrs. Langtry donned; but otherwise her ideas were esthetically correct. The White Art, as the French critic termed sculpture, is a modern art; — the sculpture of the old Greeks was not white, nor were their cities all 'white-pillared,' as modern poets declare. Color entered far more largely into Greek arts than is popularly supposed — almost as much, perhaps, as it did into the art of Egypt. To the Greek mind an endless succession of purely white architectural masses would have seemed spectral, weird — perhaps even shocking. The temples and public buildings of the Hellenes were not only painted, but painted with divers strong, warm colors — so that the uniformity of stone

[1] *Times-Democrat*, June 8, 1884.

effects might be agreeably relieved or broken by
the polychromatic decorations. Their statues
were never left in the condition which modern
sculptors consider complete; they were painted
or varnished in illusive imitation of flesh —
particularly those which were classed as iconic
statues, or likenesses of real persons, such as
winners at the panhellenic games. In colossi,
ivory was often used for the face, hands, feet,
and such parts of the flesh as were represented
undraped; and there is good reason to believe the
ivory was exquisitely painted. The exact color
of the eyes was imitated in various ways; sometimes a pupil formed of jewels and enamel was
laid upon an eyeball of silver; and silver or other
material was used also in imitation of the nails.
Although some of the most perfect nude statues
do not seem to have been painted in the strictest
sense of the word, they were overlaid with an
encaustic varnish, partly formed of wax and oil,
which produced a startling imitation of pale
transparent flesh. The marble having been
carefully chosen with a view to tint and grain,
and the surface worked minutely in imitation of
human skin, the effect of this varnish may be
imagined. Such statues might well deceive the
senses, and have provoked such singular instances of mental aberration as are recorded by
Pliny and others — or that love of the impossible
which found a crystallization in the charming

myth of Pygmalion. To the eye that gazed upon them they seemed to live, and to be distinguishable from mortality only by the holiness of their beauty, the magic of their perfectness.

A perfect white statue would certainly have seemed to the Athenians of the best epoch something ludicrous or something not to be examined — an unfinished model, a sketch half-made. It must not be forgotten that Greeks were as they still are, an olive-skinned race — who would have marveled at the sight of what we consider a fair person not less than the Romans marveled at the white skins and blue eyes and rutilant hair of the northern barbarians. Even their conception of divinity had a *tint* — they dreamed indeed of luminous beings, but not of white ones: — Aphrodite or Apollo were bright only with a brightness as of gold — or gold-colored flame. There was very probably a Creole color about the Greek ideal of flesh; — the men who laughed at the white skins of Persian prisoners (surely the Persians were never of the fairest), and who rejoiced to bathe their bodies daily in the strong sunlight, could hardly imagine marble-white flesh as natural, beautiful, or healthy. Therefore they painted in warm tints even the figures of the temple pediments, the frieze designs upon the temple façades.

It was reserved for another age and another people to find beauty in perfect whiteness; and perhaps it is not too much to aver that the spirit of Christianity had much to do with this. The new religion taught the world the very reverse of what the ancient believed — taught that the earth alone and its joys were not sufficient to satisfy the heart of man, and should rather be despised by him. The joyous, materialistic, sensual Greeks had occasionally heard of those who felt the 'world-sickness,' who found little delight in natural enjoyment, and longed for things beyond their reach; but such men were deemed to be the victims of a strange malady — were looked upon as men enamored of phantoms. Even the divinities were beings in the likeness of men and of women — beautiful beings of flesh, ichor-veined indeed, but warmly real — loving, wooing, warring like mortals. 'The gods,' said an old Greek writer, 'are *deathless men.*' As the material ideas yielded to the influx of vast spiritual conceptions, and new arts took the place of the old ones — White impressed itself upon the world in a new form; — to the Color that typified material pleasures succeeded the Colorlessness that symbolized the infinite and the formless. For more than a thousand years that simple word *White* has been connected with our spiritual ideas and holy traditions; it has become sacred as a tomb, awful as a ghost. Sanctified by the speech of the prophets and their visions, it has been applied to the raiment of angels, the robes of the blessed dead, even to that great Throne from the face of whose occupant 'the heavens and the earth fled away, and there was found no place for them.' When sculpture arose again from its pagan tomb, it arose only as a ghost; — its spiritual whiteness alone earned it the permission to return to earth. But so returning, there followed in its train countless beauteous things that had slumbered with it under the ashes of dead altar-fires; and the art-world of the past bids fair to obtain another period of splendid existence in the nineteenth century. The exhibition of the tinted Venus in London was a significant fact; — it heralded, perhaps, an esthetic return to the humane and joyous materialism of antique art.

HOT BATHS IN THE MIDDLE AGES[1]

HISTORY is being now studied with a minuteness and precision which would have seemed impossible during the last century; and new light is being thrown upon many obscure questions. The writing of history has in fact risen above the mere domain of art — it has become a science; and everything almost which was once considered standard authority is being reconstructed after the new system. Extraordinary work of this sort is being contributed to the leading foreign reviews, especially the *Contemporary* and *Fortnightly* in England, and the *Revue des Deux Mondes* in France. In the latest issue of the last-mentioned magazine the historian A. Lecoy de La Marche has taken up the subject of life in Europe during the Middle Ages, with the idea of showing that, however deficient in mental culture the people of the thirteenth century may have been, they were not by any means so miserable as the writings of Michelet depict them. M. de La Marche has studied a multitude of little-known archives and records of the century in question, and succeeds in presenting us with a very scintillant picture of the gorgeous toilets of the aristocracy. He bases his

[1] *Times-Democrat*, August 14, 1884.

argument upon the fact that the dress, the habitations, and the food of a nation are a fair index to the standard of civilization; and he succeeds in showing that the nobility of the thirteenth century, the clergy and the well-to-do bourgeois, dressed elegantly, lived in comfortable and even splendid houses, ate royally, and drank excellent wine. His account of ancient *trousseaux* and mediæval furniture is simply dazzling; and he shows that luxury in wearing apparel was occasionally carried to such extremes as to compel laws to restrain it, like the sumptuary laws of the Romans. But the most curious feature of his article is a critique upon a certain famous passage in Michelet's 'Sorcière.' Michelet was what Dr. Johnson called 'a good hater'; and in spite of his sincere efforts to be just, his personal feelings show through much that he wrote. Now Michelet hated the Middle Ages above all other ages — hated the errors of histories about them — hated the absurd eulogies uttered by sectarian writers concerning them; and never spared an opportunity of denouncing everything relating to them — customs, amusements, arts, even Gothic architecture, which he considered a false and fantastic style. Michelet's errors and exaggerations may well be pardoned for the sake of his truths, and the sincerely liberal enthusiasm of his labor — not to speak of his vivid and powerful style; but one of his warmest admirers might certainly feel inclined to join M. de La Marche in questioning the accuracy of so sweeping an assertion as this:

'The war which the Middle Ages declared against cleanliness necessarily bore fruit. . . . No bath for one thousand years. You may be sure that none of those famous knights, none of those ethereal dames — neither Parcival, nor Tristram, nor Iseult — ever washed themselves.'

M. de La Marche shows that in Paris there were not only multitudes of public baths — warm-water baths — but actually a large guild or labor-association of *estuveurs*, bath-house men. Furthermore he proves the existence of baths in other cities, and the existence in almost every comfortable residence of the *cuve à baigner*. He quotes even the 'cries' of the bathing-men of the time, who awoke the lords and others to take their morning bath:

> 'Seigneur, or vous alez baingnier
> Et estuver sans délaier;
> Li bains sont chaut; c'est sans mentir.'

Finally he cites the advice of French physicians of the thirteenth century as to bathing — such as Arnauld de Villeneuve, who flourished about A.D. 1300, and who wrote in quaint French to the effect that when a tired traveller reached his inn, he should first rest an hour, and then enter and remain in a warm-water bath until his skin became soft and pink.

M. de La Marche, in this and other matters, sustains his position excellently; but it must be observed that he takes good care to tell us very little about the serfs and peasantry of the thirteenth century, who bore the entire burden of the Middle Ages and enjoyed none of its luxuries whatever. And the reader may also remember that at a far later day when the peasantry of France could not afford even to eat white bread and salt, high dames among the aristocracy were powdering their hair with gold dust. Neither are many persons likely to agree with M. de La Marche that dress, habitations, and food are always indices of civilization. The rulers and princes of some extremely barbarous races have lived and still live in luxury and splendor.

STUDY AND PLAY [1]

WHEN M. Tchouriloff published in 1876 his treatise on the 'Cause of the Degeneracy of Civilized Races' he failed to touch upon one potent cause of physical weakness among civilized peoples. General causes for the alleged inferiority are obvious to any thinker — the comparative comfort of social conditions which render severe hardships unnecessary — the care afforded to the weakly and ailing who, in a savage society, would inevitably perish — the confinements of city life, and especially the immuring of industrial operatives for the whole period of daylight in illy ventilated prisons of brick and mortar. Happily the bulk of any industrial nation is engaged in agricultural and open-air pursuits, which are conducive to health, hardihood, and longevity; but the millions of city dwellers have much to suffer from civilized conditions which barbarians never experience. This is less the case in the United States than in Europe; but in all civilized countries it is considered debatable whether the nations of the nineteenth century are not, as a whole, inferior to their ancestors in physical vigor and endurance. The question is much disputed by physiol-

[1] *Times-Democrat*, August 24, 1884.

ogists, even in France, where the general opinion affirms degeneration. According to one eminent member of the Académie de Medicine, who believes the French nation is becoming less physically vigorous every year, one cause of their bodily deficiencies is to be found in the educational system. The hours of study in French schools and colleges, whether private or public institutions, are not properly alternated with hours of recreation and exercise; — children are kept for a whole morning or a whole afternoon in one classroom, often badly ventilated and lighted. This, too, is at the very period when young boys and girls most need air, light, hearty romping, the pleasure of running, shouting, and leaping. All young creatures need exercise and diversion to expand their strength or activity, to toughen the limbs, to make supple the muscles, to give quickness to the eye and ear, to develop perception and agility. Exercise makes the boy or girl a fine man or woman; while study may make them nothing. In the upper schools and universities the situation is worse. Already accustomed to violation of nature, to sit dully for long hours hooped over a desk, the high-school or university student resigns himself to a still harder course of uninterrupted study, which ends by dwarfing the body and weakening the eyes. Ophthalmia is frightfully on the increase; and no small number

of the young men annually excused from military
duty on the ground of physical disqualifications
are believed to have been thus dwarfed and
weakened by the school régime. Moreover, it
has been found that assiduous intellectual study
tends to deteriorate certain organs in especial
— such as the teeth, the lungs, the kidneys.
A curious special treatise on the diseases of
teeth due to school life appeared in the *Revue
d'Hygiène* of October 20, 1883. In short, the
French physician above referred to, M. Lagneau,
claims that the puny stature, poor dentition,
short sight, weak lungs and weak backs of
millions of Frenchmen must be attributed to
their school régime.

The French school system is peculiarly abom-
inable in these respects, whether the school is
public or private. The students have generally
only a large yard to play in, and rarely go out to
walk except in solemn procession, accompanied
by masters. They enjoy none of the liberty
of English or American schoolboys, nor those
athletic sports which excite physical emulation
and build up the whole muscular system. A
single trapeze is often the only means for
physical exercise afforded to the French pension-
naires. With a view to reform a vast mass of
documents are now being collected. M. Hippeau,
another French scientist, who published at
Paris in 1872 quite a large work on public educa-

tion in the United States, was naturally quite delighted with our public schools. There is no school in the United States, he says, where singing in chorus, military marching, and gymnastics do not form a necessary part of education. But MM. Demogeot and Montucci, whose work on British educational establishments appeared long before, were much more delighted with the splendid English public schools. 'These physical exercises,' they observe, 'are a diversion indeed, not strictly speaking from study — but they give a relaxation to the mind, and a stimulus also. It is impossible not to admire those beautiful young bodies, so large and so well-knit, those muscles so well filled and so lithe — those delightful colors of health. A single glance at those virile young faces tells of the habit of braving fatigue and danger — of simple and noble courage.' M. Lagneau also quotes from the *Revue Politique et Littéraire* — to which he contributes his opinions — the words of an English teacher of note: 'When none but intellectual tastes are imparted to lads without training them to exercise themselves in games of strength, it is impossible to develop in them that moral force of character, that energy and firmness which alone enables men to win in the battles of life.'

It is probable, however, that much as our public educational system is superior to the French, there is room for improvement in this direction.

THE HYPOCRISY OF THE FACE [1]

An Italian author, Signor M. P. Mantegazza, Professor of Natural History at the museum of Florence, has just contributed a very remarkable volume to the scientific series of works published by Felix Alcan, of Paris. Mantegazza's work is devoted to the subject of human physiognomy and the expression of the emotions; it deals very amply with one very interesting question — whether it is possible to mask one's feelings by force of will so completely as to deceive the keenest and most experienced observer. Civilized, and even uncivilized peoples, have been steadily training themselves to master all outward signs of emotion as far back as history records; — the fashionable man of Paris, London, or St. Petersburg tries to appear impassive as a god; — the American, less hypocritical, aims nevertheless to cultivate something of Indian gravity and stoicism. What are the results of the long-continued effort of man to master feeling and to hide what Nature seeks to express under all circumstances? They are sometimes very wonderful; but M. Mantegazza does not believe they are ever wholly successful — notwithstanding that the capacity for self-conquest

[1] *Times-Democrat*, October 19, 1884.

may have increased steadily through generations. Woman succeeds, indeed, better than man; and the uninitiated may be deceived by either, but the experienced physiologist can never be wholly duped by the immobility of a face or the tearlessness of an eye.

Gesture and expression are due to the efforts of a centrifugal current, emanating from the brain and spinal marrow, and in the ordinary course of nature, certain muscular contractions or relaxations should always correspond to certain emotions or psychical conditions. But human feeling is not always thus betrayed. Even at the very moment that a certain emotion is seeking to express itself through a certain group of facial muscles, muscles of the members or the trunk — other influences intervene to moderate or modify expression or gesture. These are influences of will — inspired by courage, by pride, by fear, by various motives. Still, all false expression can be classed under two types: — First — the exaggeration of a feeble emotion, or simulation of an emotion which does not exist; second — the attenuation of gesture or expression, or the attempt at total dissimulation thereof.

The studied exaggeration of gesture — in the attempt to make others believe we feel what we do not, sometimes produces strange consequences under the pressure of extraordinary emotion.

M. Mantegazza cites the case of a woman who had just inherited a fortune through the death of her brother, and who suddenly burst into a violent fit of laughter even while dashing her head against the walls of the room in simulation of the wildest grief. All such studied exaggeration may generally be detected by its violence, its disorderly gesture, the regular *intermittence* in its expression. But the eye is the great traitor. The muscles of the trunk and the limbs are those most docile to our will; the muscles of the face are less so; those of the eye are most independent of all. Says M. Mantegazza:

'Sometimes by force of hypocrisy or of heroism (for the physiologist may not take account of the moral state of these phenomena) we succeed in mastering all the muscles of the face and limbs, in making them keep our secret by substituting false gesture and expression for the real ones. We are saturated with humiliation and bitterness; and nevertheless we laugh, joyously move our hands or feet or necks; — all the body expresses absolute contentment; the eye alone resists the great avalanche of falsehood. Suddenly two large tears roll down the cheeks, and tell of the dolorous battle that is being fought within. Great painters and great dramatic artists know how to express all the hidden beauties of these sublime scenes; but we, who are neither artists nor actors, must study such disorders to profit thereby in real life.'

But there are men and women who obtain complete control even over the eye — either in the suppression or feigning of expression; — there are veritable artists in hypocrisy who can shed tears when they please. There is something much more difficult to control than the eye, however — the vasomotor nerves, which are very seldom kept in subjection by even the strongest wills. Even when the countenance, the voice, the eye tells nothing, the vasomotor nerves tell all, by their creations of sudden pallor or sudden flush. 'In the middle of an animated conversation in a theater or ballroom,' says the Italian writer — 'if the man who is loved suddenly enter, the beloved woman will certainly blush in ninety cases out of a hundred — or else, what is less common, she will turn pale. No mark of surprise, no smile, no gesture greeted the arrival — except perhaps the eye, which half closed, the lid which lowered its fringe to hide the sudden brilliancy of the soul's mirror; but the vasomotor nerves were forced to obey the emotion, and make the face pink or pale.'

Still, there are extraordinary exceptions to the rule; there are both men and women who hold even their vasomotor nerves in complete subjection, and.keep firmly closed all the safety-valves of expression — often at the serious risk of injury to the nervous centers. But the feelings of even these persons are betrayed by nervous agitation; — some limb or member is almost always seized with a rhythmic convulsion; — leg, arm, or finger begins to beat time to some imaginary tune.

The remarks of M. Mantegazza on the danger of suppressing emotion under certain circumstances are of the utmost importance; and some of his explanations of more familiar psychical phenomena are amusingly curious. We close with a specimen thereof, translated from the *Revue Politique et Littéraire:*

'Often the effort made to dissimulate emotion is so great, that should it last long it would bring about profound disturbances in the nervous centers. The mimic force, unable to find exit by way of the muscles, rushes to the region of thought, and therein arouses novel and puissant manifestations.

'A man enters a drawing-room; the woman he loves betrays no emotion; — but from having been silent, she becomes all at once excessively talkative; or, if she had been previously conversing indifferently, now she talks enthusiastically; — the very sound of her voice is changed, and may become very musical. Oftener it happens that she forgets the topic of conversation altogether; and by some strange bizarre association of ideas, she begins to chat about a hundred other things which bear no relation to the question in hand, nor even to the surroundings. Unexpected kisses for a child she had not noticed before; sudden enthusiasm for a picture or other object that she had already seen a hundred times without paying attention to it; — these are very precious and positive signs which assure us that her emotion was very strong, and that, not being able to pour itself out in natural expression it invaded the domain of thought and sensation, to excite all suddenly therein an unwonted and confused activity.'

THE PUNISHMENT OF SILENCE [1]

THERE is now a movement in France to abolish the penalty of solitary confinement. This punishment does not appear to have been attended with happy results — especially since the penalty of *travaux forcés* (hard labor for life in chain-gangs of the *bagne*, which long retained its mediæval name, the 'galleys,' after galleys had ceased to exist) has been practically abolished. All those wonderful and terrible books about penitentiary life, in which we read of men chained together for life, two by two, and compelled to work in quarries, on public roads, upon military fortifications, etc., describe conditions that have passed away. The republic is more humane than the empire in theory; but were criminals allowed to choose between the old-fashioned *bagne* and the modern *maison de réclusion*, there can be little doubt they would choose the former.

Nominally there are three great penalties inflicted by the French law; — death, *travaux forcés à perpetuité* (hard labor for life) and 'reclusion.' The latter is considered the least penalty, and yet it must be almost worse than death. It is not exactly solitary confinement, because the criminals can see one another, but it is more horrible. The prisoner must never open his lips

[1] *Times-Democrat*, October 28, 1884.

from the time of entering the prison; he cannot even talk to himself; he must work in perpetual silence, shut out from sun and air in a great hideous room, behind gates and gratings of iron. The man who commits a murder, and yet escapes the guillotine is condemned to *travaux forcés;* the burglar or sneak-thief who breaks in and steals is condemned to reclusion. In former times the sentence to hard labor for life meant something terrible; but it did not impose eternal silence and darkness; the convicts worked under the open sky; they could speak, they could amuse themselves at certain hours, they could smoke and occasionally earn money by manufacturing curiosities. Modern reclusion is infinitely worse; and it is far more dreaded. If a prisoner is now sentenced to hard labor for life, he does not enter a chain-gang; but is shipped to New Caledonia; if he is only sentenced to reclusion he is condemned to a living tomb; he is absolutely buried alive between four walls. It is not surprising therefore that hundreds of murders and other crimes were committed in those atrocious prisons by convicts who thus hoped to obtain either the swift mercy of the guillotine or transportation to Noumea. And in 1882, it was actually found necessary to pass a new law, which was printed and posted up in all the houses of reclusion, warning convicts that attempts to take life would thereafter be punished, in the case of those condemned for life, by death; and in the case of those condemned only for a term of years by a prolongation of the term. Nevertheless attempts were certainly being made upon the lives of keepers and guards. Men prefer to die rather than to be forbidden to speak, to think, to see the light of heaven, to behold perpetually a thousand faces around them and yet be prohibited to exchange a glance or an idea with their own kind. Women — and it is shocking to observe that women are nearly always condemned to reclusion when a heavy sentence is passed upon them — women become insane under the infliction. In the infernal silence of the great working-rooms sometimes a frightful shriek is heard, followed by bursts of laughter and violent vociferation. The guards approach to punish the breaker of silence, and find that her reason is gone; — that the nervous centers have broken under the awful strain. Edmond de Goncourt, the great naturalistic novelist, did much to provoke the present demand for the abolishment of such cruelties by his terrible book—'La Fille Elisa.'

Of course the reforms demanded will not solve all the difficulties of the penitentiary problem; but while it is recognized that such punishments do not by any means change criminals into saints, it must also be recognized that they are uselessly cruel, and a disgrace to the humane century in which we live.

THE LEGEND OF SKOBELEFF[1]

A VOLUME of personal reminiscences of the late
Russian General Skobeleff, which has created
the greatest interest in Europe and has already
been translated into various European languages,
sheds much new light upon the political mysteries
in which he took part, and adds no little luster
to his memory as a hero and a noble man.
Certainly there never was any question as to
Skobeleff's personal valor, nor as to his abilities
as a soldier; but his speeches in Paris and elsewhere, shortly prior to his strange death, did
justify some doubt as to his personal frankness.
Were those fiery words of his simply uttered for
policy — either to gratify anti-German sentiment at home or to effect, by imperial desire, a
feeling of insecurity in Germany? The public at
large, outside of Russia, were divided in opinion
in this regard. Some tolerably wild theories
were expressed. The most remarkable was that
Skobeleff, acting as the mouthpiece of one
political party only, really injured Russian
political interests to such an extent that it was
privately resolved to do away with him as soon
as possible; and the brief time that elapsed
between his incandescent speech to the deputa-

[1] *Times-Democrat*, November 23, 1884.

tion of Servian students and his enigmatic death, seemed to many an irresistible argument. In Russia itself, where Skobeleff's private character was widely known, there was never any doubt as to why that speech was made. It was fully recognized as the frank, bold utterance of private feeling; but the soldiery and peasantry long believed and still do partly believe, that it brought about the death of the gallant General.

Nemitovitch-Dantchenko, a scholarly journalist of much reputation in his own country, who followed the army during the Turko-Russian campaign in the capacity of correspondent, has undertaken to enlighten Europe somewhat as to Skobeleff's apparent political attitudinizing. Although written in a few days, the work of this fine writer glows with generous beauty, revealing at once the genius of the author and the sincerity of impressions still warm from memory. It might be claimed that admiration for the General had exaggerated Dantchenko's portraiture; but a man who shared Skobeleff's tent in his long campaigns, and who visited his home in the time of peace, was certainly likely to know him well and to judge him justly.

In order, however, to understand Skobeleff's position, one must also understand something of the foreign policy of Russia, as reflected in party sentiment at home. Panslavism and Slavophilism have been more or less confounded; but they are totally different parties. The Panslavists simply represent and maintain the imperial policy; they form a great power in St. Petersburg; they are the champions of Russian aggrandizement, universal Russian conquest, but especially of the forcible annexation to the empire of all countries inhabited by people of Slavic blood. The Slavophiles, on the other hand, represent only the patriotic sympathies of the people; they are the natural allies of the poor and weak; they desire the development of Slavic nationality — not through territorial aggrandizement, but through mutual aid; and hold it a sacred political duty to aid any Slavic people to obtain political independence. This party differs but slightly in point of liberalism from another — the true Muscovite party of liberalism. The Slavophiles are not popular nor in great favor with the chiefs of Russian policy, but they are well thought of by the Emperor, and have their organ, the *Gazette of Moscow*, and their leader, Absakof. This was essentially the preferred party of General Skobeleff, and when he expressed his hatred of Germany, he actually expressed the feelings of 20,000,000 of patriot Russians and Slavophiles.

Skobeleff was essentially a man of the people, and naturally a Slavophile. He was prouder of his humble origin, as great-grandson of the peasant Ivan Skobeleff, than of his relationship

by marriage to the imperial family — his sister
having married Prince Eugene Romanoffsky,
cousin of Alexander III. His democratic and
liberal tendencies won him prodigious popularity
and lent him vast influence; the lower classes
revered him almost to idolatry, and from all
parts of the empire letters poured in upon him
from every poor person who thought himself or
herself unjustly treated. These letters he never
failed to answer.

Ardent in everything, Skobeleff was also the
most ardent of Slavophiles, and as such became
naturally a furious hater of Germany and of
Russian official policy, too, in whose narrow
sphere were to be found the only men by whom
he was ever personally disliked. The great
Slavophile hatred of Germany began with the
treaty of Berlin. That treaty might have been
considered in England the triumphant work of
Disraeli; but it was perfectly well known in official circles to have been much more the work
of Bismarck. Russia might indeed have defied
England, but she could not defy the mighty
European coalition led by the Genius of modern
diplomacy.

And yet, how had not Russia schemed and
plotted for the conquest of Constantinople —
that ancient Byzantium, capital of the Greek
emperors, originally the Rome of that Catholic
faith professed by eighty millions of Russians?

Insurrections in Turko-Slavic provinces had been repeatedly encouraged and aided; torrents of blood had been shed; thousands of Russian military Slavophiles had volunteered to aid the Slavs long ere war had been officially declared by the empire. Then came the great moment when Russia put forth her strength, and the fond dream of centuries seemed on the point of being realized. Skobeleff's division passed from Kasanlik to Adrianople, leading the way over the Balkans, with incredible rapidity — a legendary, an epical passage which left its vast wake of dead behind it. No soldier in the army doubted the fate of Constantinople — assuredly none of Skobeleff's men; for the White General himself had said it — who ever led the van in a white uniform, mounted upon a white horse, and irresistible as the pallid Rider of the Revelation. And at last, from the elevations of Tchalaldja, the first vision of the ancient capital burst upon a hundred thousand Russian eyes:

'We stood before the very gates of the city,' says the biographer; — 'and our officers assembled upon the shores of the Bosphorus, beheld from afar the fairy-like Stamboul, whose minarets rose glittering into a cloudless sky. There was a magical calm. At our feet the sea of Marmora broke its waves in musical rhythm. All white, the pharos towered up from the foam; and further off, islands, deep flowered and palm-shadowed, gleamed in pacific splendor. And yet still further off we could view the Asiatic shore, with far ranges of snowy peaks, so faintly white that they seemed clouds. Ay, there before us was indeed Byzantium which all Slavic eyes have been turned to — rightfully or wrongfully — for fourteen hundred years! There was the realization of our fondest dreams! There was that Rome for which so many tears had been made to flow, and which belonged to us, indeed, by the right of our blood poured out.'

Already the Christians of Constantinople were preparing wreaths and bouquets for the conquerors; already the Turks were persuaded that the ancient tradition was about to be accomplished — that the infidels would indeed enter the holy city by the long walled-up gate, to arouse from his dusty slumber of four hundred years that strange priest who bides within the walls of Saint Sophia, awaiting the moment to finish that mass interrupted by the triumph of Mahomet. There was a vast saturnalia in the Russian camp. Wine flowed in rivers; strange women from the Continent were welcomed by the legions of the Empire. Suddenly the news of the armistice came! 'What can the Emperor hesitate for?' cried Skobeleff. 'I have forty thousand men here only waiting for a sign! My God! my God! what does it all mean? Is it possible we shall not be allowed to advance upon Constantinople?' And he burst into tears.

It seemed to him the fatherland was betrayed, the armies of the Empire disgraced. But the cup of his humiliation was not yet full. He was soon to learn that all the blood which flowed in the Bulgarian war had been shed in vain — that Austria was to hold Bosnia and Herzegovina until such time as all three should pass under the iron yoke of Germany; that Macedonia was to be yielded up to Turkey; that the whole fruits of the Russian conquest were snatched away from the conqueror by one stroke of the pen. Never could Skobeleff nor any Slavophile forget or forgive the bitter deception. The memory of it beshadowed the rest of his life, and doubtless hastened his death — straining the great, brave heart that beat only for Russia and for humanity.

THE ROAR OF A GREAT CITY [1]

WHEN Hogarth painted his story of 'The Enraged Musician,' whose music was drowned in
the thousand cries and noises that surrounded
him; when Chambers described 'The Roar of a
Great City,' the blending of a thousand noises,
it was of the city of the past they told. Since
then this roar has been growing louder and
louder, until now, miles away, even before you
see the smoky coronet that surrounds the modern
city, you can hear a wild growl like that of some
enraged beast. Neither Hogarth nor Chambers
dreamed of the fierce whistle of the steamboat
and locomotive, of the rattle of engine and machinery, of the cannonade as a cotton float flies
over the granite pavement, of the stunning noise
of the New York Elevated Railroad. All these
have come of late years.

The electric light, the telephone and telegraph
wires have added new music to our city. When
the winds blow at night one can hear a somber,
melancholy music high up in the air — as mysterious as that of Ariel himself or the undis-
covered music of the Pascagoula. If you want to
hear it in perfection go some of these windy
nights we have lately enjoyed to Delord or Dry-

[1] *Times-Democrat*, November 30, 1884.

ades, or some of the streets in the neighborhood of the electric light works, where the wires are numerous and the houses low, and where there is a clean sweep for the wind from the New Basin to the river. There the music becomes wild and grand indeed. The storm whistling and shrieking around some sharp corner never equalled it. Above, around, in every direction can be heard this music, sighing, mourning like the tree-tops, with a buzzing metallic sound that almost drowns your conversation. There is something in it weird and melancholy — it is like the last wail of a dying man, or the shriek of the angel of death as he clasps his victim to him.

If such it is to-day, what have we to hope for in the future? If the city is already a monstrous spider web, a great Æolian harp, what is its destiny with several new telegraph and telephone companies, and thousands of new poles, and millions of new wires promised us? If this aerial music increases, this shrieking and wailing and moaning will reach such a pitch that we will greet the rattle of the floats and tinkle of the street cars as tending to drown this new noise, and welcome the roar of the city as likely to muffle its meaning.

DEATH AND RESURRECTION IN THE SOUDAN [1]

WERE the newspapers of all civilized countries by common agreement to suppress all telegrams concerning the Mahdi until such time as the Khartoum relief expedition accomplishes, or fails in, its mission, the news-world would certainly not be the loser. Although several telegrams have been published in countless journals since the Mahdi became a huge and menacing colossus in the Oriental world the desperate fact remains that we know to-day just as much about this marabout as we did some years ago — and no more. In each flash of telegraphic lightning he appears in a quite different aspect — though always more mysterious than the Veiled Prophet of Khorassan.

When a great English review first seriously announced that the army of the Mahdi might even swell to half a million or a million — that it was even positive he might so agitate the long-slumbering deeps of Islam as to roll an earthquake wave of destruction right around the world, the writer simply showed his ignorance of the real condition of the lower Soudan; and we know now that the Prophet never had an army of

[1] *Times-Democrat*, December 9, 1884.

three hundred thousand fighting men, nor anything like it. The Arab and Berber tribes are too much disunited by antique feuds and religious dissensions to attempt a supreme effort; and even such a supreme effort would not bring a quarter of a million good men in the field. But let us suppose, for the sake of argument, that the Mahdi can summon to battle an army of a million — if any reliability can be placed on telegraphic reports from Egypt he has already lost much more than that. For the past twenty-four months his troops have been dying of smallpox, dysentery, cholera, plague, and innumerable other disorders — at such a rate that we could not dream of placing the total death-roll below 200,000. Secondly, all the powerful tribes are said to have deserted him, one after the other, which would represent a loss by desertion of some 500,000. Thirdly, he must have lost, according to account, at least 300,000 men in his numerous pitched battles with the English and the Egyptians. Gordon and the Mudir of Dongola are reported to have got away with about 10,000 more. Intestinal wars between the tribes terminated the lives of at least 20,000. Finally, the position of Suakim seems to have proved a sort of death-trap for the destruction of these fanatical swarms; every week or two a night attack has been repulsed with tremendous slaughter; — but the Moslems will nevertheless continue to rush on the place, like insects committing suicide against an electric light. Suakim must have cost the Mahdi — on British official word-of-honor — about 75,000 men.

And still the smallpox is ravaging the Mahdi's camp; and still the plague prevails; and still dysentery and cholera work in partnership with Azrael; and still the tribes are deserting him by thousands; and still his lieutenants are going over to Gordon; and if his primitive army had been as vast as an audience of the Last Judgment, it ought to have been annihilated by this time. A few days ago we heard the Mahdi was dead and his army gone; yesterday he was terribly lively, and marching on Khartoum with lightning speed. Gordon has already died or been taken prisoner fifteen or twenty times, and might have gone on dying indefinitely had not General Wolseley compelled him to communicate and to stop dying. But it is not the Mahdi's turn — a man who cannot be compelled to communicate when he does not feel like it, nor be prevented from dying as often as he deems it the right and proper thing to do.

There is evidently something extraordinarily wrong in all these accounts, and it were now exceeding rash to hazard any opinion about anything south of Wady Halfa, until our understanding be further enlarged and fully illuminated. All we know positively is that the English are try-

ing to walk to Khartoum, or at least to that part
of the world at which Khartoum is ordinarily supposed to be, if it has not already ceased to exist.
While they are getting down there, telegrams
from Gordon, Mahdi and Company are to be
taken with salt.

THE STORY OF AN ORIENTALIST[1]

THAT the indifference manifested by the United States in regard to the French Republic's superb gift of Bartholdi's colossus is a national disgrace, most intelligent Americans are willing to admit. Indeed America has satirized its own remissness in this regard with unsparing pen and pencil; and the press of the United States has certainly done even more than its duty in striving to bestir the nation into a proper spirit of interest and pride in their gift. 'We, the People of the United States' can always afford to criticize ourselves, but, like all other nations, we are apt to resent the criticism of neighbors. An excellent opportunity of indulging in such resentment is now offered by the peculiar circumlocutionary action of the French Government in regard to the Musée Guimet. French newspapers have been so unsparing of late in their animadversions upon us, that an American journalist feels justified in yielding to a slightly malicious pleasure upon reading the history of M. Guimet and his work.

M. Émile Guimet is the founder, and as yet the proprietor, of one of the most remarkable museums in the world; and has done more than any other private individual ever did toward the

[1] *Times-Democrat*, December 21, 1884.

European dissemination of knowledge regarding Oriental religious literature. More celebrated scholars there have certainly been than Émile Guimet; but no man ever devoted such a large private fortune to similar ends with equal success. Moreover, he does not profess himself to be a great Oriental linguist; he is, strictly speaking, only a dilettante, yet there are few Orientalists in the world who have not been largely indebted to him. He has spent a large part of his industrious life in travel, and brought back with him from India, China, Ceylon, Thibet, Japan, Persia, Arabia, Northern and Western Africa, and other countries, enormous collections of curiosities and documents, at a cost of considerably more than one million of dollars. Besides these things, he has also made a wonderful collection of North and South American antiquities, relating to the folk-lore, superstitions, and religions of the aborigines. These treasures are contained in a museum at Lyons, which M. Guimet himself constructed at a cost exceeding $200,000 in our money. The museum is divided into two principal departments. One contains all objects — (images, idols, bas-reliefs, hierophantic emblems, lustral vessels, censers, paintings, altar-ware) — connected with the various cults of Asia, Africa, and America, ancient or modern. This part of the museum is unique in the world. The other department is devoted to Oriental ceramics, and is of incalculably greater value than the sum-total of the prices paid by the traveller for each object.

But while these form the two great divisions of the museum, neither of them, perhaps, constitutes its most really remarkable feature. This seems to us to be the famous private library connected with the institution, filled with rare Oriental manuscripts, not to be found elsewhere, and forming a sort of college for Oriental translators. Some of the most extraordinary and valuable translations from Oriental manuscripts ever made have been written in that library — including versions by Garcin de Tassy, Léon Feer, F. Chabas (the Egyptologist), Ph. Ed. Foucaux (the world-famed Sanscrit scholar), and others whose names are guarantees of learned precision. But the most remarkable undertaking of M. Guimet was the importation of Brahmins from India, of Buddhist priests from Thibet, China, and Japan, to translate for him. In the library some strange and often beautiful faces might always be seen, whose aquiline regularity and golden complexion told of purest Aryan blood, or whose oblique black eyes and shaven forehead recalled to the visitor some Chinese figures of Buddha which he had just observed in the adjoining room. Here, among other distinguished Orientalists, brought to France and salaried out of M. Guimet's private purse, were the Japanese Ymaizoumi, Tomli, and Yamata.

The translations, essays, or treatises written under the supervision and instigation of M. Guimet, were collected into handsome volumes appearing at intervals under the title 'Annales du Musée Guimet' — some eight of which have been issued. These comprise many totally new translations of religious works from the Thibetan, Japanese, Chinese, Sanscrit, Pali, Hindostani, etc., and include Feer's celebrated extracts from the Kandjour, or Thibetan Buddhist collection. The catalogue of the museum alone covers some six hundred large pages.

With the approach of old age M. Guimet naturally felt anxious for the future of the institution to which he had devoted his life, and desired to anticipate all risk of his magnificent collections ever being brought under the hammer and dissipated by auctioneers. He might have presented it to the city of Lyons; but Paris is the great center of Oriental studies, and after Guimet's death the municipality of Lyons might not prove worthy trustees of a gift requiring much more than a mere knowledge of political economy to maintain. So he offered what had actually cost him about a million and a half, but what is worth infinitely more, a free gift to the State — asking only that the institution should be removed to Paris, and that he should be permitted to direct it until his death. Any of the other European governments would have paid an enormous price for it; and Guimet offered it for nothing. But two years were spent by him in fruitless efforts to induce the government to listen to him! It was not until all the Orientalists of Paris in a body strongly petitioned the authorities to open their eyes, that the proposition was accepted. Now the collections will be transported to Paris; and the government has even undertaken to build a special palace for them, on the Place de Jena, where M. Émile Guimet will resume his superintendence, and continue to direct the Brahmins and the Buddhists in their translations from various Oriental tongues into French. It seems to be much more facile for these Eastern scholars to learn a European language perfectly, than for a European to master Sanscrit, Chinese, or Cinghalese.

Assuredly the reproaches about the Bartholdi Statue come with bad taste from a nation so slow to accept so princely a gift as the Guimet Museum. A French critic observes in this connection: 'Administrative formalities actually render it now more difficult to perform a useful public action in France, than to commit a crime!'

A MEMORY OF TWO FANNIES [1]

NATURALLY the foreign journals and reviews are just now brimful of anecdotes and reminiscences of the great Fanny Elssler — whose name will long continue thus to glimmer through the pages of periodical literature. The prettiest, and perhaps the saddest fact published in connection with her memory abroad, however, is one relating to another beautiful dancer, who in public at least also bore the name of Fanny, but who yet lives in some quietly elegant little city of France.

It was quite rational that a woman like that wonderful Elssler should have exercised an extraordinary influence upon the imagination and the affections of men — first, indeed, because she belonged to that rare type of personages who exert a far more intimate rule over their fellow-beings than real monarchs — a sway due wholly to the esthetic sense, which is so vast an influence to any complex and refined civilization; — secondly, because she seemed also to contradict all universally accepted aphorisms regarding the impermanency of beauty and the evanescence of grace. The Muses of that art of which she was high-priestess seem to have rewarded her exposition of their doctrines with the gift of im-

[1] *Times-Democrat*, December 28, 1884.

mortal youth. The frosts of age never touched
her looks, and her beauty remained unwrinkled
as the face of an antique marble. In this she
somewhat resembled that great actress, Made-
moiselle Georges, who always appeared to Théophile Gautier like a vivified deity that had suddenly descended from the Greek pedestal upon
which her feet had rested through the centuries
— but the actress never attained the years of the
dancer. Elssler might almost have been taken
for a supernatural being. Needless to repeat how
greatly she was idolized — how many a sword
would have been drawn against the least criticism upon her. We have only to speak of one of
her idolators who worshiped her in a peculiarly
strange and romantic way — that way of all
others most worthy of her.

This adorer was an Italian officer in the service
of France — named Cerrito. He had passed
through all the horrors of the Russian campaign,
and escaped with some honorable wounds. Among
the military men who were the most enthusiastic
applauders, and most constant attendants at
Naples during Fanny's triumph there, was Captain Cerrito — who watched her with such ven-
eration as one might feel who believed that he beheld before him a divinity incarnate. Night after
night he came; and night after night he prayed
heaven for only one favor — that he might some
day have a daughter who could dance like Fanny

Elssler. The odd but beautiful prayer was heard; a little daughter came into the world for him. He naturally wished to call her Fanny. But the mother — perhaps through a natural feeling of tender jealousy refused, and insisted that the child should be called Francesca. But the great public whom she frenzied in after years only knew her as Fanny — Fanny Cerrito.

The strangest thing about the child's talent was its absolute naturalness; she danced from her very infancy, and, curiously enough, mastered the most difficult elements of the art without having to undergo the severe discipline of the Italian schools, and the torture of the bar. Supple as a reed, and almost as typically fragile, the great Italian manager Lanari, who first brought her out, long hesitated to make the venture. He feared the slender blonde fairy had no such strength of constitution as was required for the fatigues of the career. This Fanny was in everything but art the very antithesis of the other — her father's divinity, tall and of a beauty as solid as the majesty of a Caryatid. But the new Fanny soon proved that she was not so weakly as her appearance indicated; and her career was scarcely less brilliant, though briefer, than that of her august prototype. Lords of Rome harnessed themselves to her carriage — among whom was the Prince Torlonia. At Venice the dead splendors of the ancient oligarchy were momentarily

resurrected to do her homage; — from the theater to the Danielli palace, a bridge of gondolas
was built for her slim feet; and attired in the
robes of a Dogess of other days, surrounded and
followed by an escort of Venetian noblemen, she
passed to the scene of her triumphs under a vast
blaze of torchlight, through a rain of flowers, amid
the welcome of a hundred bands of music, playing
the airs of the ballets in which she excelled. The
present Emperor of Germany — then only crown
prince — was glad to bring her with his own
hands, at Berlin, a cup of soup after a fatiguing
exhibition of her skill. Alexander II of Russia
paid her honors, and rewarded her genius with
imperial gifts of jewels; and Queen Victoria did
not scruple to show her especial favor, even in the
face of the great Taglioni — who, to her eternal
honor, showed no symptom of jealousy when the
Queen detached her own diamond brooch to pin
it upon the young dancer's shoulder.

At thirty years of age, however, her career was
broken. . . . There is something so aerial, so fairy,
so ethereal, so imponderably graceful about the
motion of these beings, that it suggests the flight of
some splendid butterfly, besprinkled with dust of
gold; — but alas! even like such beautiful insects
the ballerina sometimes comes too closely in con-
tact with the lights about which she hovers.
Fanny burnt her wings at last, says the narrator
of her biography; — a thousand hands aided to

quench the flame, and the dancer received but slight external injuries. But the shock affected her heart; — and she never wholly recovered. Immense engagements were broken off; wonderful prospects were shattered, and that marvelous genius, too, which had not even then fully reached its blossoming. She lives, still, however, with her glories, not forgotten yet by the public and especially by the public of the great art city of the world, Paris, where may be seen her exquisite bust in marble — the daughter of the other Fanny, not indeed by blood, but by art and the love of her Italian father for that art and its empress-hierophant.

NORODOM THE LAST[1]

THE article translated from the *Figaro* of Paris, which appears in another column, naturally created much sensation abroad at the time of its appearance — especially as it bears the semblance of having been written by an eye-witness of the semi-tragical, semi-grotesque episode described. It was well known in Europe that the last Norodom had sold his birthright only by compulsion, but the full details of the occurrence had not found publicity prior to the *Figaro's* article. Published by a journal bitterly opposed to the government, the narrative must nevertheless be received, not with doubt, but merely as one page of a record whose title and introductory chapters are still missing. The truth is probably there, and nothing but the truth; yet we have not *all* the truth. As the bare narrative of the eye-witness stands, the action of the French governor strongly resembles a case of highway robbery, with few attenuating circumstances; and such ruffianly manner of treating a king would be under any circumstances disgraceful. But there can be little doubt that the French authorities had good reason for determining that nothing short of absolute French sway could suffice for

[1] *Times-Democrat*, January 4, 1885.

European interest in Cambodia — that the monarch was incapable of accomplishing his share of the duties of government; and that the monarchy must be converted into a province of the republic.

Great Britain has found it occasionally expedient to depose Oriental rulers incapable of fulfilling their bargains with her, and retired such personages with a handsome pension. France proposes to do the latter; but her representative deemed it better policy to suddenly terminate a royal dynasty altogether, than to take the trouble of establishing a new one. A veritable Red Republican of the old school, that Thomson, who forces his way into a royal sleeping-room, and menaces its occupant with the penitentiary. One cannot help thinking of Louis XVI and the mob at the Tuileries.

Assuredly M. Thomson is no archæologist. An archæologist might have been awed by the traditions of the land. However shadowy the power of the monarch of that phantom Kingdom of Cambodia, he represented to learned imagination a dynasty of kings ranging back in colossal file far into the night of centuries, and the majesty of one of those antique civilizations so august and mighty that they seemed to weigh down the face of the world. The Cambodia of antiquity was imposing as Egypt, gigantic as Assyria; — a hundred kings of the further East worshiped at her enormous shrines; her cities swarmed with populations that might be numbered by millions only. Over the tropical marshes and through the green night of forests immemorially old, high causeways worthy the genius of Roman engineers extended from metropolis to metropolis, binding the great cities together in magnificent commercial brotherhood. All that is now Siam, and most of what is now Annam or French Cochin-China was then subject to kings of Cambodia. To-day the traveler in those fever-haunted and forest-grown solitudes reaches with difficulty the site of the ancient splendors of Ongkor-Thom or Ongkor-Wat; — tropical nature seeks to hide the grave of that forgotten civilization. But those who make their way to the deserted cities, through leagues of giant forest and perilous jungle, are astonished at the dead magnificence before them; — the mighty temples whose courts are a thousand feet in breadth, and whose statues, too monstrous for removal, seem still awaiting worshipers; — the silent palaces, guarded only by dragons and lions of stone, inhabited only by apes and by serpents; — the bas-reliefs, picturing the splendor of festivities as luxurious and as wanton as the debauches of Babylon or Nineveh; — the inscriptions in tongues no longer spoken; — the cyclopean terraces of kingly halls; — the colossal stairs now leading only into labyrinths of forests unexplored. So wondrous these strange places are that the modern Cambodian will tell you these places were built by spirits, even as the modern Arab regards the temples and pyramids of Egypt as the work of Genii. Yet some of those halls and Buddhist temples of Cambodia ceased to echo human footsteps since the seventeenth century only; and the kingdom shrunk into provincial insignificance only within a couple of hundred years. The bayadères who danced in the presence of the French governor only last June, might have claimed direct descent from those who dance in stone upon the bas-reliefs of Ongkor-Thom — all with finger-nails sheathed in gold, with slender ankles encircled by serpent-anklets or rings wrought in likeness of double-headed dragons — all nude-limbed and feather-crowned and smiling a mysteriously voluptuous smile with eyelids languorously closed.

SOME FOSSIL ANTHROPOLOGY [1]

A GENTLEMAN writes to this paper asking for information regarding the scientific position of Professor A. de Quatrefages on the subject of evolution, as presented in his most recent volume 'Hommes Fossiles et Hommes Sauvages' (1884). The question, we fancied, might interest others than the correspondent in question.

M. Quatrefages has not, as yet, entered the ranks of the Evolutionists. In a former work, 'The Human Species,' published in the *International Scientific Series*, while giving full recognition to the immense value of Darwin's works, he expressly stated that he could not give adhesion to the theory of descent until positive proof should be given of the fact that 'physiological species can be produced by selective crossing.' This is the same doubt which Huxley has also advanced in his expression of the reserve under which he accepts the Darwinian hypothesis. There is, however, this difference in the position of Quatrefages and Huxley. While the latter considers the Darwinian hypothesis of descent as by far the most rational yet offered in explanation of the origin of species, Quatrefages does not hold the same high opinion of it, even while declaring

[1] *Times-Democrat*, January 18, 1885.

that he agrees in other respects upon all that Darwin has said in regard to the Struggle for Existence and Natural Selection. This position M. Quatrefages has not abandoned, according to his last work; but he has plainly stated that his doubts are based wholly upon scientific investigations. He does not condemn those who differ from him and simply asks for more light. Those who have read his former small work will recollect that in regard to the origin of species he takes a position of pure agnosticism — printing the confession I DO NOT KNOW in small capitals.

M. Quatrefages' new work deals with fossil man of the tertiary and quaternary epochs, the persistence of certain fossil types among modern races, and the consideration of the condition of fossil races as compared with those of modern savage tribes. In the latter relation he gives us a series of very curious and entertaining papers upon the Malays, Negritoes, Polynesians and the Todas — a beautiful and singular race of Indian mountaineers who practice polyandry, and neither cultivate the soil nor hunt, living wholly by means of their herds. In the first part of the work the author presents a full summary of scientific discoveries and investigations concerning primitive man; acknowledges his errors in combating the first statements advanced concerning the existence of human races in the tertiary epoch; acknowledges likewise his error in formerly denying that the oldest human remains belong to a dolichocephalic or long-headed race; but for his opinions on the transformation theories of Haeckel and Darwin still refers the reader to his essay of 1870. The following discoveries rather tend to support than to weaken M. Quatrefages' position in regard to the origin of species:

1. That the earliest men of the tertiary period existed contemporaneously with apes much resembling extant anthropomorphic species.

2. That the craniology of those fossil races with which we are most acquainted reveal a high cerebral development, and in some cases a brain capacity superior to that of the average modern adult. (For example the skull of the Old Man of Cro-Magnon has a capacity of 1590 cubic centimeters — or 119 centimeters more than the average Parisian skull of the nineteenth century.)

3. That ample evidence has been gathered to show that the men of certain fossil races possessed religious beliefs as well developed, at least, as those of savage races to-day.

4. That from a purely physical point of view fossil man was not a human type inferior to existing types, but one in many respects superior.

Were there any geological indications of a human type having existed which presented indubitably apish characters — the idea that the present human race had been developed from quadrumana at all resembling existing species, might claim scientific proof. But man has been traced back to the age of mammoths and other monstrous mammalia which have long been extinct, and he ever remains man. Some day other links may be found; but at present the Haeckelist can only theorize as to human origin. Recent discoveries have not, however, at all seriously affected these theories. In one respect they rather aid them; for in proving so vast an antiquity for man, they also seem to account partially for that wondrous evolution of brain power which gives to him the mastery of the world.

SHAPIRA [1]

THE whole history of the most stupendous archæological frauds ever perpetrated has just been given to the world by M. Clermont-Ganneau, the French savant who twice unmasked Shapira. Some of the principal details were published two years ago in the leading journals of the world; but the extraordinary obstacles with which M. Clermont-Ganneau had to contend will only be appreciated after a perusal of his admirable little book, which is enriched with many explanatory illustrations. It seems that the audacity of the counterfeiters was encouraged by the violent aggressiveness of various German savants, who felt furious at the mere idea of being duped, and whose position in regard to M. Clermont-Ganneau was stiffened by self-interest and professional jealousy.

It was in 1872 that two English men of letters, commissioned to make an archæological and topographical exploration in Palestine, first saw the celebrated collection of *Moabite potteries* made by the Jew Shapira, in the house of the latter at Jerusalem. These consisted of urns, vases, tablets, figurines in terra-cotta, covered with what appeared to be Phœnician characters — and in-

[1] *Times-Democrat*, March 15, 1885.

cluded many specimens of an art both grotesque
and obscene. The obscenities, however, seemed
to emphasize the authenticity of the objects; the
characters were more or less decipherable; and
the English travelers, deeming the collection of
indubitable antiquity, made water-color drawings of the whole, and sent them to London,
where they were privately exhibited at the office
of the Palestine Exploration Fund. M. Clermont-
Ganneau visited the office, and was asked for his
opinion. Without a moment's hesitation he pronounced the potteries all frauds; and even stated
the name of the artisan who had manufactured
them. It was not Shapira himself — who claimed
to have disinterred them in the ancient land of
Moab — but a certain Selim El-Qari that had
been employed by Ganneau to copy the Stela of
Mesa — one of those Arab stone cutters capable
of so well imitating Egyptian scarabæus, hieroglyphics and all, that few scientists could distinguish the imitation from the original carving.
M. Clermont-Ganneau had, by close observation,
detected certain peculiarities in this man's work,
which he also found traces of in the pretended
Moabite potteries. It was privately agreed not
to give the matter publicity; but England was
thus saved from mystification. M. Shapira,
finding no encouragement from the British savants, turned his attention to Germany.

The Germans were thoroughly duped — a fact

that speaks very strongly for the dangerous character of Shapira's frauds, and the remarkable
talent of their inventor. Herr Schlottman, one of
the leading archæologists of the empire, actually
wrote a tremendous panegyric about these potteries, especially certain vases inscribed with the
Song of Songs, or something closely resembling
it. The government was moved to negotiate
with Shapira, and *seventeen hundred objects* were
purchased for the imperial museum at Berlin.
The sum disbursed is supposed to have been
immense; but owing to the discovery of the
frauds the government has never allowed the
world to know just what was paid, nor did it
ever suffer the potteries to be exposed in the
glass cabinets of its museum.

Shapira began to make new collections, of
course; and meantime Clermont-Ganneau was
sent upon an archæological mission to Palestine.
Shapira did not wish to admit him to inspect the
Moabite antiquities, when he called upon him at
Jerusalem — for the excellent reason that Shapira
had been warned by Selim El-Qari, the manu-
facturer! But Shapira was finally compelled by
the insistence of several English archæologists
to let M. Ganneau in. The latter at once recognized the frauds; — the earth used was an earth
almost peculiar to Jerusalem; the imprint of a
cotton-texture was visible on some of the terra-
cottas, and the cotton had been woven by mod-

ern machinery. Clermont-Ganneau said nothing
to Shapira, but immediately started on the track
of the potter — an ignorant and simple-minded
man, who told the visitor that he used to bake
statues and other things for Selim El-Qari, who
made them. Other potters doing similar work
for Selim were also found; — and the French
savant soon obtained all possible details as to the
method of manufacture — even to the details
of how the terra-cottas were impregnated with
saltpeter so as to produce efflorescences capable
of deceiving experts. And all these things having
been discovered, the facts were sent to the *Athe-
næum*, and published therein. There was a tremendous excitement at Berlin; and the government ordered a counter-investigation. Clermont-
Ganneau's witnesses were bulldozed or bought
up by Shapira and his friends. Selim was arrested by sole authority of the German consul,
and imprisoned in the consulate. Shapira played
a desperate hand by buying up the jury, and terrifying the potters. These swore by Allah and
the beard of the Prophet that Ganneau had paid
them to say what was not true; Selim swore that
the French archæologist had offered him two
thousand francs to bear witness that the potteries
were manufactured by order of Shapira. Unfortunately for themselves, the perjurers over-
shot the mark. At the time when, according to
Selim and others, M. Clermont-Ganneau had

made these offers, that gentleman was in Europe! The frauds became visible to the universe; the immense and awfully learned volume in folio, to be entitled 'Corpus inscriptionum moabiticarum,' was never completed; and in 1876 Professor Mommsen boldly confessed the errors of his fellow-scholars before the Prussian Landstag.

How Shapira could have subsequently had the colossal impudence, in 1883, to carry that pretended original manuscript of the Bible to the imperial museum at Berlin, which he had already so badly duped, is a peculiar mystery. When Berlin ignored him instead of arresting him, he offered it for sale in London; and, strange to say, the English savants seemed to have forgotten their former experience. Specimens of the manuscript were exhibited in the British Museum; and a great German Hebrew scholar, Dr. Ginnsberg, was appointed to investigate its authenticity. While he was publishing wearisome and nonsensical reports in the *Times*, Clermont-Ganneau suddenly came out with a clear exposition of the whole fraud. He had analyzed both sheepskin and ink; the sheep that furnished the parchment had lived only a few years before! Shapira, who expected a million for his manuscript, committed suicide. Why so impudent a man should ever have thought of committing suicide is another wonderful mystery.

Not the least noteworthy thing about the

whole scandal was the revelation it entailed of
human pettiness, even in the person of highly
distinguished and learned men. The vanity of
the duped German scholars would never permit
them to acknowledge the services of their French
rival; while the great Dr. Ginnsberg, who had
been enthusiastic over the fraudulent manuscript
of the Bible for months, seized upon M. Clermont-Ganneau's exposition immediately after
its appearance, and rather than acknowledge a
superior, recopied statements, and published the
real discoverer's observations as the results of his
own study! But the learned world is much less
liable to be duped by such duplicity as this, than
by the uncommon talents of such scoundrels as
Shapira.

THE RISE OF THE MAHDI[1]

At this exciting period in the history of the great
Arab revolt in the Soudan, a brief sketch of the
history of its leader will have some opportune
interest. What the title of Mahdi means, its
origin, and the high rôles played by some who
have borne it, our readers may have learned from
our review in last Sunday's issue, based upon the
scholarly lectures of M. Darmesteter before the
Sorbonne. The same writer has communicated
to the public some facts of importance connected
with the Mahdi of the Soudan.

Still it may be well to observe at the outset,
that comparatively little is known about this
personage. The distances, the deserts, and the
dangers which separate his country from civilization, have made it for Europeans a mysterious
land; and even the brutal pachas who ruled it
mostly remained cautiously walled up in strong
cities during their stay, and collected taxes
chiefly by means of mercenary tribes, who allied
themselves with Bashi-Bazouks and other Turkish soldiery in consideration of such generous pay
as the plunder of half a dozen provinces alone
rendered possible. Even the names of the great
families of those regions are not generally known.

[1] *Times-Democrat*, March 29, 1885.

Travelers have written many books about what they have seen, and traders about what they have heard; but with all this, and many Turkish official documents of importance, much remains to be learned before the geography and ethnology of these regions are definitely ascertained and mapped out.

There are only two trustworthy sources from which information about the Mahdi has been obtained; — one is the recent correspondence of Mousa Peney, a Frenchman born in the Soudan, son of Dr. Peney, the first European explorer who ever made his way to Gondokoro; and the statements obtained in writing by M. Clermont-Ganneau from the Ulemas of El-Azhar mosque (greatest of Moslem universities) at Cairo. These Ulemas or Mohammedan doctors were gently, but firmly, compelled by a mandate from the Sultan of Turkey to obtain all possible information about the Mahdi's history and pretensions, and to anathematize him as a theological impostor.

According to all that has been learned in this way, the Mahdi, whose name is Mohammed Ahmed, was born at Dongola in 1843 (1260 of the Hegira); his father's name being Abdallah and his mother's Amina — these also being the names of the father and mother of the Prophet. These coincidences have an immense value in the Moslem world; for they are according to the prophecy upon which all claims to Mahdiship are based. Furthermore the boy had three parallel marks on each cheek — 'the beauty-spot which is the Seal of prophecy.' Abdallah and his wife being profoundly religious people, doubtless encouraged their son to believe that his destiny was a great one; and their encouragement was probably sincere. In times of great despair, human helplessness finds relief in faith and the promises of prophecy; and this poor Arab couple might well have felt happiness in the dim hope that their child would prove the Master of the Hour, who was to free the land from the oppression of the infamous Turks. The old man never lived to see his dream take material form; but his ideas were received and nourished by his two grown-up sons, Mohammed's elder brothers, who followed the trade of boat-builders upon the White Nile. At twelve years of age, Mohammed knew the Koran by heart, and showed wonderful predisposition to study; his brothers determined to send him to study at a celebrated Moslem ecclesiastical seminary, or *Medrassa*, conducted by two learned religious doctors — Abdel Dagim and El-Gourachi. This was an excellent beginning for the youth. Although the Mussulmans have no religious hierarchy in precisely the same sense implied by our word 'church,' the vocation of a marabout, or religious teacher, is not an unenviable one in the Orient. A man who can expound the Koran, settle disputes, give good advice, and obtain a reputation for sanctity according to Mohammedan dogma, may readily obtain an excellent position. Attached to a tribe as its spiritual leader, he receives large perquisites in the form of alms and gifts; the best tent is at his disposal, and the daughters of chiefs are proud to marry him. Scholars trained for such a life, who are unable to find a vacancy at home, boldly go forth as missionaries — and often far to the south — toward the region of those great lakes which are the reservoirs of the Nile and were familiar to Moslem eyes centuries before the birth of their European discoverers. Thus were many black Moslem kingdoms formed in the Southern Soudan; and should other civilizing powers not intervene, it is almost certain that Mohammedanism will be successfully spread throughout the heart of Africa.

But Mohammed Ahmed believed too much in his special calling to dream of becoming a missionary among the blacks. After studying for twenty-five years, during which time his mother also passed away, he settled in the little island of Aba in the White Nile; and began to devote himself wholly to fasting, prayer, and meditation — living in a sort of burrow in the earth. There he dwelt fifteen years — precisely the same time that Mahomet the Prophet spent meditating upon his vocation before he began to preach.

For he who believes himself the Mahdi must imitate the life of Mahomet in all things; and not go forth upon his mission until his fortieth year. But long before that year, the ascetic of Aba had made his influence felt. Venerating him as a saint, believing his every word inspired by the Spirit of God, the mighty tribe of the Baggaras proclaimed him their marabout. When his fortieth year arrived, he was received by them as a prophet; and found himself already a potentate in the land.

It was for the faithful a momentous era. Had not the prophecies foretold that in the 1300th year of the Hegira (1883) Islam should triumph? The Mahdi believed firmly that the hour was approaching; he sent missionaries to the Sheiks of all the tribes to announce the event, saying that he was indeed the Master of the Hour — that the Shadow of Mahomet had visited him in a dream, and had told him that the dominion of the Turk should cease — that by Allah's will the men of the Soudan would arise — that when the infidels and the traitors should be driven forth, he, the Mahdi, should go to Mecca, and there make himself recognized by the Grand Shereef as Prophet and Caliph of all the Moslem *world*. The spaces of desert separating the tribes were broad; — some missionaries traveled for many months to deliver their messages. But for one year these summonses had been continually sent out before a suspicion of what was going on found its way to the Turkish authorities at Khartoum. Admirably shrewd in the policy of repression, the Turks immediately resolved to end the danger by seizing the Mahdi. Aba was only three days' sail from the Nubian capital; and Reouf Pacha sent two hundred men to the island for that purpose. They reached it unobserved in the midst of a rainy night; and after groping among the trees arrived before the cabin of the Prophet, where a band of Dervishes whirled in their sacred dance with arms extended — calling upon the name of Allah. Immediately the adjutant-major fired into the group and killed a dervish; — he supposed no doubt that a panic would follow. But the result was the very reverse — with a hideous roar all the Dervishes rushed upon the Turks with only their naked hands for weapons; and a thousand Arabs, answering their cry, came rushing from the groves like savage lions. Not a Turk escaped; — it is said that every man in the expedition was torn limb from limb.

That was in May, 1881. The first spark had been ignited; the conflagration spread; the flame of the new faith flashed through all the Libyan desert — and eastward beyond the Nile and the naked hills to the surges of the Red Sea — and far south into the black provinces of Waday and Darfour. The Soudan uprose as though lifted by the very breath of Allah. Meantime the Mahdi had retired to Mount Gadir; and Reouf Pacha thought there was yet time, despite the gathering of the nomads. He sent expedition after expedition; and the corpses of the soldiers were given to the hyenas and the jackals of the mountains. Then, made rash by fear, Giegler Pacha withdrew from Senaar, Fachoda, and Kordofan, the Turkish garrisons, in order to muster a force strong enough to send against the prophet; and, as the troops departed, the country behind them burst into insurrection. Seven thousand disciplined troops were sent, however, to Mount Gadir; and were unexpectedly surrounded by 50,000 Arabs, under command of the Mahdi's two brothers — Ahmed and Mohammed. The brothers died like heroes; but of the Egyptian army only one hundred and twenty men escaped. Senaar declared for the Prophet (who made El-Obeid his capital January 17, 1883); and Hicks Pacha sought to stay the ruin. Needless to recount the fate of his army, nor of the forces under Baker Pacha. As the Shadow of Mahomet had predicted to the Mahdi, Turkish dominion was a thing of the past.

No less important an event for the holy cause was the death of Gordon. The English press did not correctly reproduce the announcement of his decease in the telegraphed words of the Prophet: 'We have killed the *traitor* Gordon.' The Arabic word was *Deddjal*, which means 'Antichrist'; and it is one of the duties of the Mahdi's mission to kill 'Antichrist.' To the Arab mind Gordon was more than man — he was supernatural — a demon-spirit incarnated — the veritable Antichrist himself.

So far the career of the Mahdi proves him a great man and a good general. His plan has been to starve out fortified places; and to weary armies by a succession of short, sharp fights, cutting off stragglers and harassing convoys, until the enemy is sufficiently weakened to justify a desperate attempt to crush him by overwhelming numbers. Meantime the anathema of the Ulemas has not moved the faith of the Soudanese in their Savior; the Mahdi has proved his mission to them by the annihilation of six armies.

The tribes of Arabia watch in excited expectation the course of events beyond the Red Sea; but the English fleet bars the way to Mecca; and the Mahdi cannot yet visit the Holy City. Such a visit would be indeed fraught with peril to Asiatic Turkey.

Politicians but half understand the nature of the rising in the Soudan. A few hard-won victories will not settle the country; — the tribes will resist bravely until exterminated. We have read in the dispatches how even the women fought and died. This is the heroism of a deep faith — call it fanaticism if you please; and such a spirit is not checked by disaster. The Lord has promised that his angels shall aid; and when the

next great battle comes, many a glazing Arab
eye will fancy it beholds at the head of Islam's
warriors the luminous cavalry of heaven — or
perhaps the grand figure of that mighty captain,
Khaled, who of old shattered the power of
Rome — or even the blessed phantom of Sidi
Abdel Kader El Djalani, who yearly crosses the
desert upon a ghostly steed, to watch over the
children of Mahomet. Dreams indeed! — but
these are the dreams that shake the world, and
make men laugh in the face of death, and see
eternal peace and joy and the soft black eyes of
houris beyond the lightnings of the English guns.

L'ARLÉSIENNE [1]

ONE of the greatest of recent theatrical successes in Paris is the lyrical drama entitled 'L'Arlésienne' — the joint creation of Alphonse Daudet and of his lamented friend Bizet, the author of 'Carmen.' As the work will doubtless be widely appreciated in this country, our readers may be interested in the history of the composition — a history at once romantic and pathetic, and curiously illustrative of the fickleness of public favor. Several foreign journals have narrated the story, but none so prettily as *Le XIXe Siècle* in its issue of May 6.

The history of 'L'Arlésienne' carries us back thirteen years to the period of depression immediately following the tremendous shock of the Franco-Prussian war, and the convulsions of the Commune. The world of artists and writers had suffered severely in those great struggles; some of the most celebrated names in the French literature of the century found place upon the endless roll-call of the dead; many a mighty painter and sculptor had been swept away by the wind of battles; and the surviving members of the grand companionship of art and belles-lettres mostly found themselves ruined. Among these were

[1] *Times-Democrat*, May 31, 1885.

Alphonse Daudet, the novelist; and César Bizet (who always signed himself George) the musician — both already illustrious. Bizet at the age of *eleven years* had taken the solfeggio-prize at the Conservatory; had in his nineteenth year won the great prize of Rome; and had subsequently given to the theater two audaciously original and exquisite compositions, 'Les Pécheuses de Perles' and 'La Jolie Fille de Perth.' Daudet had published a number of dainty and delightful little things, 'Les Amoureuses,' 'Le Petit Chose' (said to be partly autobiographical), the uniquely humorous 'Tartarin de Tarascon,' and the 'Lettres de mon Moulin' — charming sketches which have found translators in almost all European countries. It was in the latter work that first appeared the story entitled 'L'Arlésienne' — the story of a young Provençal who dies for love.

Both the novelist and the musician, whose last pecuniary resources had been wrested from them by the hard necessities of the war, began to look about them anxiously for a chance to repair their losses by good work. Both had families to care for, and the situation was desperate. Publishers refused to risk their capital in any undertaking; the newspapers, seriously affected in their finances, could not or would not pay a respectable price for fiction; and the bookstores had little patronage to encourage them. Only one way to success seemed still open — the theater; and Daudet proposed to his friend Bizet an opera based on the story of 'L'Arlésienne.' Bizet readily acceded; and produced in a short time one of the most delicately beautiful musical creations ever composed — full of passionate Southern melody, of strangely delightful variations upon quaint Provençal themes.

Everything seemed propitious. Great critics believed the music would enthuse Paris. Admirable actresses had been found for the leading parts — many of whom have since become famous. The directors were hopeful; the support of the press seemed assured. . . . 'L'Arlésienne' was performed for the first time at the Vaudeville Théâtre, on October 1, 1872.

It was a momentous evening for both Daudet and his friend; the first had everything to gain, the latter much to lose. As the French journalist who describes the events of that evening remarks, nothing is so utterly a failure as the failure of a theatrical piece. There is often some hope for an unpopular book; — if it contains aught of real talent, it may work its way slowly but steadily into public notice; it may be suddenly resurrected from dusty oblivion by some timely sensation, some great social excitement about the very theme upon which it treats. But the theatrical failure is apparently irremediable, and the petty whim, malice, or mere indifference of critics, or of audiences, may bring about such a failure. Even literary giants have been driven from the stage forever, and masterpieces hopelessly damned by nothing more than popular ill-humor. To Daudet a failure meant the closure of all theatrical doors against him for long years, and the destruction of a hundred projects — among which was a drama in preparation founded on the theme which afterwards was to form the plot of that admirable novel, 'Fromont Jeune et Risler Aîné.'

There was a large audience, but a strange one — an assembly made somber of aspect by the multitude of mourning robes — an assembly wearied to nervousness by the long strain of the war, saddened by memories of death, anticipating in a visit to the theater rather the consolation of social distraction than the pleasure of studying a rare and charming art. The music was admirably performed; but no one seemed to hear it; — the text was faultlessly declaimed, yet no one appeared to listen. People with programmes upon their knees were discussing politics in whispers; others, who had met as if by chance, thought and spoke only of their bereavements. The vast gloom of the war seemed to fill all the theater; and the ghosts of a thousand haunting sorrows drew away the gaze of the spectators from the stage. The audience seemed to have forgotten the mock drama, and to remember only the terribly real drama in which all had taken part; they stared without seeing, as in dream; they felt no passing emotion; they uttered no applause. 'L'Arlésienne' was concluded in a great buzz of indifference; and its close was marked only by a moment of icy silence — as though all present had suddenly awoke to the knowledge of the fact that a lyrical drama had just been performed of which they had not heard a word.

Daudet went home in despair, destroyed the manuscript of his unfinished play, and after awhile bravely sat down to write the novels which were destined to make his fortune. It was slow work but sure success. Bizet wrote 'Carmen'; but the public waited for his death to admire it.

... Thirteen years passed by; and Daudet's name had become familiar to the whole civilized world. Fame smiled upon him, and wealth; translations of his novels appeared simultaneously in England, Germany, Spain, Italy, Russia, and America;—his 'Sapho' reached a sale of eighty thousand copies within a few months of its appearance. Bizet was long dead; but his marvelous music had conquered indifference, had mastered criticism, had compelled the enthusiasm of a thousand audiences. And suddenly the fickle and forgetful public, moved by some strange souvenir, remembered 'L'Arlésienne'

while remembering Bizet. So it happened that
on the 5th of May, 1885, a great concourse of
people found themselves in the Odeon, madly
applauding the music they had refused to hear
thirteen years before, weeping at the spectacle
that had left them unmoved in 1872. There were
new decorations, new costumes, and other actors;
but the words and the music were the same, and
'L'Arlésienne' was a triumph!... Daudet, sit-
ting alone, watched the tumultuous pleasure
of the crowd; but never smiled; — doubtless he
saw beside him the Shadow of the dead musician,
the beloved friend, gazing as one that seeks to
speak in vain, yearning for the utterance de-
nied to those who dwell forever in the Place of
Silence.

A NEW POMPEII[1]

TARENTUM, the modern Taranto —which in both ancient and recent times gave its name to the vast and beautiful gulf upon which it looked — was in the era of old Greek civilization one of the mightiest cities of Magna Græcia; — in military power worthy to rival Crotona; and in luxury, Sybaris. Until very lately, however, all we knew of the antique city was from the descriptions and histories of Greek and Roman authors. Except a multitude of coins of exquisite beauty, and some few broken columns and shattered stones, time seemed to have effaced all traces of the mighty town which could once send from the gates a disciplined army of 34,000 athletes. It was Tarentum which invited Pyrrhus to attack Rome; it was Tarentum which Hannibal besieged for years in vain before it was betrayed into his hands; it was Tarentum which yielded avenging Fabius Maximus a booty larger than that of Syracuse or Corinth. Still, the traveler Swinburne wrote some years ago: 'Never was a place so completely wiped out of existence.' The great classical encyclopedias give many columns indeed to Tarentum; but they definitely state that no remains exist to give us any idea of

[1] *Times-Democrat*, November 1, 1885.

the topography, the plan, or the magnitude of
the city.

But Tarentum has suddenly proved to be a
mine of archæological riches scarcely inferior to
Pompeii. It was the late François Lenormant —
(author of 'Chaldæan Magic' and the 'History
of the Ancient Peoples of the Orient' — one of
those princes of philology who aided in the interpretation of the Assyrian inscriptions) — that
first intimated that Tarentum had never been
so utterly destroyed as was generally believed.
Enabled by her wonderful position to survive
not only the horrors of the Roman decadence,
but all the miseries of the Middle Ages, Tarentum, under her modern name of Taranto, was
beginning for the first time in history to venture
beyond the narrow boundaries of her ancient
walls; and while the new quarters were being built,
Lenormant complained of the negligence of the
Italian government in not having superintended
the work of excavation. Later on, he stated,
such negligence might prove irreparable, and all
hope of discovering the plan and extent of the
Greek city be annihilated. Moreover, he made a
statement that startled the learned world. He
declared that Tarentum must have been, according to numerous hints thrown out by ancient
authors, one of the greatest art-markets of old
Italy. This granted, it was almost certain that a
special and unrivaled Greek school of art must

have flourished there; and the Tarentine vases
found elsewhere in Italy manifested a grace and
perfection of workmanship that gave them a
particular stamp. Finally he even ventured to assert that the excellence of that school must have
been such as to influence all Italian art, through
all the centuries of Roman luxury.

The archæologists of Italy were moved to action; and Signor Viola, one of the most learned
in the world, was sent by the government to
superintend the excavations at Taranto. Lenormant died before his predictions were verified;
but verified magnificently they have been!
Underneath the modern site Signor Viola found
the remains of the Roman city, which were not
rich; but under the Roman city, again, lay the
treasures of the *Parthenians* — the Spartan
colonists of old Tarentum — and their descendants. But that was not all. Under the old Greek
city, again, lay the remains of a town absolutely
prehistoric — containing objects of a character
even more archaic than the quaintest relics
among Cesnola's Cyprian collection.

Then it was found that Lenormant's belief in
the supremacy of the Tarentine art-school was
absolutely correct. Thousands upon thousands
of statuettes, of lamps, of figures, of votive offer-
ings, of dainty vases, of utensils in metal and
composition, were soon unearthed. More than
five thousand figurines of women alone were

found — each bearing a quadruped, bird, or
some other creature in her arms. Strange
grotesques were also discovered; and mystic
gods oddly resembling the divinities of India
and of China. There was considerable inferior
work; but there were also figurines of women of
exquisite beauty, the grace of whose attitudes
can be compared only with the finest statuettes
of Tanagra. For the time being, these discoveries are deposited in the Convent of San-Pasquale,
but the great building has become so filled with
them that it is almost impossible to go up the
stairs or along the corridors without crushing
gods and heroes. It will be years before all can
be classified and studied.

Wonderful intuition of genius! . . . Alone in his
Parisian study, the great Lenormant, awaking
from some mysterious meditation like the fabled
Merlin, sat down and wrote to the savants of the
entire world: '*You are all wrong! — you have indeed been there: I have not; but Tarentum exists
beneath the ashes of centuries. I know her buried
gods; and the secrets of her art are mine!*' . . .
And Viola, obeying the indication, brings to light
a world hidden for twenty centuries — a Roman
city seated upon the corpse of a Greek city, lying
again upon the skeleton of a metropolis so old
that all history is silent about it, and that the
very name of its people has been lost forever in
the night of ages.

ARCHÆOLOGY IN CAMBODIA [1]

THE year 1885 has witnessed much archæological progress of a most important sort. We spoke last week of a memorable discovery in Italy; — the *Journal des Savants* furnishes us now with complete details of a much greater discovery in the extreme Orient, accomplished by the grand labors of M. Aymonier, rewarded a few months ago by one of the greatest recompenses within the power of the Academy of Inscriptions to bestow. Before touching, however, upon the labors of Aymonier, it will be well to review briefly the history of Cambodian exploration.

Centuries ago, rumors of extraordinary remains in Indo-China were brought to Europe by Portuguese navigators; and more recently it was known that during the thirteenth century Chinese officials had not only visited these mysterious cities, but had published recitals of their travels thither. Still the recitals of the Portuguese of the fourteenth century, and the accounts of the Chinese travelers were forgotten before France had made her first conquests in Cochin-China. The oblivion into which the Chinese narratives had fallen was natural enough. When Abel Rémusat in 1829 translated the texts, the

[1] *Times-Democrat*, November 8, 1885.

learned world was not yet familiar with the histories of Buddhist missionaries, and had not yet learned that to a great extent the marvelous accounts of those voyagers dealt rather with real facts than fictions. Consequently the Chinese narration appeared from its novel character a work of imagination, and the cities described were deemed mere creations of fancy — like the cities of the Thousand and One Nights. But in 1861, Mouhot, the French naturalist, having ventured as far as the great lake whose waters overflow into the Mekong River, suddenly discovered in a tropical forest the truth of all that the Chinese writers of the thirteenth century had described. An enormous structure, which suggested 'a combination of the Louvre, the Tuileries, the Pantheon, Notre Dame, and Saint-Sulpice, but offering a plan much more harmonious than such a combination could be,' rose before him, half-veiled by monstrous creepers and tropical foliage. This was Angkor-Vat, or Ongkor-Wat, the colossal temple whose form has since been made familiar by countless engravings and photographs. Mouhot carried his explorations further into the twilight of the forest; and visions still more fantastic and vast appeared to him. He found the huge dead city of Angkor-Thom, inhabited now only by birds, apes, reptiles, and tigers; — visited only at long intervals by herds of wild elephants. But in spite of the lianas, the creepers, the insertion of roots between the joints of the masonry — in spite of the fact that the tropical forest had invaded and conquered the city for many hundred years — the grandeur of its architecture, the weird beauties of its sculptures, had withstood the passing of time. There were the gate-towers, whose summits are four faces, turned to the four winds of heaven and crowned with tremendous tiaras of stone; — there were the prodigious moats, traversed by bridges in the form of seven-headed marble dragons, and supported by long files of carven giants whose feet rested beneath the crocodile-haunted waters. . . .

This discovery awakened intense interest; and between 1863 and 1866, Lieutenant Doudart de Lagrée was sent to Cambodia upon a two-fold mission — diplomatic as well as scientific. Having succeeded in securing the recognition by King Norodom of the French protectorate, Lagrée thoroughly explored several provinces of Cambodia, made a multitude of new discoveries, and prepared a magnificent volume on the ancient monuments. Dying in 1868 — unfortunately before the publication of his works — he was succeeded in his archæological labors by Francis Garnier, Lieutenant Delaporte, Dr. Harmand, and Captain Aymonier — besides several English and German scientists, including the great architectural authority, Fergusson, and the eminent Dr. Bastian.

In the first burst of amazement caused by the spectacle of these remains, which exceeded anything previously dreamed of in regard to splendor, the explorers did not notice or seek for any inscriptions. Angkor-Vat simply took their breath away — a work realizing the Arab fables regarding the constructions of genii — a marvel whose grotesque beauty seemed a vision of Pandemonium. But in a little while more attention was paid to details; and Lagrée found that all the monuments were speckled with inscriptions, which he was the first to copy. Then another puzzle presented itself. The sculptures at first supposed to be all of Buddhist origin, revealed in some respects a still earlier inspiration. The prodigious seven-headed serpents whose bodies, supported by giants of stone, bridged the broad moats, belonged to the mythology of Vishnu. The terrific quadruple Faces upon the towers revealed a kinship with Brahmanic idealism. Finally the interminable reliefs cut upon the palace-walls, represented, not the gentle legends of Gautama, but the wilder stories contained in the awful epics of the 'Ramayana' and the 'Mahabharata.' Buddha, nevertheless, smiled there with his mysterious smile, and all the unmistakable attributes of his divinity. What problem was this? Certainly one to be solved only by the discovery of the history of a civilization long dead and buried under the roots of serpent-plants, in the green gloom of unknown forests.

If Aymonier did not solve all the problem, it is at least to him that the world owes most of its knowledge concerning ancient Cambodia — the empire whose vanished existence had scarcely been suspected twenty years ago. The inscriptions discovered and copied, and latterly published at Paris with types especially cast for the purpose, were found to be in many languages and various alphabets — in *Khmer* or ancient Cambodian; in Pali; in Sanscrit; in Laotian; and in Siamese. As for the antique Cambodian texts, the modern bonzes of the kingdom could not interpret them; but Aymonier, with wondrous patience, succeeded in reconstructing the dead tongue by the aid of his knowledge of modern Indo-Chinese idioms. The characters bear a close resemblance to those in the ancient palm-leaf Pali books. But the honor of first translating the Cambodian Sanscrit inscriptions belongs to the Indianist, Kern, who by his uncommon familiarity with the old Indian alphabets was able to decipher these unfamiliar signs. The mystery of the monuments became partially comprehensible; — it was now certain that both the civilization and the religion of ancient Cambodia had an Indian foundation — and a Brahmanic one — which afterwards continued to flourish side by side with a form of Buddhism totally unlike that of Annam or China — nor yet resembling that of

Burmah and of Siam, which latter are importations from Ceylon, and represent the 'Southern School.' The Buddhism of the modern Cambodians is similar to the Buddhism of the Burmese and Siamese; but that of the ancient Cambodians has been found to be the Buddhism of the North, whose sacred language was not Pali, but Sanscrit.

By 1883 Aymonier, besides translating a number of legends, texts, and other epigraphy, had sent to France a whole vast literature copied from stone. It comprises four hundred lots or collections; — many single documents, reproduced in Roman characters, occupying each twenty large quarto pages. By the time that all of these have been translated, we shall have a collection larger than that comprised in 'Records of the Past'; and the whole mystery of Cambodia shall be revealed.

Still, Aymonier's work did not end here. He is still busy in the Orient — busy with a new and marvelous discovery, dating, we believe, from the present year. One great puzzle in regard to the ancient Cambodian civilization, was the enigma of its destruction. How could savage tribes have ever paralyzed the power of so colossal a civilization? How could the immense vitality of a people who made the very walls of their cities dance with sculptures — whose towers were shaped like gods — whose bridges were dragons — whose piers were dæmons of marble — be extinguished by barbarian force? To believe this was impossible! — the power that brought about the decadence of Cambodia must have been an extraordinary one. Aymonier solved the riddle. Cambodia, it seems, had a rival as mighty as herself, and dowered likewise with the arts, the sciences, and the religion of India — the vast and vanished empire of Tchampa, extending once over the greater part of Eastern Indo-China. The last vestige of the language of that empire, the Tcham language, lingers now only in the most southerly district of Annam, which is called Binh-Thuan. It is there that M. Aymonier now is. He has already announced the discovery of a great number of ancient monuments covered with inscriptions both in Sanscrit and in Tcham, that are soon to be reproduced in French scientific prints. The fact that Tchampa had existed was indeed first surmised from the translation of various Cambodian texts discovered by the intrepid explorer; but he was the first to prove the surmise correct; — just as he was also the first to obtain for us some knowledge regarding the history of those kings, '*whose toe-nails*' (the inscriptions tell us) '*were perpetually illuminated by the flashing of the jewelled diadems of vassal monarchs, who came in multitudinous procession to kiss their feet!*'

'SOLITUDE'[1]

THE very strange study by Maupassant, entitled 'Solitude,' which appears upon another page of this issue, contains a thought worthy of more consideration, perhaps, than the author himself has cared to bestow upon it. One of the strongest characteristics of this prince of story-tellers is lavishness; — he compresses into a few pages the materials of a whole novel, and appears to have such confidence of creative power that he can afford to pluck all his literary fruit while yet green. He has thrown out to the world scores of undigested plots, any one of which might have made the fortune of a clever novelist — scorning to develop the theme according to any romantic precedent. There is, perhaps, no other living writer who could so well afford to do this; — Maupassant appears to afford it with an ease not less wonderful than his strength of style; for every six months he can present the public with a fresh volume. All his stories, indeed, are not stamped with the peculiarity referred to; — some are mere photographs of life taken at random — incidents of an afternoon or evening — studies in a railroad car or a *diligence* — anecdotes gleaned at receptions or balls — scenes

[1] *Times-Democrat*, February 14, 1886.

rapidly sketched upon a boulevard or at the foot
of an Opera-stairway. But aside from these, he
has written a wonderful number of sketches as
unquestionably original, and yet at the same
time so suggestively incomplete, so tantalizingly
abrupt, that the reader experiences a sort of
pained surprise at finding such riches flung
abroad as carelessly as beggars'-coin. This
Rothschild of modern French fiction seems to
have no time to work as others have worked before him and must continue to work after him;
— the fertility of his resources is such that life
appears too brief for any attempt to utilize them
fully. Zola would have written a five-hundred-
page novel upon such a theme as 'Solitude';
Maupassant writes ten and produces an equally
durable effect upon the reader's mind. That is
the difference! It is lamentable, indeed, that so
prodigious a talent should ever waste itself upon
subjects tabooed by morality and good taste; and
that nine tenths of its production must always
remain untouched by English translators.

But in 'Solitude' we have an idea worth dwelling upon — an idea which seems sufficiently well-
preserved for study in our hasty English version
of it, although the sketch loses greatly by translation. Inspired, apparently, by the recital of some
curious hallucination, and developed merely into
a conversational fragment, the thread of thought
so abruptly terminated by the ingenious writer

himself might be taken up at either end and
pursued to very startling lengths. Following the
clue backward would lead us into the most extraordinary realms of medical psychology — into
secret chambers of mentality, whose windows
look out upon the infinite. Pursuing it in the opposite direction, from the point at which the
writer dropped it, would lead us to the much
more vapory but not less interesting realm of
philosophical speculation — to the extreme limits
of that idealism circled by the Unknown. In fact
behind the strange mask of madness, or pessi-
mism, or aberration, which the figure of the story
wears, there is an idea so subtle that Maupassant
might have been afraid to develop it himself. It
could only be developed by men thoroughly capable of following his suggestion to either ex-
tremity — the profound Western physician, or
the profound Eastern philosopher; and either end
of the line touches the verge of the Unknowable.

There is a peculiar nervous mental affection,
demophobia — the horror of crowds — or of con-
tact with people in general. The affliction of
Maupassant's solitary is the antipodes of this
form of aberration, and yet represents such a returning of the mind upon itself as must eventually develop it. One question to consider is
whether the first condition could be possible as
a *permanent state* of mind; but it is a question
which belongs to the alienist. Another question

is whether one phenomenal human mind may not develop certain functions or ideas incomprehensible to all other human minds. This might, we think, be answered in the affirmative; for such men as the Mezzofantis and Magliabecchis and certain mathematical prodigies manifested the possession of powers of a totally unfamiliar order, through results to be obtained only by mental processes which the ordinary man has no knowledge of, and could not understand any more than a man blind from his birth could understand the sensation of color. But the possession of such faculties would not necessarily render the possessor miserable through any feeling of mental isolation.

Maupassant's intellectual hermit does not, however, suffer from any sense of an incomprehensible and undivined superiority. He claims simply to have discovered the fact that 'nobody can understand anybody' — *personne ne comprend personne!* It is true that we know each other only by inferences — analogies. Now, are these wholly trustworthy? Have there ever been in this world two minds precisely alike — two voices with exactly the same *timbre* — two blades of grass absolutely indistinguishable — two grains of sand in all respects similar? No! Then there is a vague truth, is there not, behind the assertion that *personne ne comprend personne?* Exaggerate the nature of this differentiation as madness might exaggerate it, or as a nightmare might distort it, and the sense of total solitude becomes comprehensible. But in sober moments could a man reason thus against himself, or fail to recognize, if he did, that such isolation as his individuality gives him is simply the reason of his existence!

Now, however, comes in a possible fancy which seems to me the most interesting suggestion of the sketch — an application of the evolutional law to this sense of isolation, faintly existing in every thinker; for there are moments in all lives when one suffers, or fancies that one suffers, from not being understood. According to the law of progress this sense of self-isolation would tend to become incomparably stronger in the future, as individuality must be enormously intensified. No conservative forces are conceivable which would check this development of personal differentiation; neither educational systems, beliefs, pursuits, social customs, nor climatic and geographical influences. The whole tendency of the age is toward specialism. Imagine this differentiation of individuality developed to the highest possible pitch, and strive to picture the possible result! Would it be such a result as the Maupassant sketch hints at? — each man dwelling in a mental desolation impenetrable to all but himself, and longing for his absorption into nature, through death, as the only means of escaping from his solitude?

OVER–EDUCATION IN GERMANY[1]

NOT long ago Ernst Eckstein, a well known German author, complained in the *Magazin für die Litteratur* that latter-day German imaginative literature evoked no interest abroad. Except in Holland, he declared, and the Scandinavian countries, nobody cared to know anything about new German books — much less to buy them. Why the French did not care, Herr Eckstein maliciously hinted that anybody could understand; — besides, it was 'well known that the French had little liking for any literature except their own.' But in Spain, in Italy, in Portugal, in Turkey (*sic!*), in Roumania, German literature was equally ignored. While the show-windows of the booksellers were filled with English or French literary novelties — either in the original language or in translations — it might be actually said that no German novel was ever to be seen there. What could be the reason? — asked Herr Eckstein.

The reason he himself suggested was anything but flattering to Germany. 'The part played abroad by any literature,' he asserted, 'is invariably an echo of what it plays at home.' But the rôle performed by German literature in Germany

[1] *Times-Democrat*, March 28, 1886.

was absolutely insignificant. Publishers scarcely
deigned to look at original manuscripts; they preferred translations of French novels. A similar
unpatriotic partiality for French literature was
manifested by newspaper managers and theatrical directors; — they wanted Parisian *feuille-
tons* or Parisian plays. Never could Germans
hope to win fame abroad until they could succeed
in making something resembling a reputation at
home.

Allowing that it is at least probable that Herr
Eckstein's complaint was provoked by some personal discomfitures or disappointments, it is
nevertheless absolutely certain that he states a
great deal of unpleasant truth. Not perhaps
when he declares that the French — who devour
Tourgueneff, Tolstoi, Gogol, Dostoievsky — who
know Dickens, Thackeray, Bulwer, Brontë,
Eliot, Scott, Reed, Collins, Marryat — who
worship Poe, admire Hawthorne, appreciate
Bret Harte and Mark Twain — who have produced the finest editions ever issued of certain
English and American authors — are insensible
to foreign literature. There he is grievously
wrong; for there is scarcely an English, American,
Russian, Italian, Spanish, Greek, Turkish, Roumanian, or Scandinavian author of note who has
not found a French translator; and those wealthy
Paris firms who make a specialty of translations
— such as Lévy and Hachette — do not print

books which are likely to prove failures. To be printed, there must be a certainty of their being read; and if Herr Eckstein had simply glanced over the columns of titles of foreign novels in the most recent French catalogues, he would have found reason to modify his outcry. But it is awfully true that in those same catalogues of fiction, he would have found scarcely half a dozen living German names. Still less is German fiction appreciated in the other Latin countries.

It remains to ask why? Herr Eckstein could only answer as any French laborer might answer if asked why his countrymen were defeated by the Germans. He speaks of lack of patriotism, of literary betrayals and traitors. This does not by any means explain why the French literature has vanquished the German at home, nor why German novels are little read and seldom translated abroad. The fault must lie in the literature itself! If the Germans prefer English, American, or French fiction to their own, it is assuredly because they find their own to be inferior. Why should it be inferior?

Herr Eckstein himself would not grant the assumption, we fancy; it is not therefore at all surprising that he should not attempt to answer the question. Another writer in the *Magazin für die Litteratur* foolishly sought to explain it by 'the injury caused to writers by circulating libraries'; — the experience of England, America, and France amply proving to intelligent observers that circulating libraries rather aid than decrease the financial success of an author. Carlos von Gagern, another eminent German writer, who died very recently, seemed to throw more light upon the subject when he called attention to the fact that authorship is not a profession, but a vocation; that one must become an author, not by study or intention, but by accident; and that the extraordinary number of writers in Germany has produced a competition which results in the establishment of a scale of prices for literary work which no ordinary man could hope to live upon. It does not follow that writing to make money should bring about happier literary results than writing for an art-principle; — indeed the contrary is the general rule! — but it would seem that where there is enormous competition, small pecuniary encouragement, and a broad level of mediocrity in taste, literature withers. The essential point to note is, that the prices paid for literary work in Germany are so paltry that authorship can only be pursued as a relaxation in the intervals of practical labor — of a very different sort. That prices are so low is in itself a proof that competition is vast; and the latter fact, again, indicates that mediocrity is extraordinary.

But what is such mediocrity? — what does it signify? It is not a contemptible subject for consideration; — it signifies a remarkably high general level of intelligence, of culture, and consequently of education. Mediocrity in literature is that stratum which lies between great talent and vulgar commonplaceness. It is rarely despicable; but it is never admirable; — it may be praiseworthy, but it is never inimitable. It is like the work of a man who knows how to do too many different things to be able to distinguish himself at any particular craft; he has never found the time or the self-denial or the patience necessary to devote himself successfully to any specialty. We would surmise, though we could scarcely dare to assert it positively — that the decadence of popular literature in Germany is the result of *over-education*. And in support of this hazarded opinion we might cite the indisputable fact that in the deeper sciences for which only the very highest education or the most profound study fits a man — the Germans stand easily first among all the nations of the world.

Some years ago a writer in the *Atlantic* enunciated a truth which probably deserves more consideration than it received — viz.: that it is not at all desirable that an author of romance should be a learned man. Outside of criticism — and the critic himself is rarely a creator — this fact is well exemplified in our own American literature. None of our really popular authors are learned men. The same is true of English writers, of French writers, of Spanish writers, of Russian writers — scarcely excepting the flash of true genius that lightens the world once in two or three hundred years.

Perhaps the reason is that, like the poet, the novelist is most successful when he appeals most strongly to the emotional feeling; and the tendency of the higher learning is to suppress emotionalism. To the philosopher passions are follies, trivialities — to the scientist they are mere physiological phenomena. But the poet and the novelist must appeal to those trivialities and to those phenomena in order to succeed; and their appeal, moreover, must be a sincere and mighty one.

Now, in Germany there is a very craze for learning; and the extraordinary educational facilities of the Empire have developed it to lamentable extremities. On this subject we recommend to our readers the perusal of the remarkable article entitled 'Pauperism in German Universities,' which appeared in No. 1064 of the New York *Nation*. It tells us of the marvellous endowments of the great institutes of learning — of the 283 bursaries which Vienna disposed of even in 1874 — of the associations which supply the means of living to poverty-stricken students — of smaller universities so well provided with benevolent funds that they do not know how to dispose of them! Armies of young men go there to study the professions, the sciences, the dead languages, the Oriental tongues; — and thousands return to the world only to starve. The vast Order of Begging-students, which died with the middle ages — after bequeathing to the world nothing better than love-ditties and drinking-songs — seems in a fair way of being revived; but the modern mendicant student has none of the emotion of the mediæval one; — study has only mummified his heart without sufficiently disciplining his brain. As private tutor, music-teacher, country-doctor, twenty-fourth-class architect, interpreter, translator, clerk, copyist, newspaper contributor — he starves in the streets of a hundred cities, and cries out against public inappreciation in vain. It is a serious question whether high educational facilities should ever be extended to those whom nature has gifted with no strongly marked aptitudes therefor.

CHINESE BELIEF IN GOD [1]

AN eminent Chinese scholar — the Marquis d'Hervey-Saint-Denys, translator of the 'Chi-King' (or, as English readers are more accustomed to see the title spelled, the 'She-King'), of the poets of the Thang dynasty, of the 'Kin-Kou-Ki-Koan,' and other Chinese classics, recently delivered a lecture of uncommon interest before the French Institute on the subject of Chinese religion. In a country like the United States, where almost every large city has its Chinese element, and where more is supposed to be known in a general way about the Chinese than is known in European capitals, the lecture of M. de Saint-Denys deserves very considerable attention, because it completely contradicts many current opinions in regard to Chinese faith. A full account of the religions of China, their evolution, their interrelation and interblending, would require a labor so colossal that no man, in the present state of linguistic science, could hope to attempt it successfully; and M. d'Hervey de Saint-Denys has frankly announced his incapacity for so vast a task. But the underlying spirit of all Chinese religion, ancient and modern, may be pursued by a consummate scholar through the

[1] *Times-Democrat*, December 26, 1886.

long course of that literature, which for enormity and uselessness has been forcibly compared by Williams to the Great Wall of the Empire. This is the duty the Marquis has undertaken; and the result of his researches throws a new and very pleasing light upon the subject of Chinese belief.

Like some of those Oriental fabrics, whereof the texture is wholly concealed by grotesque embroideries in gold thread and multicolored silks, primitive Chinese faith in the Supreme has become so covered up by the imagery of fantastical superstitions and idolatrous rites as to have been hidden even from the discernment of Christian missionaries learned in the language of the country. What the Three Religions are was not made any plainer to Occidental comprehension by Confucius' tolerant observation that they were really all one and the same; the symbolism of the strange Trinity was too conflicting to be harmonized by any superficial examiner. How Buddhism, with its philosophy of illusion, could be made to harmonize with the practical ethics of Confucius — how Taoism, with its demonology and witchcraft, could unite with the pure worship of Chang-ti, the Sovereign Lord, was long a riddle to Western minds. And the riddle has not been easily solved. Books and monographs innumerable have been written by sinologists for the purpose of establishing some positive position for Chinese faith in general, but

these writings, interconfused and antagonistic,
left only a chaos of mystery in the mind of the
reader, who felt himself totally unable to decide
whether the Chinese ought to be considered athe-
ists, polytheists, or materialists. As in Chinese
music the philosophy of that art is totally at
variance with the practice thereof; so, in Chinese
religion, the worship of ancestors and the rites
of sacrifice, and the observance of multifarious
superstitious customs, seemed totally at variance
with the general materialism of Chinese life.
And as that music, although rich in melody, is
wholly void of harmony, so it seemed the Chinese
ethical system, while replete with philosophical
excellence, totally lacked the basis of all great
religions — belief in a universal God. Finally,
through the writings of zealous but ill-informed
missionaries, and the writings of specialists also,
whose studies had been directed through too narrow a channel, we were taught to regard the
Chinese as a curiously contradictory race, full of
gross superstitions, and yet otherwise atheistical.
By confuting this wide-spread error, the Marquis
d'Hervey-Saint-Denys has done no less a service
to the science of comparative religions than to
the Chinese nation itself.

The most striking fact about the Marquis's
essay is that it upsets the popular idea of Confucius as the founder of a new religion. Confucius was simply the reformer, or rather the con-

servator, of a preëxisting faith and an ethical system dating back to at least the twentieth century before our era. Confucius, coming upon the world's stage in the fifth century before Christ, found Chinese literature and philosophy in a period of decay. It was a decay of material so vast that only a very wonderful scholar could hope to sift out and preserve the few sound remains of great learning and healthy thought from the boundless heap of rotting philosophy and decomposing art. Confucius thus discovered and preserved for us those noblest monuments of Chinese antiquity — the two 'King,' the 'Chi' and the 'Chou.' Between the doctrines of those most ancient books and his own, there are no differences of ethical or religious belief. If Confucius wrote little of his own ideas of God and of a future life, it was because he wrote only as a conservator — as an editor. He did not think it necessary to prove beliefs already deeply rooted in the Chinese mind, nor could he dare to vary from creeds whose hoary age seemed to him a proof of their eternal truth.

Now these very canons — the 'King' — preserved and rejuvenated by the learned labor of Confucius, bear testimony the most positive of Chinese belief in a Supreme Being, an omnipotent Creator, an All-Father — to borrow the grand Scandinavian term. For example, in the 'Chi-King,' which takes us back three thousand years, we find the following lines upon the founder of the Tcheou dynasty:

'Wen-Wang now dwelleth in the upper spaces;
Oh! how great is his glory in heaven!
Whether he riseth (to the highest of the celestial spheres)
    or whether he descendeth (to the regions of earth), —
He remaineth ever at the right and at the left of the
    Sovereign Lord.'

[*Chi-King*, Part III, Ode I.]

It will be observed that this simple declaration of faith in God, is coupled with an equally strong assertion of belief in the immortality of the soul.

Again we read:

'Heaven (*tien*), who placed upon the throne the virtuous
    ancestor of the dynasty of Yn,
Hath not permitted his (degenerate) descendants to keep
    the Empire. . . .
Wen-Wang, who served the Sovereign Lord (*Chang-ti*)
    with a pure heart, was filled with blessings, and received
    the mandate to govern the nations.'

[Ode II, Part III.]

And here is a third touching extract from the same ancient scripture:

'Oh! how great is He! — how vast is He! — the Sovereign
    Lord (*Chang-ti*), the Master of the World!
How terrible is He! — how awful his judgments are!
Heaven (*tien*) created man, but not in order that man
    should rashly use the privilege of life.'

[Ode XXI.]

These paragraphs leave no doubt whatever in the mind regarding the signification of the Chinese words *tien* and *Chang-ti;* — the former is used as we use the word 'Heaven' in religious writing; the latter as a name of the Supreme. Yet another example:

'I cannot forbear to do that which Heaven (*tien*) commands;
I cannot disobey the Sovereign Lord (*Chang-ti*).'
[*Chou-King:* Chap. *Ta-Kao*, or 'Great Warnings.']

Nor could any other meaning be taken from the following lines, in which the words 'Heaven' and 'Lord' are used as explicitly as in the Christian Bible:

'Of old, when Tching-tang took possession of the throne, his minister, Y-yu, was inspired in his counsels by august Heaven. . . . Also in the reign of the King Tai-ou, the ministers Y-chi and Tchin-hou received inspiration from the Sovereign Lord.' [*Chou-King.* Chap. *Kiun-chi.*]
'The Sovereign Lord (*Chang-ti*) first gave warning to the King of Hia by many Calamities.'
[*Chou-King.* Chap. *To-fang.*]

And as he did not mend his ways, we hear that 'Heaven (*tien*) chose one more worthy than he to whom to confide the government of the nations.'
Again we read:

'Sovereign Heaven cannot err, — cannot be deceived.'
[*Chi-King*, III; Ode II.]
'Heaven loves us with the love of a father and of a mother; — Heaven is the Master of the World.'
[*Chou-King:* '*Hong-fang*.']
'Heaven has given power unto Kings to preserve nations and to teach them: they are the ministers of the Sovereign Lord.'

[*Chou-King:* '*Tai-chi*.']

'The Sovereign Lord caused Tching-tang to be born.
By his unceasing piety, Tching-tang surpassed even all
    those who had gone before him;
Daily the brightness of his merit went up, as a homage, to
    Heaven.
The Sovereign Lord was touched by the fervent worship
    thus paid unto Him.
He gave unto Tching-tang the government of all the states
    of the Empire.'

Eleven hundred years before Christ, the idea
of God had not altered, as the following hymn-
verses of the Tcheou period show:

'The Most High and Sovereign Lord looks down upon the
    earth:
Majestically he contemplates the passing of events;
Attentively he watches all the regions of the Empire;
He wishes that the nations be righteously governed.'

And the Chinese commentators of the Imperial College, reëditing the 'Chou-King,' thus
at a later date expressed their conception of the
Almighty in language well worthy of the Hebrew
Psalmist:

'How great, how sublime, how profound He is, — the
August Heaven! His justice is infallible; — His penetra-
tion is absolute; His intelligence hath no limits. He hath
no ears; — yet all things are heard by Him; He hath no
eyes; — yet all things are seen by Him. Whether in the
rulings of a prince, or in the life of any private person, there
is no good or evil action that escapes Him. For Him there
are no obscurities, nor any secret chambers. He knows all;
He observes all things; nothing may be ever hidden from
Him.'

The French scholar successfully traces out the same belief, the same faith, all through the long evolution of Chinese literature and dogma, and even into our own day—faith in One God—faith in the immortality of the soul; and he points out with great force that in no known Chinese book can a profession of materialistic belief be discovered, and that there are no Chinese characters to express the idea of *atheist* or of *atheism*. Furthermore he assures us that the Buddhist idea of *Nirvana* — of the total end of the soul — never has taken root in China! This is a very interesting statement, especially when we recollect that De Rosny, in his recent work upon Japanese literature ('Bibliothèque Orientale Elzevirienne') shows that in Japan Buddhism changed character, and became a religion in which the doctrine of a future life obtained much poetical and touching expression. The reason for this state of things in China appears especially to be that the worship of ancestors, the family duty of reverence to the dead (which forms so profound a principle in Chinese religion that the Jesuit missionaries found it inexpedient to oppose it), could never exist side by side with the doctrine of total annihilation.

The monotheistic dogmas of the Religion of the Learned, as Confucianism is called, could not be easily understood, perhaps, by the more ignorant millions of China — to whose grosser

imaginations the outward practices and pomps
of Buddhism and of Taoism offered a readier
religious inspiration.   But the purity of the antique cult prevails among the educated classes
still — side by side with the harmless and beautiful religion of ancestral worship, whose shrines
are in every household; and still the Emperor
publicly bows in homage before that Supreme
Lord, to whom no altar is erected, because His
altar is the Universe, with its myriad million
suns for taper-lights — to whom no temple is
ever built, because His temple-roof is the blue of
the infinite and eternal heaven.

ARTISTIC VALUE OF MYOPIA [1]

PROBABLY more than one reader, on coming to page 15 of Philip Gilbert Hamerton's delightful book, 'Landscape,' was startled by the author's irrefutable statement that 'the possession of very good eyesight may be a hindrance to those feelings of sublimity that exalt the poetic imagination.' The fact is, that the impressiveness of natural scenery depends a great deal upon the apparent predominance of *mass* over *detail*, to borrow Mr. Hamerton's own words; the more visible the details of a large object — a mountain, a tower, a forest-wall — the less grand and impressive that object. The more apparently uniform the mass, the larger it seems to loom; the vaguer a shadow-space, the deeper it appears. An impression of weirdness — such as that obtainable in a Louisiana or Florida swamp-forest, or, much more, in those primeval and impenetrable forest-deeps described so powerfully by Humboldt — is stronger in proportion to the spectator's indifference to lesser detail. The real effect of the scene must be a *general* one to be understood. In painting, the artist does not attempt microscopic minutiæ in treating forest-forms; he simply attempts to render the effect of

[1] *Times-Democrat*, February 7, 1887.

the masses, with their characteristic generalities of shadow and color. It is for this reason the photograph can never supplant the painting — not even when the art of photographing natural colors shall have been discovered. Mr. Hamerton cites the example of a mountain, which always seems more imposing when wreathed in mists or half veiled by clouds, than when cutting sharply against the horizon with a strong light upon it. Half the secret of Doré's power as an illustrator was his exaggerated perception of this fact — his comprehension of the artistic witchcraft of *suggestion*. And since the perception of details depends vastly upon the quality of eyesight, a landscape necessarily suggests less to the keen-sighted man than to the myope. The keener the view, the less depth in the impression produced. There is no possibility of mysterious attraction in wooded deeps or mountain recesses for the eye that, like the eye of the hawk, pierces shadows and can note the separate quiver of each leaf. Far-seeing persons can, to a certain degree, comprehend this by recalling the impressions given in twilight by certain unfamiliar, or even by familiar objects — such as furniture and clothing in a half-lighted room. The suggestiveness of the forms vanishes immediately upon the making of a strong light. Again, attractive objects viewed vaguely through a morning or evening haze, or at a great distance, often totally lose artistic character when a telescope is directed upon them.

In the February number of *Harper's Magazine* we find a very clever and amusing poem by the scholarly Andrew Lang upon this very theme. The writer, after describing the christening-gifts of various kindly fairies, tells us that the wicked one said:

> 'I shall be avenged on you.
> My child, you shall grow up nearsighted!'
>   With magic juices did she lave
> Mine eyes, and wrought her wicked pleasure.
>   Well, of all the gifts the Fairies gave,
> *Hers* is the present that I treasure!
>
> 'The bore, whom others fear and flee,
>   I do not fear, I do not flee him;
> I pass him calm as calm can be;
>   I do not cut — I do not see him!
> And with my feeble eyes and dim,
>   Where *you* see patchy fields and fences,
> For me the mists of Turner swim —
>   *My* "azure distance" soon commences!
> Nay, as I blink about the streets
>   Of the befogged and miry city,
> Why, almost every girl one meets
>   Seems preternaturally pretty!
> "Try spectacles," one's friends intone;
>   "You'll see the world correctly through them."
> But I have visions of my own
>   And not for worlds would I undo them!'

This is quite witty and quite consoling to my-opes, even as a cynical development of Philip Gilbert Hamerton's artistic philosophy. Still, it does not follow that the myope necessarily possesses the poetic faculty or feeling; — neither does it imply that the presbyope necessarily lacks it. If among French writers, for example, Gautier was notably nearsighted, Victor Hugo had an eye keen as a bird's. It is true that a knowledge of the effect of short sightedness on the imagination may be of benefit to a near-sighted man, who, possessing artistic qualities, can learn to take all possible advantage of his myopia — to utilize his physical disability to a good purpose; but the long-sighted artist need not be at a loss to find equally powerful sources of inspiration — he can seek them in morning mists, evening fogs, or those wonderful hazes of summer afternoons, when the land sends up all its vapors to the sun, like a smoke of gold. Baudelaire in his 'Curiosités Esthétiques,' made an attempt to prove that the greatest schools of painting were evolved among hazy surroundings — Dutch fogs, Venetian mists, and the vapors of Italian marsh lands.

The evolutionary tendency would indicate for future man a keener vision than he at present possesses; and a finer perception of color — for while there may be certain small emotional advantages connected with myopia, it is a serious hindrance in practical life. What effect keener sight will have on the artistic powers of the future man can only be imagined — but an increasing tendency to realism in art is certainly perceptible; and perhaps an interesting chapter could be written upon the possible results to art of perfected optical instruments. The subject also suggests another idea — that the total inability of a certain class of highly educated persons to feel interest in a certain kind of art-production may be partly accounted for by the possession of such keen visual perception as necessarily suppresses the sensation of breadth of effect, either in landscape or verbal description.

COLORS AND EMOTIONS [1]

THE evolutionary history of the Color-Sense, very prettily treated of by Grant Allen and others, both in regard to the relation between fertilization of flowers by insects, and in regard to the æsthetic pleasure of man in contemplating certain colors, has also been considered in a very thorough way by American thinkers. Perhaps the most entertaining and instructive paper yet published on the subject was one contributed by Dr. L. Webster Fox and G. M. Gould, A.B., to the *American Journal of Ophthalmology* last September. It has just been reprinted in pamphlet form, under the title of 'The Human Color-Sense as the Organic Response to Natural Stimuli'; and contains a remarkable amplification of theories, rather suggested than laid down by the author of 'Physiological Æsthetics.' Of course the reader whom the subject can interest, comprehends that outside of the mind no such thing as color exists; and that the phenomena of colors, like those of sound, are simply results of exterior impressions upon nerve-apparatus specially sensitive to vibrations — in the one case of ether, in the other of air. Everybody, moreover — even those totally ignorant of the physiology of

[1] *Times-Democrat*, May 8, 1887.

the eye, knows that certain colors are called primary or elementary. But it has probably occurred to few to ask why — except in regard to mixing of paints in a drawing-school.

The theories of Gladstone and Magnus that the men of the Homeric era were color-blind, because of the absence from the Homeric poems of certain words expressive of certain colors, have been disproved by more thorough modern research. The primitive man's sense of color, or the sensitiveness of his retina to ether vibrations, may not have been as fine as that of the Roman mosaic-worker, who could select his material of thirty thousand different tints, nor as that of the Gobelins weaver, who can recognize twenty-eight thousand different shades of wool. But the evidence goes to show that the sense of color is old as the gnawing of hunger or the pang of fear — old as the experience that taught living creatures to discern food and to flee from danger. There is, however, reason to suppose, from certain developmental phenomena observed in the eyes of children and newly born animals, that the present condition of the color-sense has been gradually reached — not so much in any particular species, as in all species possessing it — just as vision itself must have been gradually acquired. Also showy colors must have been perceived before tints could be discerned; and even now we know through the spectroscope that the human eye is not yet developed to the fullest possible perceptions of color. Now the first colors recognized by the first eyes must have presumably been just those we call primary — Yellow, Red, Green, Blue. Yellow, the color of gold, is also the color of our sun; the brightest daylight has a more or less faint tinge even at noon, according to the state of the atmosphere; — and this tinge deepens at sunrise and sunset. Red is the color of blood — a color allied necessarily from time immemorial with violent mental impressions, whether of war, or love, or the chase, or religious sacrifice. Green itself is the color of the world. Blue — the blue of the far-away sky — has necessarily always been for man the color most mysterious and holy — always associated with those high phenomena of heaven which first inspired wonder and fear of the Unknown. These colors were probably the first known to intelligent life; and their impressions are to-day the strongest. So violent, indeed, have they become to our refined civilized sense, that in apparel or decoration three of them, at least, are condemned when offered pure. Even the armies of the world are abandoning red uniforms; — no refined people wear flaming crimsons or scarlets or yellows; — nobody would paint a house or decorate a wall with a solid sheet of strong primary color. Blue is still the least violent, the most agreeable to the artistic sense; and in subdued form it holds a place, in costume and in art, refused to less spiritual colors.

It might consequently be expected there should exist some correlation between the primary colors and the stronger emotional states of man. And such, indeed, proves to be the case. Emotionally the colors come in the order of Red, Yellow, Green, and Blue. Red still appeals to the idea of Passion — for which very reason its artistic use is being more and more restrained. Very curious are the researches by Grant Allen showing this fact of the sensual use of red. In Swinburne's 'Poems and Ballads' (the same suppressed work republished in this country under its first title 'Laus Veneris'), the red epithets appear 159 times, while gold, green, and blue words occur respectively 143, 86, and 25 times. In Tennyson's beautiful poem, 'The Princess,' the red words occur only 20 times, the gold 28, the green 5, the blue once. With all his exquisite sense of color, Tennyson is sparing of adjectives; — there is no false skin to his work; it is solid muscle and bone.

Next to Red, the most emotional color is Yellow — the color of life, and of what men seem to prize next to life — Gold. We fancy we can live without green sometimes; it comes third; but it is the hue associated with all the labors of man or the earth, since he began to labor. It is the color of Industry. Blue has always been, since man commenced to think — associated with his spiritual senses — his idea of many gods or of One — his hopes of a second life — his faith, his good purposes, his perception of duty. Still, all who pray turn up their faces toward the eternal azure. And with the modern expansion of the Idea of God, as with the modern expansion of the Idea of the Universe, the violet gulf of space ever seems more mystical — its pure color more and more divine, and appeals to us as the color of the Unknowable — the color of the Holy of Holies.

THE FASCINATION OF CRIME [1]

THAT crime and criminals exercise a strong
fascination upon a certain class of people is an
undeniable fact. Our exchanges give an abundant proof of this, in their accounts of the at-
tentions lavished on men who have been imprisoned for the committal of atrocious deeds.
A wife-murderer who, perhaps, slaughtered his
victim with pitiless ferocity, is almost buried
under a load of floral tributes from sentimental
persons. We read of a negro who, with the aid of
an accomplice, had killed an old woman for the
purpose of robbery: his cell was filled with offer-
ings of fruit, pound-cake and candy, though
whether as a reward of merit, or as a consolation,
we are not told. It is stated that he seemed
'contented and happy' — small blame to him!
Doubtless, to his ignorant mind, soothed by
these influences, the vision of the gallows had
vanished into the dimness of improbability.
Had he pursued the straight and narrow path of
virtue, he would have toiled and sorrowed and
gone down to the grave, 'unwept, unhonored
and unsung.'

Going a step farther, it is not an uncommon
thing for these sentimentalists to wish to link

\ [1] *Times-Democrat*, July 27, 1887.

their destinies with that of the criminal. The mere fact that a man has been imprisoned seems to add some mysterious charm to his personality: witness the struggles of a handsome young woman to marry Spies. This peculiarity, however, is not confined to any nationality. When the Count de Molen, after brutally maltreating his wife, and trying to shoot her and his father-in-law, was sentenced to ten years' hard labor, a Roumanian girl was moved to offer him her heart and hand. In the case of Pranzini, it was announced that he received at least fifty impassioned love-letters, many addressing him as 'Unhappy persecuted one.' One of the fair scribes promised to follow him to New Caledonia, and marry him. Perhaps it may add a pang to the punishment of malefactors to have it supposed that they would be willing to ally themselves with such feeble-minded creatures.

But it is not only members of the fair sex who are fond of making pets of jail-birds. In several instances, women arrested for poisoning their husbands have received numerous offers of marriage; apparently on the strength of their evil notoriety. The motives which may actuate such proceedings form an interesting problem. It may be that the adventurous spirit cherishes the vague theory of the familiar superstition that lightning never strikes twice in the same place, and that, by marrying a woman who has disposed of one husband, he secures immunity forever from the poisoned bowl. Or, perhaps, it is a love of excitement and a desire to avoid the ordinary stagnation of domestic peace and happiness.

Even petit larceny is not without its charms, as is proven by the career of Hannah Sykes, a girl who has figured frequently in the police courts. There was a period when she was one of the loudest shouters of the Salvation Army, but was afterward arrested for stealing a dress. On her way to the station, she attempted to escape by leaping from a bridge. When her case came up, Thomas Gray, a New Yorker, asked permission to marry her, although he had never seen her before; so, after he had paid her fine, they were made man and wife. Being questioned with regard to his motives, Mr. Gray replied that he thought she would make a lively wife. No doubt she will.

THE END